CHIANG KAI-SHEK

CHIANG KAI-SHEK

ROBERT PAYNE

WEYBRIGHT AND TALLEY

NEW YORK

Published in the United States by
WEYBRIGHT AND TALLEY, INC.
3 East 54th Street
New York, New York 10022

Published simultaneously in Canada by
CLARKE, IRWIN & COMPANY LIMITED,
Toronto and Vancouver

Library of Congress Catalog No. 68-17754
PRINTED IN THE UNITED STATES OF AMERICA

PHOTO CREDITS

Page 1 CAMERA PRESS *from* PIX: *Page 2* CAMERA PRESS *from* PIX: *Page 3* CAMERA PRESS *from* PIX: *Page 6* CAMERA PRESS *from* PIX: *Page 7* WIDE WORLD PHOTOS: *Pages 8 and 9* WIDE WORLD PHOTOS: *Page 9 top,* UPI: *Page 10* UPI: *Page 11* UPI: *Page 12* UPI: *Page 13* WIDE WORLD PHOTOS: *Page 14* WIDE WORLD PHOTOS: *Page 16* CAMERA PRESS *from* PIX.

CONTENTS

CHIANG KAI-SHEK

INTRODUCTION

IN THE EARLY YEARS of the nineteenth century guerrilla chieftains who rose to power in Mexico and South America would sometimes adopt the title of Generalissimo. The word had pleasantly romantic associations, and the chieftain who assumed the title would attempt to live up to his romantic reputation. Sometimes the title was adopted by more distinguished military leaders. Count Alexander Suvorov was known as the Generalissimo during his Italian campaign, and the same title was adopted briefly by General Franco when he took command of the Nationalist forces in Spain.

Although Chiang Kai-shek has been known in the western world for forty years as the Generalissimo, it is not a title for which he has ever displayed any enthusiasm. It has no exact equivalent in Chinese. It was used once by Dr. Sun Yat-sen and then forgotten, only to be revived by the journalists who accompanied Chiang Kai-shek on his march from Canton to Shanghai in 1927. Thereafter he was never able to escape from it. The word rang like an alarm bell, and in the context of the Chinese wars it acquired a special meaning, for it implied triumph, victory, and domination. Since Chiang Kai-shek was eventually to go down to disastrous defeat, history, which does not judge people by their titles, added to the word an ironical question mark.

Nevertheless, it is likely that historians a hundred years from now will continue to remember him as the Generalissimo, as though no other Generalissimos had ever existed. A rather dry, precise man, devoted to the Confucian virtues and totally incapable of flamboyance, he will continue to be known by a title for which he is wholly unsuited. The quiet, self-absorbed scholar will continue to wear a romantic halo; and when they speak of the Generalissimo, they will mean Chiang Kai-shek and no one else.

Austere and passionless, Chiang Kai-shek dominated Chinese history for two generations, and then became a footnote in the history of the island of Formosa. The sudden fall from grace was not an accident and was not due solely to the brilliance of Mao Tse-tung; it lay in the character of the man himself. From a very early age he saw himself as a "superior man," one of those chosen celebrants of the Confucian mystery, his mind revolving ceaselessly around a fixed point, his behavior circumscribed by fixed laws and therefore predictable. According to Confucius the "superior man" is stern, high-minded, unyielding in his sense of propriety, ruthless, and incorruptible. Chiang Kai-shek was all of these except the last. Power corrupted him, as it corrupts all men, and he came to regard himself as essential at a time when his usefulness was at best dubious. Early in his career he wrote that he was determined to leave his mark on history. He succeeded beyond all his expectations, but the Chinese people have little reason to be grateful for his success.

Yet it is necessary to observe that he possessed qualities of character which were admirably suited to a Chinese leader in a time of crisis. Like Confucius' "superior man," he was never deflected from his purpose and did not permit his affections to disturb his judgment. The face he presented to the world was always the same: calm, detached, unemotional, the faintest of smiles hovering around his lips. Reserved and unwilling to share his counsels with others, he acted as though he alone knew the answer to the innumerable problems which confronted the Chinese people; and since they were incapable of finding their own answers, his singular detachment and his ability to convince others that he was the destined leader served sometimes to bring a sense of balance to a people living under intolerable strains. In his legend they found relief from their own insecurities. There were times when he merged imperceptibly into the figure of a Chinese emperor, credited with mysterious powers received from Heaven. At other times he wore the mask of the heroic captain who alone can cut a way through the massed troops of the enemy. Whatever role he played, it was always played with high seriousness. It never seems to have occurred to him that there were elements of desperate comedy in the tragedy.

"Fame," wrote Paul Valéry, "is merely the sum of the misunderstandings which have accumulated around a name." So it was with Chiang Kai-shek. Misunderstandings crowded around him throughout his life. He appeared to be strong, but was often weak; he appeared to be continually making decisions of far-reaching importance, but they were often made for him by historical forces; he was regarded as inflexible when he was drifting with the tide. His followers saw in him the modern man who had broken completely with the past, but at times of crisis he always behaved according to patterns established in remote ages. When he was arrested at Sian by his own officers, he behaved exactly like one of the princely warriors of the age of Confucius, daring his adversaries to kill him and taunting them with oracular utterances derived from the sages. He did not know that he owed his safety to his most determined adversary. Irony was his constant companion, but he never seems to have observed her presence.

A biography of Chiang Kai-shek presents unusual difficulties. Many of the documents concerning his early years have been lost or tampered with. His private dealings with the world are largely unknown, and we have only a few letters written to his sons to show that he was capable of private emotions. Only three times has he been known to show emotion in public. He wept unrestrainedly at the time of his mother's death, and again at the death of General Tai Li, the head of his secret police, and he was visibly shaken by his arrest in Sian. At all other times, so far as we know, he maintained a calm and unruffled composure, like the quiet of an inland sea.

Some part of the difficulty of writing about him derives from that unruffled calm. His mind never leaps, new ideas rarely penetrate it, and his speeches tend to be the same speech. The same ideas are continually repeated, and the writer of a biography is in constant danger of accepting him on his own terms. He will say in 1968 exactly what he said in 1938, as though there had been no catastrophes and upheavals in the interval. The writer, dazzled by the tenacity of a single idea, may be tempted to applaud him for consistency.

He was a man dedicated to the virtues he had learned at his mother's knees, and it never occurred to him that virtues that are admirable in a mother might be dangerous in a dictator. In the end he was destroyed by his virtues and by the legend of infallibility which his propagandists constructed at his bidding. In time he came to believe in his own legend, and this was fatal.

In the following pages I have attempted to divorce Chiang Kai-shek from the legend, to see him as he was and not as his propagandists saw him. I have said very little about Madame Chiang Kai-shek, because I find little evidence that she took any effective part in his decisions. She attained the rank of commander-in-chief of the Chinese Nationalist air force, but I suspect that the air force would have acted as well, or as indifferently, without its commander-in-chief.

I have studied Chiang Kai-shek's childhood and youth at some length, because it seemed to me important that we should observe the springs of his character. Many pages have been devoted to his arrest in Sian, because it was a historical event of some magnitude and because he showed himself there to his best advantage, naked, stripped of all authority except the moral authority he derived from a prolonged study of Confucian tradition. I have said very little about the battles with the Chinese warlords in the twenties; today they have assumed the dimensions of tribal skirmishes. I have opened the book with an account of the Emperor Kuang Hsu's abortive revolution in 1898, which took place when

Chiang Kai-shek was eleven years old, in order to set the stage. For a few months the young Emperor had it in his power to divert the course of Chinese history. Almost alone, without any following, he wrestled with the dark powers of medieval corruption, and was defeated by them. Because he risked his life for his beliefs, there was high tragedy in his downfall.

Chiang Kai-shek's downfall belongs to another order of things. It came about inevitably as a result of his own weakness and remoteness. Great gifts were granted to him at his birth; he possessed virtues denied to most men; vast opportunities presented themselves to him, and he squandered his gifts and threw away his advantages. Fate gave him the opportunity to lead a brilliant and industrious people into the twentieth century, but instead he attempted to lead them back to the age of the Confucian kingdoms. In this way he led China to destruction.

Chi Kang asked Confucius concerning government, saying: "What do you say about killing the unprincipled for the good of the principled?"

Confucius replied: "Sir, in carrying on your government, why should you use killing at all? Let your desires be for what is good, and the people will be good. The relation between superiors and inferiors is like that between the wind and the grass. The grass must bend when the wind blows over it."

ANALECTS OF CONFUCIUS

THE END OF AN EPOCH

IN 1643 THERE DIED in Mukden a man who was to have an extraordinary influence on Chinese history. His name was Abahai, and he was chief of the many chieftains who ruled over the Manchu tribes. A heavily built man, with a quick and fiery temper, he had given himself one aim in life—the conquest of China. To this end he bent all his energies, and he was so certain that he would one day sit on the Dragon Throne that he solemnly proclaimed himself Emperor of China under the reign name of Tien Tsung, even though he had conquered no Chinese territory. He had once attacked Peking, but it was scarcely more than a foray, and he retreated under the fire of the Portuguese guns mounted on the city walls. Nevertheless, he acted and behaved as though he were the real emperor, wore the ceremonial robes of Chinese emperors, and presided over a court modeled on the court in Peking.

Abahai was one of those barbaric geniuses who arise from time to time to plague the people of China. He was a man without any scruples whatsoever, ferociously determined to conquer. He trained his army for the day when it would cut like a knife through

China, and he instilled in his people the spirit of conquest. He had calculated exactly how the conquest would be brought about, and he left a testament in which he commanded the Manchus, who lived by hunting in the forest clearings behind the Great Wall, to live as lords in the cities of China. Within a year of his death the Manchu Bannermen occupied all of northern China and his infant son was proclaimed emperor in Peking. A new dynasty had been founded. Abahai had already given it a name. It would be known as the Ching, or Pure, dynasty, and it would endure for two hundred and sixty-seven years.

As Abahai well knew, China was ripe for the plucking. Famine, wars, treachery, and corruption had so weakened China that she was incapable of putting up a sustained resistance. In addition there were peasant rebellions and provincial warlords with private armies. When the Manchus broke through the Great Wall, they had no difficulty setting the Chinese warlords against each other. The Chinese in the south were in no mood to accept the Manchu barbarians as their overlords, and continued the struggle for many years. But there was never any doubt that the Manchus had come to stay. The last Chinese emperor hanged himself on the Coal Hill within the walls of the Forbidden City, leaving a message in which he proclaimed his guilt before Heaven and his hope that the Chinese people would not have to suffer for his sins.

The pattern of conquest was a familiar one, for in much the same way the Mongols had descended upon China from the north, setting warlord against warlord, employing subversion and corruption whenever they were unable to take a city by storm, suffering dangerous reverses only when they reached out into south China. The Japanese invasion of China followed the same principles, and their armies marched along the same roads. And when Mao Tse-tung conquered China, he too emerged from behind the Great Wall and his army followed the roads of earlier conquerors.

Abahai had commanded his tribesmen to hold themselves aloof from the Chinese. They ruled as conquerors, maintaining themselves in garrisons in strategic cities, adopting Chinese culture but setting themselves apart from Chinese society. For a hundred and fifty years they were able to maintain undisputed control over

China. Under the reigns of two remarkable emperors, Kang Hsi and Chien Lung, whose combined reigns totaled one hundred and thirteen years, the Manchu empire reached its greatest extent. Tibet was conquered. Japan, Korea, Annam, Nepal, Burma, Indochina, and the provinces of Central Asia acknowledged the suzerainty of the Manchus by sending tribute to Peking. It was the greatest empire on earth, stretching from the Siberian forests to the Indian Ocean. Throughout this long period the Chinese lived in a settled calm. Chien Lung died in 1796, and with his death the years of calm came to an end.

In the nineteenth century the Ching dynasty gradually collapsed. There were no great emperors capable of holding the empire together; one weak and self-indulgent monarch followed another. The Opium War, forced on China by the British, and the Taiping Rebellion, led by a strange sect of Christian converts, were cataclysmic events, shaking the foundations of the dynasty; and while the Opium War cost few lives, the Taiping Rebellion brought about the deaths of many millions, with whole provinces drowned in blood. Both the war and the rebellion arose from the pressure of foreign ideas. The Chinese way of life had been a settled one, circumscribed by immemorial custom, Confucian in dealing with practical affairs, Buddhist and Taoist in its attitude toward religion and the world of the spirit, with a delicate and precise balance between the three forces which worked so satisfactorily on the Chinese mind. The introduction of western rationalism, and particularly of western science, and the presence of Christian missionaries, had a shattering effect. All the old Chinese values were questioned. Steamships sailed unchallenged down the Yangtse river, and cast anchor in Chinese ports crowded with sampans which had not changed in a thousand years. The telegraph, the newspaper, the Maxim gun and the heavy cannon of the marauding ships confronted the Chinese with a way of life which was demonstrably more powerful and swifter than their own. Right up to the end of the nineteenth century the Chinese were fighting their border wars with bows and arrows.

The Chinese way of life was rounded and complete; it did not permit assimilation. If one value was questioned, then all the

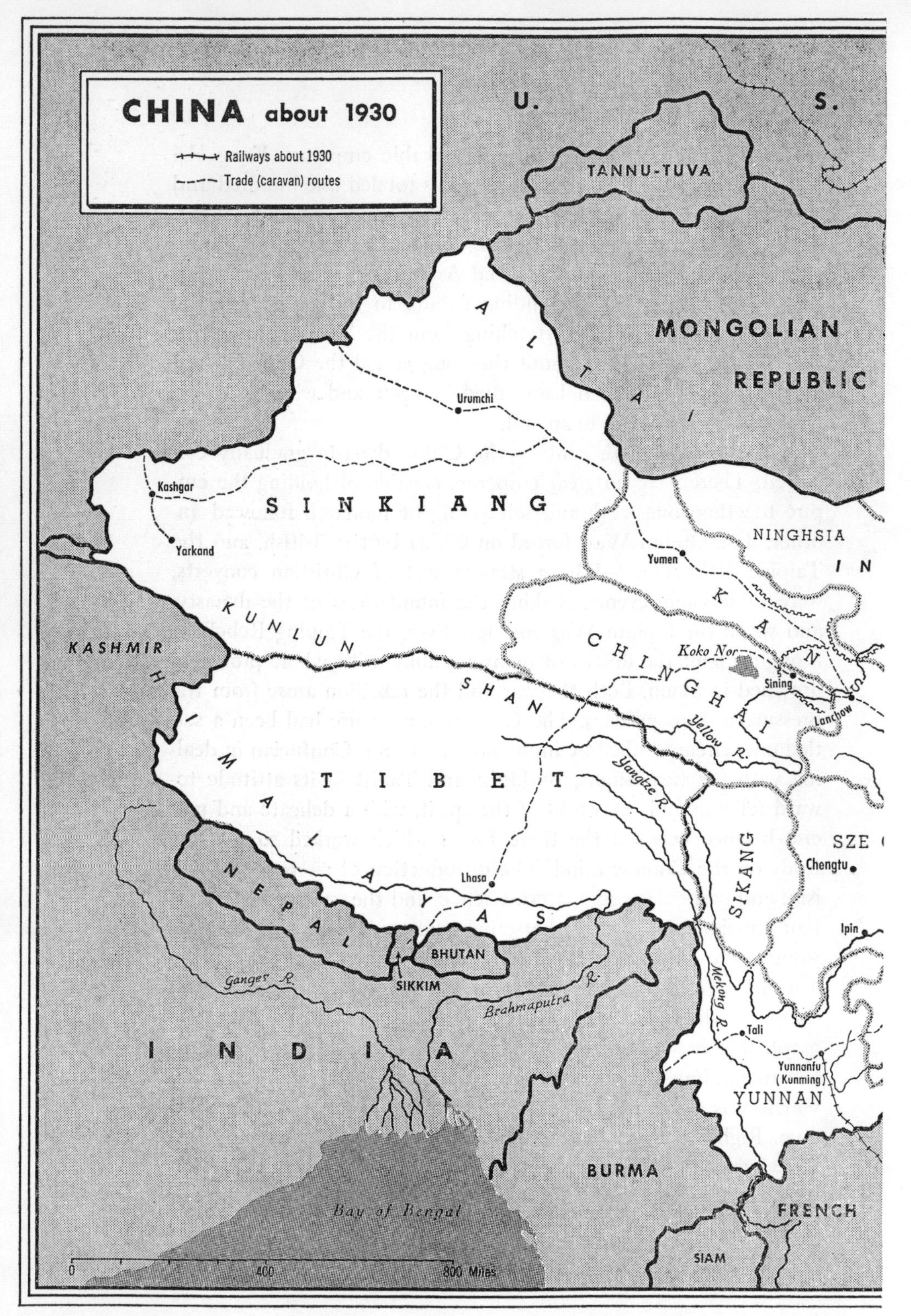
CHINA about 1930
Railways about 1930
Trade (caravan) routes
U. S.
TANNU-TUVA
MONGOLIAN
REPUBLIC
ALTAI
Urumchi
Kashgar
Yarkand
SINKIANG
NINGHSIA
Yumen
KANSU
KASHMIR
KUNLUN SHAN
CHINGHAI
Koko Nor
Sining
Lanchow
Yellow R.
Yangtze R.
TIBET
HIMALAYAS
SIKANG
SZE
Chengtu
Lhasa
NEPAL
BHUTAN
SIKKIM
Ipin
Ganges R.
Brahmaputra R.
Mekong R.
Tali
Yunnanfu
(Kunming)
YUNNAN
INDIA
BURMA
Bay of Bengal
FRENCH
SIAM
0
400
800 Miles

S. R.
Amur R.
TRANS-SIBERIAN RAILWAY
HEILUNGKIANG
Manchouli
Tsitsihar
Harbin
KIRIN
Ulan Bator
PEOPLE'S
MANCHURIA
Vladivostok
Changchun
LIAONING
Sea of Japan
MONGOLIA
CHAHAR
Erhlien
JEHOL
Mukden
KOREA
JAPAN
SUIYUAN
Chengteh
THE GREAT WALL
Kalgan
Paotow
Peiping (Peking)
Dairen
Port Arthur
INNER
Tientsin
Chefoo
Weihaiwei
HOPEH
Taiyuan
SHANTUNG
Tsingtao
SHANSI
Tungchang
Tsinan
Yenan
Yellow R.
SHENSI
Haichow
KIANGSU
Hsuchow
Chenghsien
Wei R.
Sian
HONAN
East China Sea
Nanking
Shanghai
Wuhu
ANHWEI
CHUAN
HUPEH
Hankow
Hangchow
Ningpo
Yangtze R.
Chikow
Chialing R.
Ichang
Kiukiang
CHEKIANG
Peipei
Chungking
Nanchang
Wenchow
Changsha
KIANGSI
HUNAN
Foochow
FUKIEN
Kweiyang
Kanhsien
Pacific Ocean
KWEICHOW
Kweilin
Amoy
TAIWAN (FORMOSA)
Shiuchow
KWANGSI
Canton
Wuchow
Swatow
Nanning
KWANGTUNG
Hong Kong (Br.)
Macao (Port.)
Hanoi
INDOCHINA
HAINAN
PHILIPPINE IS.
V. Gray

others must similarly be questioned; if one domino fell, then all the others would fall. The intricate rituals of the Confucians, the prayers of the Buddhists, and the gentle nihilism of the Taoists were all ineffective against the march of western science. The Chinese were faced with the prospect of having to refashion their culture from top to bottom, or going down to defeat as a colony divided up among the western powers.

Many foreigners living in China urgently hoped for the awakening of China. They hoped that in some mysterious way the Chinese would accept western values and become powerful enough to ward off the encroachments of foreign powers. When Sir Robert Hart asked the imperial minister Tso Tsung-tang his opinion about western influence on the Chinese mind, he was told: "You are all too anxious to awake us and start us on a new road, and you will do it, but you will regret it, for once awakened and started, we shall move faster and farther than you think; much faster than you want."

In Japan the Meiji restoration was in the process of bringing about a modern state fully equipped to resist foreign aggression. Such things had happened before. Peter the Great had single-handedly changed the face of his country, given it purpose and direction, pouring into it all the resources of his energy and transforming it into a modern state. There occurred what the Romans called a *renovatio*, a renewal and rebirth. The old Muskovy perished, and a new Russia was born.

Toward the end of the nineteenth century Chinese intellectuals were demanding a similar *renovatio* in China. The times were out of joint. The Manchus were no longer governing effectively. One after another the western powers had wrung concessions and spheres of interest out of a supine government. When two German missionaries were murdered in 1897, the German government exacted as the price of martyrdom the ninety-nine year lease of the port of Kiaochow. Russia, not to be outdone, secured the lease of Port Arthur and Talienwan, and within a few weeks the French secured the lease of Kwanchow-wan in Kwangtung, while Great Britain acquired the port of Wei-hai-wei "for so long a period as Port Arthur shall remain in the occupation of

Russia." France acquired a sphere of influence in Hainan and the provinces bordering French Indochina, Great Britain acquired a sphere of influence over the provinces of the Yangtse river, Germany claimed Shantung, Japan claimed Fukien, and Russia claimed the territory north of the Great Wall. The pattern of colonization was becoming clear. The living body of China was about to be torn apart by beasts of prey. There had never been greater need for a powerful emperor who would defy the foreign powers and pour new energy into a dying culture.

On the throne of China there sat the twenty-seven-year-old Emperor Kuang Hsu, the nephew of the Empress Dowager Tzu Hsi, who had abruptly stepped down from the throne nine years before. Kuang Hsu had the delicate features of Manchu royalty, with heavy lids, fine cheekbones, a feminine mouth. He was no Abahai, from whom he was descended, but he possessed gifts of charm, intelligence, and courage. Suffocating among the ceremonies of the Manchu court, surrounded by eunuchs and in great fear of the formidable Empress Dowager, who possessed the instincts of domination and practiced murder as a fine art, he was seeking vainly for a way out of the impasse. Through Weng Tung-ho, formerly the Emperor's teacher and therefore held in high respect, he had been hearing about the reforms proposed by a brilliant thirty-nine-year-old Cantonese scholar called Kang Yu-wei, who had passed the literary examinations with high honors at a very early age. He had been writing pamphlets advocating basic reforms which, if carried out, would shake the foundations of Chinese society. Through Weng Tung-ho, the Emperor made contact with the revolutionary scholar. He collected the revolutionary's pamphlets, studied and annotated them, and finally on January 3, 1908 he commanded Kang Yu-wei to present his ideas at a conference of ministers of state. Although the Emperor was not present, the conference was held under his protection and auspices, and a full report of it was delivered to him.

During the following days the implications of Kang Yu-wei's speech at the conference were discussed in the Forbidden City. The speech had lasted for three hours, and the ministers had listened in awed silence as he demanded nothing less than a *reno-*

vatio, a new China, the old effete China to be thrown away like a broken toy. Kang Yu-wei began quietly by demanding a change in judicial procedures, and then he went on to demand the reorganization of the entire structure of government. With the laws and the administration changed—so changed that they could never be restored—he demanded that the entire educational system should be remodeled on European lines, and that it should no longer be necessary for a man desiring a high government appointment to submit to the ferociously difficult literary examinations. New railways, new roads, a new navy, a new army, a new people. China must become westernized; it must adopt the policies of the west in order to fight the west; foreigners must be encouraged to flock to China to teach the western sciences to students brought up to memorize the Chinese classics. Unless China did this, she was doomed.

On that cold winter day, while the ministers huddled in their fur-lined gowns and warmed their hands over bronze braziers, the fuse was being lit. For six months it would burn slowly, and then the powder keg would explode.

During those six months the Emperor maneuvered behind the scenes. He had no illusions about the task confronting him. Those unlikely bedfellows, the Emperor and the revolutionary, were in league to bring about a sudden and violent change in the nature of Chinese society. They knew they were taking terrible risks, and they also knew that if these changes were brought about gradually their enemies would have time to consolidate their forces and organize a counterattack. Only a policy of great boldness had a chance of success. For various reasons the Emperor thought that the summer would be the best time for the revolution. Meanwhile he remained in continual communication with Kang Yu-wei through Weng Tung-ho, who occupied the position of Grand Secretary. Altogether six memorials to the Emperor were written by Kang Yu-wei in impeccable classical Chinese, and all were pondered and marked with the Vermilion Pencil. The six memorials constituted a blueprint for revolution by a series of shattering decrees, whose effects were unpredictable, for there was no area of

Chinese society which would remain unchanged if they were put into force.

On June 16 Kang Yu-wei was summoned for the first time to an audience with the Emperor, which took place in a reception room in the Palace of Heavenly Purity in the Forbidden City. In the customary fashion the Emperor was led in by two eunuchs and took his place on a throne padded with an imperial yellow cushion. A long low table with two candlesticks stood in front of him, and throughout the two-hour audience Kang Yu-wei remained kneeling on the bare wooden floor. There were cushions scattered over the floor before the throne, but only great ministers of state were permitted to kneel on them. It was dawn, the usual hour for audiences, and the candles were glowing on the pale face of the Emperor, who looked unusually strained and careworn. The Russians had occupied Port Arthur and Talienwan only a few days before.

When the eunuchs were dismissed, the Emperor spoke quietly about the pleasure he had derived from Kang Yu-wei's writings, and sometimes he would look up toward the fretted windows to make sure that no one was listening outside, for he was afraid of treachery and knew there were many potential traitors in his court. Kang Yu-wei spoke about the necessity of introducing those sudden and sweeping reforms which would revolutionize China. Peter the Great had revolutionized Russia, the Emperor Meiji had revolutionized Japan, sweeping the medieval forms of government away and giving high positions to young men, thus transforming Japan into a modern state respected by the west. "You, the Emperor," he said, "I would ask you to remove yourself from the seclusion in which you live. Come forth boldly."

The old arguments were repeated to the lonely Emperor, who knew them by heart. He had summoned Kang Yu-wei into his presence because he wanted reassurance before he made the final, irreversible decision. There was still time to turn back.

"What is needed," Kang Yu-wei continued, "is that all the laws, and the entire political and social system, shall be changed. It is not enough that we change a little here and there. Meanwhile the four barbarians are all invading us and they are gradually attempting to partition the country."

"Yes," the Emperor said. "All this is the fault of the conservatives."

At that moment he may have remembered that just before the audience with Kang Yu-wei, there had been another audience with the imperial minister Jung-lu, who had been appointed on the previous day commander-in-chief of all the troops in the empire and concurrently Viceroy of Chihli, the province in which Peking stands, all these titles and powers having been bestowed on him at the command of the Empress Dowager. Jung-lu was a conservative, vigorously opposed to any changes in the government. During the audience he had pointedly remarked upon the dangers of reform and attacked Kang Yu-wei. Since he now commanded the army his opinions inevitably carried weight.

"What can I do?" the Emperor asked. "They are doing everything possible to hinder me."

"You can use your imperial authority to carry out the reforms," Kang Yu-wei replied, "and even if all the necessary reforms are not carried out, then at least the most important ones can be made into law. As for the ministers of the Grand Council, they are all so old and conservative that they are incapable of understanding foreign affairs. If Your Majesty should wish to rely on them to bring about reform, it would be like climbing a tree to seek for fish."

"True," the Emperor said, "and what is worse is that they are inattentive to their work. They do nothing."

"But something must be done, and done quickly. Let the old ministers remain for a little while longer, but let the executive power go to younger men appointed by Your Majesty. But if Your Majesty issued decrees, then there could be no question of anyone opposing or criticizing them. If you desire to strengthen the determination of the officials and to encourage the people, then Your Majesty should issue decrees 'with grief and heartbreak,' and so bring about the reforms."

In this characteristically Chinese fashion, Kang Yu-wei pleaded for immediate reform, always returning to the central point—the need that the reforms should be brought about by the imperial decree, because there was no other way —while the Emperor said little, nodding or saying "Yes" and sometimes sighing, for a Chinese Emperor could indicate many things with a cultivated sigh. In the course of Kang Yu-wei's long monologue, for it was nothing less, many other subjects were brought under review, but the most important thing—the terrible danger in which the Emperor was placing himself—was never mentioned. The Emperor knew that his throne and perhaps his life were at stake. The destiny of China was at stake. He was living at that precise moment when it was possible to change the direction of an entire civilization, and it was in his power to do so. But the very setting of the interview, with the revolutionary kneeling below the throne, his head bent low, always averting his face from the Emperor, showed that China was still bound by ancient conventions.

Although they never spoke about danger, they were both deeply aware of it. The truth was that among the people who were closest to the Emperor, only a few were wholeheartedly behind the reform movement, and they could be counted on the fingers of one hand. A revolution, to be successful, needs the dedicated cooperation of thousands of men and a general staff of brilliant political organizers. There was only this small handful of men hoping to bring about a revolution by throwing the immense prestige of the Emperor into the struggle. If the reforms failed, the Emperor would be the first victim.

By the time Kang Yu-wei had left the audience chamber, retreating backward on his knees from the throne, the main outlines of the revolutionary political program had been agreed upon. The executive power in the ministries would be given to young men chosen by Kang Yu-wei, and a series of imperial edicts and proclamations would be issued at short intervals, while the influence of the conservatives and reactionaries would be curbed in every possible way. In effect, Kang Yu-wei was given dictatorial powers, acting in the name of the Emperor. He wrote the decrees, and saw that they were carried out. In the space of a hundred days, twenty-seven decrees were issued in the Emperor's name, and every one of them struck at the existing foundations of Chinese society.

The first decree put an end to the arduous examinations, based on a study of the *Four Books* of Confucius and Mencius, which led to appointments in the civil service. Instead, beginning with the next examination, the tests would be based on a study of current problems. This may not appear to us as a particularly revolutionary idea, but it was in fact the most revolutionary of all. It meant that the Confucian past was jettisoned, and the study of the present day was given precedence over the study of events which happened more than two thousand years before. There followed a decree abolishing the useless ceremonies which occupied most of the time of government officials, and another inviting foreign technicians to come to China. A translation bureau was inaugurated under Kang Yu-wei's most devoted pupil, a young Cantonese called Liang Chi-chao. Ministries of agriculture, industry, and commerce were set up. There was a decree for the adoption of the western system of parliamentary government, and another for the opening up of new railroads, waterways, and other means of communication. A university was to be established in Peking, and every town and village was commanded to establish free schools for the poor, with broader schooling in the affairs of foreign nations. If necessary, temples were to be converted into schools. All sinecure appointments at the court and in the government were abolished, and the question of whether all existing government and military appointments should not be abolished was left to a board of inquiry under the presidency of the Emperor, who was also empowered to hand down a final verdict on whether Christian missionaries should be encouraged or denounced. Quite clearly the Emperor was well-disposed to the missionaries, for he demanded nothing less than the westernization of China. Chinese society was to be reshaped according to western models, and no area of society was excluded from the imperial decrees. The West was to be regarded with respect and affection, and imitated.

The twenty-seven decrees electrified China. A new spirit was coursing through the country, and the young Emperor was at the height of his power and popularity. Peking was flooded with young and eager students who wanted nothing more than to share in the revolutionary ferment of the time. In September the Emperor gave an audience to Prince Ito Hirobumi, the leading architect of Japanese reform, at that time prime minister. The Emperor had previously asked him for a full report on the reforms in Japan, and the Prince accordingly presented him with the voluminous manuscript. The decrees had also been shown to Prince Ito, and he approved of them, adding only that it was necessary that high officials should be well informed about them. It is clear from the minutes of the audience, which have survived, that the Emperor was well pleased with the way the reform movement was going.

The Empress Dowager was less pleased. She was surrounded by reactionary officials, who were now in danger of losing their positions. She adored ceremonies, and heartily disliked all western innovations. She had approved of many decrees, without clearly understanding their implications, but by the beginning of September she was plotting the downfall of the Emperor. Kang Yu-wei proposed that the Empress Dowager should be placed under restraint. He had no clear idea how this should be accomplished, and like the Emperor he appears to have underestimated her power. There was a confused plot to arrest her during a military parade, at which both the Emperor and the Empress Dowager were to be present, but the plot failed. The Empress Dowager was a forceful and utterly ruthless person; the Emperor was one of those men who are the victims of their moral scruples. He did not act quickly or decisively; and with the army against him he recognized that there was no way to enforce his reforms. He had hoped the army would remain neutral. Instead, it came out on the side of the Empress Dowager.

The Emperor was imprisoned in a small palace on an island in the North Lake within the Forbidden City. He was stripped of his powers and displayed merely on ceremonial occasions, in order to show that he was still alive. The Empress Dowager gave orders that all who had assisted him in the reform movement should be rounded up and summarily executed. A special punishment was reserved for Kang Yu-wei, who was to be cut to pieces with small knives, the ultimate refinement of the death penalty. He escaped from Peking, and with the help of Prince Ito found refuge in

Japan. But the Japanese prince could do little to help the other reformers. The "hundred days" ended in a bloodbath.

The reform movement came to an abrupt end, in terror and confusion. Of all the institutions brought into existence through the Emperor's decrees only Peking University was permitted to survive; everything else was swept away. China returned to the medieval past, and for the remaining ten years of her life the Empress Dowager continued to rule incompetently, with no understanding of the real forces at work. She despised the West, having no comprehension of its power or motives. Two years after the collapse of the reform movement, she encouraged the Boxers, a sect of fervent traditionalists, to murder Christian converts and loot Christian churches, killing any foreigners who fell into their hands. Growing bolder, the Boxers attacked the Legation Quarter in Peking, murdered the German ambassador, and attempted to sweep every vestige of foreign influence out of Peking. There was so much looting, burning, killing, and torture of foreigners that an allied army landed at Tientsin and marched on the capital. The Empress Dowager fled into the interior, taking the helpless Emperor with her. When she returned to Peking, she found it looted by an army of occupation. China was ordered to pay a vast indemnity.

For eight more years the Empress Dowager continued to reign, a ghostly survivor from the medieval past. China, she felt, was secure behind her frontiers, and the inroads of foreigners were no more than the pinpricks which must be suffered by a great and enduring nation. It never seems to have occurred to her that Manchu domination of China was coming to an end, or that the ancient medieval China was dying at the roots. She died on November 15, 1908, having left the throne to the infant son of Prince Chun, the younger brother of the Emperor Kuang Hsu. By a strange coincidence the Emperor had died the previous day. She had not wanted the Emperor to survive her, and it is possible that he was poisoned.

The old order was passing away, but on the surface there was little change. The Manchus were still ruling China; there had been an orderly succession of power; all the proper ceremonies were being attended by the court officials; and the Emperor and the Empress Dowager were solemnly buried with the panoply appropriate to ancient Sun kings. But below the surface the storms were raging. In almost her last words the Empress Dowager rebuked the students for their tendency to revolutionary beliefs, and she gave orders that everything should be done to stamp out these beliefs. It was too late. Three years later the long pent-up grievances exploded in a revolution which swept the Manchus out of power, the Chinese Republic came into existence, and China stepped falteringly into the modern age.

SUN YAT-SEN

WHEN THE EMPEROR KUANG HSU placed the great seal of the Empire on the twenty-seven decrees written by Kang Yu-wei, he knew perfectly well that time was running out and that if the reforms failed, they would be followed by a revolution which would change the face of China. He was a man of great sensitivity, with the modern spirit and the modern temper, interested in physics and chemistry, widely read in European and American history. If he had been a few years older, with more experience and more authority, he might have succeeded in carrying out his revolutionary reforms, and China would have been spared the agonizing revolutions which tore her apart during the twentieth century.

The revolution from the top had failed. Inevitably there would come the revolution from below: a long-drawn, sporadic, bloody revolution, for the Chinese are not a people who are easily organized according to new patterns. Two or three generations would have to pass before Confucianism, Buddhism, and Taoism would lose their hold on people's minds and hearts, but even if the medieval beliefs disintegrated, there would remain the problem of

Chinese provincialism, the tendency of every Chinese province to live its own life independent of the rest. Unless a man of revolutionary genius emerged to focus the revolution in himself and to "shake the dice" at exactly the right moment, the Chinese could expect to suffer a long series of inconclusive revolutions and civil wars. There would be no general conflagration. Instead there would be brush fires, bolts of lightning, volcanic explosions. The revolution would go underground only to emerge as another kind of revolution altogether. Provincial warlords would assume the disguise of revolutionaries, only to abandon the disguise when it suited their purpose. Millions would die in the name of the revolution without ever knowing exactly what kind of revolution they desired. China would split apart like the pieces of a jigsaw puzzle, and the pieces would group in strange conglomerations, and these would regroup and split apart, never coming to rest. Once the revolutionary ferment began to act on the people, there would be no settled peace. Dr. Sun Yat-sen once called China "a tray of shifting sand," and these words were as much a testimony to his despair as to his knowledge of his countrymen.

After his death Dr. Sun Yat-sen came to be known as "the father of the Republic." It was not a title he would have claimed for himself. A singularly modest man, with few illusions about himself, he was content to regard his work as merely the preliminary preparation for a revolution which was not completed in his lifetime. He was the forerunner, leaving to others the task of announcing the true gospel. He knew that if victory was ever achieved, it would come at the end of a long and exhausting process, and sometimes he seems to have doubted whether it would ever come. After the failure of the reform movement he emerged as the most powerful and dangerous revolutionary figure in China. His strength came from his belief that the revolutionary must hammer at all the doors and never give up.

He was born in the small village of Choyhung, meaning the Blue and Thriving Place, in a nest of hills some forty miles from Canton, on November 12, 1866. His father was a smallholder plowing a few acres of land, a man of some education who claimed descent from the ancient nobility of the Ming dynasty. It was not an unlikely claim, for there were thousands of peasants in Kwangtung who could make the same claim. Sun Yat-sen was born when his parents were already old, for at the time of his birth his father was fifty-four and his mother was thirty-nine. There were altogether three sons and three daughters of the marriage, and living with the family were two widowed aunts, whose husbands had deserted their farms and set out for California during one of the gold rushes. The family looked outward, to Hongkong and America, and there were people from the village who had settled in Hawaii.

In later years Sun Yat-sen, usually reserved about his private life, would speak of his childhood as an unbelievably happy period. He especially enjoyed the company of an old soldier who had taken part in the Taiping Rebellion, and it is possible that his first revolutionary dreams arose out of the old soldier's vivid stories of the days when the Taiping leader led his army across south China and in less than three years established himself as the Heavenly Emperor in Nanking, with a vast retinue and a powerful army. For fifteen years the Taiping Emperor fought the Manchus. Six hundred towns and cities were conquered, and the Yangtse valley, where most of the battles were fought, was devastated. The Taipings introduced sweeping land reforms, gave women equality with men, strictly prohibited the use of opium, tobacco, and alcohol, and showed in many other ways that they were aware of the need for revolutionary changes. The Manchus, however, were able to obtain the services of foreign military advisers, and the Ever-Victorious Army under the American General Frederick Townsend Ward and later under General Gordon fought a series of successful battles against them. At last the Taiping Emperor and princes were captured by a ruse, and there was a general massacre of the Taiping rebels. The last engagement against a Taiping army was fought in 1866, the year of Sun Yat-sen's birth.

In 1872, when Sun Yat-sen was six years old, his elder brother Ah Mei left Choyhung to seek his fortune in Hawaii. He was eighteen, strong and sturdy, with a good knowledge of farming. He worked the rich lowlands in the neighborhood of Pearl Harbor, and being frugal and industrious, he made enough money to buy some land and to send regular remittances to his father. Five years later he returned to Choyhung for a brief visit, long enough to acquire a bride and to set the village tongues wagging about the unaccountable prosperity of Hawaii. Sun Yat-sen, now eleven, was suitably impressed, and there seems to have been an agreement that he would follow his brother as soon as he obtained his parents' permission. Two years later he sailed for Honolulu, joined his brother, and was put to work in the general store which Ah Mei had opened in the small village of Ewa. In this dimly lit store, among rice sacks, fly whisks, brushes, sweetmeats, and medicines, Sun Yat-sen learned a smattering of the Hawaiian language, plied the abacus, posted his accounts, and discovered the limitations of a life spent serving behind a counter. Ah Mei thought he had acquired a good shopkeeper; the boy thought he was being imposed upon, and begged to be sent to school.

After the summer vacation of 1879 Sun Yat-sen was admitted to the diocesan college of Honolulu. All the teachers were English, for Hawaiian education was then largely in the hands of English missionaries. Everything in the school—the textbooks, the methods of teaching, the syllabus, the refinements of punishment—was English, and English history and the genealogies of English and Hebrew kings were taught as a matter of course to all the students. Sun Yat-sen was a diligent student, and it was remembered that he was a devoted attendant at Bible classes and especially enjoyed taking part in the processions from the school to St. Andrew's procathedral in Honolulu. At such processions he wore a surplice and carried a candle.

Deeply religious, he attempted to convert his brother to his newfound faith, laboriously explaining the mysteries of the Holy Trinity to a brother who was incapable of understanding the significance of the Ten Commandments. Both brothers possessed hot, sultry tempers. Soon Ah Mei was writing to Choyhung that his younger brother was getting out of hand; he was disobedient, spoke disparagingly of the ancestors, and was becoming more Western than the Westerners. Worse still, he had been baptized and was seriously thinking of becoming a missionary.

Sun Yat-sen graduated from the school, known as Iolani, in

1882 with commendable grades, receiving the second prize in English grammar. The prizes were presented by King Kalakaua and consisted of two books—a Bible bound in pigskin and a history of Christian missions in China. Armed with his prizes, he returned to Choyhung, having apparently quarreled so bitterly with his brother that it was inadvisable for him to stay in Hawaii. He was in a rebellious mood when he returned to his native village. The missionaries had taught him that idol worship, concubines, foot-binding, opium-smoking, and bribe-taking were all offenses against God; he found that these evils were practiced openly in Choyhung and with all the authority of a seventeen-year-old he proposed to set the villagers to rights. On one occasion he stood up in the village temple and announced that the gods served no purpose at all, for they could not even protect themselves. Saying this, he wrenched off the arm of one of the gods, revealing the hollow core, and went on to mutilate other gods, then calmly marched out of the temple through throngs of appalled worshipers.

In those days the village elders had power of life and death over the villagers, and Sun Yat-sen promptly found himself on trial. The punishment for rebellion against the gods was decapitation or being buried alive in a pit. Only the respect in which his father was held by the villagers saved him from an early death. He was summarily banished from the village and ordered never to return, while his father was ordered to repair the damaged temple.

Late in the autumn of 1883 he reached Hongkong, possessing no valuables except those his parents had secretly saved for him, since banishment entailed that the victim leave the village with only the clothes he wore and the tools of his trade. In Hongkong he disappeared from sight, and for three or four months nothing further is known about him. Then in April 1884 he entered Queen's College, at that time the best school in Hongkong, and in the following month he married the daughter of a farmer from Choyhung.

He still regarded himself as a future candidate for the priesthood, associated with missionaries, took part in Bible readings, and joined a small group of converts busily attempting to evangelize Macao. As an Anglican, he regarded the Archbishop of Canterbury as the supreme religious authority, and he believed that he had been given the mission to bring Christ to the heathen Chinese.

Meanwhile the French were continuing their conquests in Annam and seeking a foothold in the Chinese province of Yunnan. A French expeditionary force had crossed the Chinese frontier and French ships were raiding the Chinese coast as far as Amoy and Formosa. Annam was a vassal state which paid an annual tribute to the Chinese Emperor, and its loss to the French was regarded as an irreparable insult to the honor of China. The French retreated from Yunnan, but here too they inflicted damaging blows to Chinese pride. All over China infuriated students clamored for revenge, and Sun Yat-sen in later years liked to believe that the Franco-Chinese war first led him along the path of revolution. In his memoirs he wrote: "From the time of our defeat in the war with France, I set before myself the object of the overthrow of the Ching dynasty and the establishment of a Chinese republic on its ruins."

In fact, he appears to have spent these years preparing for a career as a medical missionary, being more interested in Christianity than in politics. In 1885 he again quarreled with his brother over his Christian beliefs. Ah Mei invited him to revisit Honolulu, ostensibly to sign some documents concerning properties in which the younger brother had an interest, but in reality to warn him against pursuing his dreams of becoming a missionary. Just before he left Honolulu, in March 1885, Sun Yat-sen told his brother: "I cannot follow in the footsteps of our forefathers. I cannot abide their old customs. I thank you for your generosity—and with all my heart I can only return the money to you. Money will never make me betray Christianity, and indeed money is a curse in China, a source of corruption and a burden to the people." Having no money, Sun Yat-sen returned to China with the help of friendly Chinese Christians who saw in the young convert a future missionary of great promise and distinction.

They liked him well enough to underwrite his expenses when in the following year he entered Pok Tsai Hospital in Canton as a medical student, where he remained for only a year before transferring to the Alice Memorial Hospital in Hongkong. The hospital had only just been founded, and he was therefore among the first students. Dr. James Cantlie, a gruff Scotsman, was one of the founders of the hospital, and Sun Yat-sen appears to have been one of his favorite students. Their friendship was to have remarkable consequences, for when Sun Yat-sen was in grave danger, Dr. Cantlie was able to save his life. What the doctor admired most in the student was a certain calm gravity of manner and an air of quiet authority. In his view Sun Yat-sen had all the makings of a good doctor.

In his memoirs Sun Yat-sen wrote: "All the years between 1885 and 1895 were like one day in my hard fight for national liberty, and my medical practice was no more to me than a means to introduce my propaganda to the world." If he meant by this that he subordinated his medical career to revolutionary propaganda, he showed very few signs of it during his early years as a medical student. He was the dedicated student, quick, adaptable, uncompromising in his search for knowledge, and there could have been very little time for propaganda until he graduated in 1892. After graduation he set up a small hospital in Macao, which he later transferred to Canton. It was about this time that his thoughts turned gradually to the problems affecting the mainland.

During this period he was far from being a revolutionary. His interest was in reform, as he demonstrated when in the summer of 1894 he set out for Tientsin with his boyhood friend Lu Hao-tung in an attempt to present his ideas to the imperial minister Li Hung-chang, one of the men who brought about the downfall of the Taipings. In the memorial presented to Li Hung-chang the main ideas were stated in sixteen Chinese characters: The *full development* of *men's abilities*, the *full exploitation* of the *earth's resources*, the *full* use of *material things*, the *unhampered flow* of *business* and *trade*. He had hoped to discuss these ideas with the imperial minister, but the minister was too busy to see him. From someone in the minister's office he obtained the authorization to raise money abroad for the study of improvements in agriculture. Accordingly, in the autumn he paid his third visit to Honolulu, where he founded an obscure society called the Hsing Chung Hui (Revive China Society), which was apparently intended to agitate for the four points mentioned in the memorial to Li Hung-chang. The society was not in the least concerned to overthrow the Manchus; it aimed to strengthen the existing government and to oppose foreign aggression. All this was somehow connected with the establishment of an agricultural association. Everyone joining the society paid a membership fee of five dollars. Members paid their first fees on November 24, 1894, and this day has usually been regarded as the day when the society was founded. The date has some importance, for the Hsing Chung Hui was the direct ancestor of the Kuomintang.

While the Hsing Chung Hui was content to pursue peaceful reforms, events in China were quickly approaching a crisis. In September 1894 there had been a battle between the Japanese and Chinese navies at the mouth of the Yalu river. As a result China, which had already lost Annam to the French, was compelled to acknowledge the naval supremacy of the Japanese. By the treaty signed at Shimonoseki China surrendered her claim to Korea, while Formosa, the Pescadores Islands, and the Liaotung Peninsula were ceded to Japan. This was a far more devastating loss than the loss of Annam. Now for the first time Japanese expansionist tendencies could be clearly observed. No one needed to possess a gift for prophecy to realize that Japan was making her first step in the long march across Asia. Already there were Japanese who spoke of a "divine mission" to colonize all Asia.

The treaty was signed in April 1895. Long before the signing of the treaty it became known that Japan would make punishing demands, knowing that China was too weak to resist. Suddenly Sun Yat-sen abandoned all hope in a program of gradual reform, and from being a devoted monarchist he became a determined revolutionary. The Hsing Chung Hui became a secret society with the aim of overthrowing the Manchu dynasty and building a republic. The conspirators met and agreed that on October 26, the day when the Chinese, following an immemorial custom, go into the country to offer sacrifices on the tombs of the ancestors, an attempt would be made to capture the yamen at Canton and to sieze control of the province of Kwangtung. Sun Yat-sen was placed in charge of the revolt, while his close friend Yang Chu-yun raised money, bought arms, and recruited men in Hongkong. By giving themselves six months to plan the revolt, the conspirators hoped to plan for all eventualities. In this way they gave hostages to the enemy, for during the six months the revolutionary organization was infiltrated by traitors.

At the last minute all their plans went awry. On the eve of the revolt the Canton authorites arrested three of the conspirators and promptly executed them. They captured the weapons of the conspirators, amounting to 205 revolvers and 80 cases of ammunition. Forty-five revolutionaries from Hongkong were arrested as soon as they arrived in Canton. Sun Yat-sen, who was living in Canton, barely escaped with his life. Three days later he succeeded in slipping out of the city, making his way to Hongkong and then to Japan with a price on his head. It was only then, when he realized the full extent of his failure, that he took the step which many others had already taken. He cut off his queue, as a sign that he had finally abandoned all allegiance to the Manchus. He grew a mustache and took to wearing Japanese clothes, so that he was indistinguishable from the Japanese in Kobe, where he was hiding.

The Manchus had their own agents in Japan, and he soon decided he would be safer in Honolulu, living quietly on his brother's estate and reorganizing the Hsing Chung Hui. Except for a single day in 1907, when he slipped over the borders of Annam and visited a revolutionary outpost in the Kwangsi mountains, he would spend the next sixteen years of his life outside of China.

He traveled round the world, making speeches against the Manchus, raising money for his revolutionary activities, quietly exerting his authority over the many revolutionary movements which were beginning to arise amid the crumbling ruins of the Manchu empire. He was not a forceful or even a convincing speaker, but he was admired for his singlemindedness and tenacity. He had connections with the Chinese secret societies and secret funds reached him from Japan, a country likely to benefit from the revolutionary ferment in China. Quiet, strangely impassive, avoiding all notoriety, he passed like a shadow across the world.

The Manchu government followed him closely. Orders were given for his arrest on foreign soil. Once arrested, he was to be shipped to China for a brief trial and a lingering execution.

On the morning of Sunday, October 11, 1896, he was hurrying along Devonshire Street in London on his way to church when he was accosted by two Chinese who gently and persistently maneuvered him into a doorway. The door opened, and he found himself a prisoner in the Chinese Legation. There he remained, while arrangements were made to charter a ship which would take him to the Chinese mainland. He threw messages out of the window, but none of them reached his friend Dr. Cantlie, who lived nearby. At last, with the help of an English boy servant in the Legation, he was able to smuggle out a letter to Dr. Cantlie, who immediately went into action. Although he was a man of great resourcefulness, Dr. Cantlie was unable to shake the apathy of the English government. He approached Scotland Yard and the Foreign Office, to no avail. *The Times* printed nothing about the revolutionary's arrest, even though the doctor called on the editor and begged him to print a brief announcement. Sun Yat-sen was saved by the English popular press, for the *Globe* newspaper printed a full account of the incident as supplied by the doctor. There were banner headlines reading: CHINESE REVOLUTIONARY KIDNAPED IN LONDON. Within two hours the Chinese Legation was surrounded by a crowd of reporters and sightseers clamoring to see the kidnaped revolutionary. On the following day, after Lord Salisbury, the Secretary of State for Foreign Affairs, had pointed out that private imprisonment was an infringement of British law, the Chinese Legation reluctantly released its prisoner. For a few days Sun Yat-sen was the most famous man in London.

This newfound notoriety did not altogether displease him. He had been a lonely figure, inspiring little warmth or affection, strangely reserved. Now he became more convivial, and as he traveled across Europe his knowledge broadened. He read Bakunin and Karl Marx, without finding in them what he was seeking. About this time he concluded that none of the European social scientists described a form of government suitable for China, and he accordingly invented a new form of democracy based on three principles: national economy, national independence, and popular freedom. His attempts to explain what he meant by the three principles were so discursive, so hedged around with evasions, and stated in such general terms, that no one was ever able to fathom his precise intentions. On more practical matters he could be very clear. What he wanted was the destruction of Manchu rule, the establishment of a republic governed by people of the Chinese race, and the equalization of land ownership, by which he meant that the increase in land values resulting from reforms and social improvements after the revolution should belong to the state and be shared equally by the people. He did not explain how the increase in land values would be calculated, or how the wealth would be shared, but he clearly intended that smallholders should be protected and that the profits of large landowners should be limited by state control. He was a revolutionary with little knowledge or understanding of social reform, and he was inclined to despise the reformers who were crushed by the Empress Dowager in 1898. "They were attempting to buttress the monarchy," he declared. "Our task is to destroy the monarchy."

Although he saw himself as a revolutionary, he never led a successful revolutionary uprising. He organized a revolt which broke out on October 10, 1900, in Waichow, close to Hongkong. His intention after capturing Waichow was to work his way through the province of Fukien along the coast in the hope of receiving help from Japanese friends in Formosa; but the help did not come, and though there were some successful skirmishes, the revolt was abandoned two weeks later. His career as a revolutionary seemed at an end, for after Waichow he had few followers. For the next five years he made his home in Yokohama, sometimes traveling to Honolulu or the United States in the forlorn hope of recouping his political fortunes. In his memoirs he wrote that he had less than a hundred followers among the Chinese students in Japan. He blamed them for their inertia and their lack of courage, but he might more reasonably have blamed himself. "On the whole," wrote one of the Chinese students who was sympathetic to him, "we regarded him as an uncultured outlaw hard to get along with." The students had more respect for Kang Yu-wei, who was more literate and knew considerably more about what was happening in China.

In the summer of 1905 Sun Yat-sen met a young revolutionary called Huang Hsing, a Hunanese, who had founded a revolutionary society in 1903 which came to be known as the Hua Hsing Hui, or Society for the Revival of China. Sun Yat-sen's conspiratorial society had its roots among the overseas Chinese; Huang Hsing's society had roots deeply embedded in China. Far more than Sun Yat-sen, Huang Hsing was in a position to throw the Chinese secret societies into the coming conflict. Unlike Sun Yat-sen, who was slight and slender, Huang Hsing was powerfully built, with a commanding manner, and looked as though he would become an effective leader of revolutionaries in battle.

The meeting between the two revolutionaries was to have profound consequences. They joined forces, and their two revolutionary societies combined to form the Tung Meng Hui, which means simply the United Society. Sun Yat-sen was elected president of the society, and Huang Hsing was elected vice-president. At the inaugural meeting one of the benches at the back of the hall collapsed, and Sun Yat-sen remarked pleasantly that this boded ill for the Manchus. There was some laughter, and then the revolutionaries resumed their deliberations concerning the fate of the Manchus, the maintenance of world peace, and the promotion of friendship between the Japanese and Chinese people.

The new society captured the imagination of the Chinese students in Japan. The growth of the revolutionary movement was phenomenal. "In less than a year the membership reached tens of thousands, and new branches were established all over China, in the Straits Settlements and in America," wrote Sun Yat-sen. "The revolutionary current became so swift that we began to watch its progress with something like stupefaction." For the first time Sun Yat-sen began to believe that he would see the overthrow of the Manchu dynasty during his lifetime.

As it happened, the overthrow of the Manchu dynasty owed very much more to Huang Hsing than to Sun Yat-sen, who wandered around the world raising large sums of money for the revolutionaries, leaving to Huang Hsing the more dangerous task of fighting against the enemy. Between 1907 and 1911 there were eight separate uprisings in Kwangsi, Kwangtung, and Yunnan provinces. Nearly all of them were led by Huang Hsing, and Sun Yat-sen was present at only one of them, and then only for a few hours. In disguise, with a price on his head, Huang Hsing traveled across China, set up his revolutionary committees, established contact with the leaders of the secret societies, and prepared for the day when, as he hoped, all China would burst into a single revolutionary flame.

The stage was now set for the revolution which would ultimately sweep away the Manchus and introduce nearly forty years of civil war. There was to be no peace. Countless generals would arise, appearing on the stage for a brief moment before vanishing into obscurity. Great cities would be sacked, great treasures would be plundered, and the wealth of China would be dissipated in useless battles. Huang Hsing would be forgotten, his body laid to rest in his native hills, while Sun Yat-sen would be buried with great pomp and ceremony in a marble mausoleum close to the tombs of the Ming emperors in Nanking. History, which smiles indulgently on the best and the worst, would offer China to the son of a small farmer in Chekiang, and after him to a young soldier called Chiang Kai-shek. But there was no stability, and China would be restless and divided during all the ensuing years.

THE EMBROIDERED STREAMS

IN CHINA when men approach death they go back to their birthplaces, or are carried there later in their coffins. The place where a man is born is more important than the place where he dies; and it is to the tutelary gods of the village rather than to the earth that he returns. The village where he is born is "the place of return," more sacred than the sacred mountain of T'ai Shan. And the Chinese historian, who may forget all the dates and most of the events of a man's life, will fondly remember the birthplace of his hero.

Chiang Kai-shek was born in the little village of Chikow, which lies in a secluded valley high up among the purple mountains of Chekiang, not far from Ningpo. Except for the fact that it contained the tomb of Wei Cheng, a relentlessly domineering prime minister during the T'ang dynasty, it was unknown to history. Farmers and shopkeepers lived in the village, which consisted of no more than three streets lying in the shadow of towering mountains, which were snow-clad in winter. Down the slopes of the mountains came rushing streams, with white waterfalls. There were so many streams that the whole district was known as Chinchi, or Embroidered Streams, and Chikow means Mouth of a Stream. Fish were plentiful, and there were immense bamboo groves. Indeed, these bamboos were especially prized, because they grew fat and tall and straight. The sea lay nearby, and in a day's journey one could reach Shanghai. Yet, like so many of the Chinese villages in the later years of the nineteenth century, Chikow gave an appearance of remoteness and inaccessibility, living in its dreams.

All the provinces of China have their special characteristics, and the people of Chekiang province are reputed for their hard-headedness and a certain dourness. There are some who say that the people in the coastal regions of Chekiang are not purely Chinese, but have intermarried with Indian, Malay, Arab, and Persian traders who settled along the coast and bred a lean, hard, golden-skinned people, farmers and fishermen and sea rovers. They are a silent people, with the silence of the sea and the high mountains, famous for their feuds and secret societies, reserved and gloomy, and often their faces are carved in the fantastic shapes of the weather-beaten blue hills. In Chekiang the winters are long and bitterly cold; the summers are tropical; only in spring and autumn is it possible to breathe freely. But even in spring the ice flows down the mountain streams, the wind howls in the bamboos, and ghosts are everywhere.

There is a story told in Chekiang of a blood feud between two families. For several generations the feud had been destroying the families, and at last it was decided to put an end to the bloodshed by marrying the son of one family to the daughter of the other. In the course of time a girl was born, and when she was seven years old she was solemnly presented to the relatives of both families. An old man, the great-grandfather of one of the families, appeared at the festivities; no one knew that he carried a heavy sword under his gown. While the seven-year-old girl stood on the altar, smiling at the assembled families, the old man drew his sword and hacked her in two. The feud began again, becoming more violent and bloody than ever.

It was a story which the people of Chekiang regarded as characteristic of their remote villages, where family loyalties and primitive beliefs survived well into the present century. They are a people disciplined to the commands of their elders. There was a hardness in them, a lack of imagination, a calm deliberation. It was a land which produced more than its proper share of bandits and generals. Three famous generals were born in Chekiang. They had only one thing in common—they were all *ko ch'i*, men who went to extremes.

There was Ch'i Chih-kuang, a general of the Ming dynasty, who put his eldest son to death for retreating in battle, exterminated bandits with the utmost savagery, and destroyed the Japanese pirates who frequented the Chekiang coast. For his success in pacifying the country, he was rewarded with the position of viceroy of Fukien. It was remembered that he talked little and made few gestures. In later years Chiang Kai-shek regarded him as a model to be imitated, and he was sometimes inclined to regard the Japanese invasion of China in his own time as comparable to the pirate raids during the Ming dynasty. Certainly the people of Chekiang were aware of the danger coming from Japanese ships.

Another Chekiang general, Huang Chung-hsi, became famous for his efforts to expel the Manchu conquerors. He fought many battles, displayed great bravery, and when the Ming dynasty finally went down to defeat and the Manchus offered to take him into their service, he retired abruptly into a life of scholarship and poverty. The third general, born in the same village as Huang Chung-hsi, was Wang Yang-ming, chiefly remembered today because of his profound influence on Chinese philosophy. He put down two serious rebellions, and for a while was viceroy of Kwangtung and Kwangsi. In his philosophy he sought to break through the opaque, formal structure of Confucianism and to embrace a rigorous ethic cultivating direct and spontaneous action, being fully aware that problems were made to be solved and not merely debated. He was a great scholar in an age of scholarship, and Sun Yat-sen paid him the tribute of saying that he was one of the fathers of the 1911 revolution. Wang Yang-ming died in 1529, but his influence can still be felt on Chinese philosophy.

In the heady air of Chekiang such scholars were rare, and

there was no tradition of scholarship in the obscure village where Chiang Kai-shek was born. Yet in the seclusion of the high mountain valleys the classics were taught and learned by heart, and the students in the village school were rooted in ancient traditions. Life followed the seasons. The small community formed a world in itself. It was as though Chikow lived outside time altogether, and a visitor from the Han dynasty would see very little to surprise him.

At the head of the Chiang family there stood the venerable figure of Chiang Yu-piao, a devout Buddhist, a man of substance, being a landowner and a salt merchant. He owned rice fields, shops, and houses, and was by far the richest and most influential man in the village. During the Taiping Rebellion he was forced to flee into the interior, and for a while suffered great hardship, but all his possessions were restored to him when the rebels were defeated. He was born in 1813, and was therefore in his fifties when he returned at last, after a long exile, to his native village. Once more he was in charge of affairs, rich and respected, with a growing family and a reputation for being so just and wise that the peasants would come to him to adjudicate their disputes rather than seek out a lawyer. It was remembered of him that he built a small tea house where the roads from the three cities of Ningpo, Taichow, and Shaoshing met, not far from Chikow. The monks of a nearby Buddhist monastery operated the tea house at his expense, and he felt that some merit in Heaven must be accorded to a man who dispensed tea freely to weary travelers.

The violence of the Taiping Rebellion had spent itself; for nearly thirteen years the province of Chekiang had suffered from marauding armies; and now once again there was peace under the Manchu dynasty. Chiang Yu-piao could now afford to build a large and comfortable house for his growing family, which included three sons. In time they would inherit his estates, but he hoped they would all live together in amity under a single roof.

The youngest son, Su-an, appears to have been his favorite, and there was some talk of letting him follow a career of scholarship, but he became a merchant and salt-trader like his father. He married at twenty-six, in 1869, but his wife died in childbed after giving him one son. He married again some years later, but there was no issue, his wife dying eighteen months later. In the spring of 1886 he married for the third time. His bride was the daughter of a farmer, Wang Ping-chai, who had some reputation for opening up virgin land near his native village of Koh-si, not far from Fenghua. In the village of Chikow people rarely married strangers from so far afield, and there appears to have been trouble from the beginning. The Wangs came originally from the province of Anhwei. In the eyes of the villagers of Chikow it was as though the new bride came from another planet.

While Su-an remains to the end a curiously vague figure, we know his wife far better. She was small and strong-willed, deeply devoted to her Buddhist faith, capable of enduring every hardship. She could embroider and do needlework; she practiced calligraphy—no inconsiderable accomplishment in a village woman at that time—and she had been brought up to love books. She was not handsome, but she possessed great dignity. With her square brow, hard chin, and high cheekbones, she was not a woman to be dissuaded easily from any path she had decided to follow. As she appeared in a faded photograph taken some years later, she has an expression of dour imperturbability. She wears a long padded gown and mittens, and sits on a conventional blackwood chair beside the conventional blackwood table. On her square face there is all the sadness of those who know they must perish or succeed by their own unaided efforts.

She gave her husband four children, two sons and two daughters. The eldest son, born on October 31, 1887, was given the name of Chou-tai—Entire Prosperity. In time, following the Chinese fashion, he would have many other names. As he grew older, he acquired a "little name," used only in the family. This was Jui-yuan—Auspicious Beginning. When he was eighteen, his mother gave him the name of Chung-cheng—Balanced Justice. Many years later, in revolutionary times, he would acquire the name of Chieh-chih—Between Rocks. In the Cantonese dialect this was pronounced Kai-shek.

At first it was a happy family, living in the shadow of the kindly old patriarch. Kai-shek grew up in a wealthy household, with servants to look after him. He suffered from chicken pox when he was three, but otherwise there were no serious illnesses. He was high-spirited and adventurous, and they tell the story that when he was three or four he thrust a pair of chopsticks down his throat "to see how far they would go." They went far enough to give him extreme pain, and for a while there was some fear that his vocal cords might be damaged. His earliest recorded words are those he spoke the next morning when he leaped out of bed: "Look, grandfather, I have not lost my voice." Once he fell into a water jar and struggled free in the nick of time. He was very close to his grandfather, whom he would accompany on long walks through the countryside, often to the little tea house at Wuling. At such times the grandfather would talk with horror about the invasion of the Taipings, and about the need to show benevolence to all strangers, and about the Buddhist Heaven which awaited all good men. Kai-shek was an apt pupil, and he was determined to model himself on his grandfather.

Of his childhood we are told that he especially liked fishing, and was perfectly happy to spend the day wandering beside the many streams near the village. He caught crayfish, and brought them triumphantly to his mother, who boiled them and served them for dinner. Hagiographers have described how he watched the fish swimming upstream, being swept back time after time by the current, but continually fighting their way to the spawning ground, and he is supposed to have said: "I must be like these fish. I must fight against all the odds of life, and never despair." But this is to grant him more imagination and more will power than he possessed until a much greater age. Except for his quick temper and his shrewdness there was very little to distinguish him from the other children of the village.

The calm, leisurely life in the Chiang household came to an abrupt end on October 24, 1894, just before the boy's seventh birthday. On that day his grandfather died. The close-knit patriarchal family immediately began to break up into its several parts. With the kingpin removed, the three sons began to fight for the succession. Su-an, the youngest son, was the least successful, for he had no great commercial ability, and he never received his full inheritance. He died during the following year, and his widow was left to bring up her four children on a pittance. From being rich and respected, she became poor and rejected. It was remembered that she was a "foreigner" from another village.

There began the long, hard years which were to have a decisive effect on the character of Kai-shek, who could remember the idyllic years of his childhood, when his grandfather was alive and all the villagers bowed to him. Little income came into the house. Kai-shek's mother inherited some rice fields and two small properties; the farmers who worked the rice fields paid little rent, and the tenants of her two properties refused to pay any rent at all, or perhaps they were unable to pay. There was worse to come, for two of her children, one son and one daughter, died of scarlet fever. The house was wracked with so much poverty and tragedy that the widow contemplated suicide.

Inevitably the widow drew on her son for comfort and support. She found comfort too in her religion, and it was related that she sometimes wandered over the countryside and lit spills in abandoned temples, and sometimes out of her hard-earned income she would contribute to the upkeep of the temples in the hope that the gods would relent. She recited the sutras, and in winter, when the mountain passes were thick with snow and the two surviving children huddled over the earthenware stove, she would speak to them of her faith in the Buddhist promise of eternal release from the bondage of the flesh. As the years passed, the attachment between mother and son became even greater. Later he was to describe his life with her in a mood more closely akin to poetry than anything else he wrote: "Widow and orphan took pity on each other as the body and the shadow."

She earned her living by the sweat of her brow. She wove cloth, gathered mulberry leaves to feed the silkworms, carried pails of dung in the fields, sowed rice, fought off the tax-gatherers, and seemed to take on the whole village singlehanded. Her son did all the work around the house, swept the floors, boiled the rice, washed the bowls, and learned to eat up the last crumb of rice. She was a hard taskmaster, and the son in turn became accustomed to hardship. Many years later those who knew him well concluded that whatever was great or small in him was determined by his love for his mother, frail in her frailty and strong because she could endure. Sometimes there are even moments when the person of Chiang Kai-shek seems to have no independent existence, and we see only the relentless old face of the mother, the private griefs, the long winters, the poverty, and the circle of indifferent kinsmen whose indifference she would somehow survive. The memory of their former grandeur was both a stimulant and a torment, coloring their lives.

In 1898, when Kai-shek was eleven years old, China was undergoing intolerable trials. Germany took Kiaochow on the Shantung peninsula, Russia took Port Arthur, France took Kwangchow-wan, Great Britain extended her holdings in Hongkong and took Wei-hai-wei. It was the year when the young Emperor Kuang Hsu embarked on his program of revolutionary reforms and failed disastrously. Historical events of vast magnitude were taking place, but these events scarcely affected the villagers of Chikow. High in their mountains, they saw no foreigners and never heard the rumble of guns.

Kai-shek showed no signs of special brilliance at school, and was said to have been better at games than at learning. There is a story that he once frightened the school bully by appearing at night with his head covered with a bamboo basket wrapped in a white cloth, and they say that he once endured stoically the punishment due to another student. They say, too, that he appointed himself commander-in-chief of the military games of the schoolboys when he was still quite young, but this would appear improbable if only because it was exactly the kind of story which would be invented later. On the whole he seems to have been quiet and rather timid, given to long periods of meditation and solitary walks beside the embroidered streams, brooding on the constant warfare between his mother and the villagers. By all accounts he was a reserved and lonely youth, who held himself a little apart from the rest.

The hagiographers, of course, have invented the usual pious legends to account for his future eminence. We are told that in 1898 a geomancer named Yu, a native of Anhwei, came wandering into the village where he remained for several days. When the villagers asked him what he was doing there, he answered that the place was highly auspicious and in a score of years would produce a man who would bring renown to the village and all of China. Then the geomancer disappeared as mysteriously as he had come, content to have found the birthplace of a hero.

It is in the highest degree unlikely that any such event occurred. There was nothing in the least legendary about Kai-shek's lonely and unhappy adolescence, lived in the shadow of an embittered woman whom he loved with a desperate and unyielding love. He wrote on the eve of his fiftieth birthday: "Whenever I returned home she would ask me where I had been and what I had been doing, and when I returned from school she would question me on the lesson of the day. She taught me how to conduct and behave myself. She would make me do manual labor in order to train me physically. In a word, all her time and energy was devoted to my well-being. In my youth I was rather mischievous and full of youthful apprehension, and could never endure any instructions of great severity. I became as helpless as a child in my early age, so that I was always ill-treated by other boys and was even once expelled from their games."

The portrait of the proud leader of a children's army is absent in his own account. Instead we see the boy rejected by his playmates, full of apprehension, with memories of "instructions of great severity," the mournful warnings and castigations of his schoolmasters. Inevitably he withdrew into himself, clung to his mother, and lived in dreams. He does not seem to have possessed any profound hatred for the villagers: he was indifferent to them and lived in his own imaginary world, in which his mother was both the center and the circumference. At least one biographer mentions with a mark of approval that when he was eleven he learned for the first time of the existence of the powerful President of the United States, and burst out: "Why do you mention his name? He is mortal—so am I! I shall be greater than he is!" It may be true. It is the kind of outburst we might expect from a sensitive and bewildered child determined to rise in the world.

Because he was so frail and so often ill, his schooling was continually being interrupted. With his mother he read Mencius, *The Great Learning,* and *The Doctrine of the Mean,* and began the great historical annals called the *Tso Chuan.* He learned many poems from *The Book of Songs* by heart, and he began to write those rather wooden poems which he was to compose at intervals throughout his life. The earliest of his surviving poems invokes the cool shade of the bamboos he knew so well:

See how the hill is abundant with bamboos:
They can produce coolness on summer days.

It is an undistinguished poem which would have been forgotten but for the charity of his biographers, but it shows a certain simplicity and directness of mind. The occasional poems written when he became Generalissimo are no better and no worse. Very early in his life he learned that he did not have the makings of a poet.

A child growing up in a remote Chinese village with the classics around him becomes the inheritor of a great civilization. To a quite extraordinary degree Confucius and Mencius sum up the energies of the past, as they portray a Golden Age when wise emperors ruled according to immemorial rites. It is a world a child can dream in, listening to the wisdom of the sages and admiring the heroic actions of the princes. Mencius describes how a great ruler often emerges from obscurity, having "eaten bitterness" in his youth, been abandoned by his friends, and suffered many privations. He lives hungry and thirsty in the wilderness, until at last, hardened by adversity, he is ready to assume the responsibilities of leadership. Such dreams have powerfully affected generations of Chinese, who consciously or unconsciously identify themselves with the great rulers of the past.

Meanwhile in Chikow Kai-shek's boyhood was coming to an end, and his dreams of a distinguished career were being eclipsed by stark reality. An uncle, from whom his mother had borrowed money, now insisted that he should be apprenticed to a trade in Ningpo. He had no liking for trade, and he hated the thought of leaving his mother. Finally, it was decided that he should continue his schooling in his mother's native village of Koh-si, where he would be looked after by her relatives. At all costs the mother wanted him to have the advantages of an education. Once she said to him: "Since your father's death I have been such a poor widow, and we have been living in such unbearable circumstances, that I really did not know how we could preserve ourselves. My only conviction has been that a fatherless child like you should be carefully brought up, otherwise we can expect no success in the world." Now, on the eve of his departure from Chikow, she reminded him again of his duty to become a great scholar or at least to follow a course of life which will bring renown to his family. She said: "Since your father's death I have suffered all kinds of hardship, and now that you are going to school I do not expect you to secure wealth or a high position in government but to render loyal service to your country and maintain the reputation of the ancestors."

Such were the words which the mother addressed to the fatherless child, and there is little doubt that they are reported accurately. This, or something very like this, must have been said at the solemn moment when the boy left his native village for the first time. A new life was opening up for him, and now at last there had come the long feared, long expected separation from the mother, who would have to remain in Chikow to look after the small vestiges of the family property.

In her parting advice she had spoken about his ancestors, reminding him of his duty to maintain the ancestral reputation. She was not speaking about her own ancestors or the immediate ancestors of her husband, who were farmers and salt merchants. She was speaking about a family tradition that the Chiangs were descended from no less a person than Tan, Duke of Chou, the great innovator, the man who founded the fortunes of the Chou dynasty in the twelfth century B.C.

Family traditions die hard in China, and it is not unusual to find people who sincerely believe they can trace their ancestry over a period of three thousand years. To claim descent from Tan, Duke of Chou, was to claim a connection with one of the greatest characters in Chinese history. He was a sage, a statesman, a warrior, a scholar. He was the reputed author of *The Great Declaration,* the oldest surviving document on Chinese statecraft, which is incorporated in the Confucian classic of history known as the *Shu Ching*. According to *The Great Declaration* the emperor rules his people as the Pole Star rules the heavens. The task of the emperor is to seek the blessing of heaven, perform the proper rites, and interfere as little as possible with the affairs of the people. He is said, too, to have compiled *The Book of Changes*, a book of prophecies and prognostications begun by his father, the famous King Wen, whose military exploits are celebrated in *The Book of Songs*. Tan, Duke of Chou, assisted his brother in overthrowing the last tyrant of the Shang-Yin dynasty, and it was remembered of him that when an infant emperor came to the throne he acted as regent, surrendering his power as soon as the infant reached his majority, an action which was regarded as exceptionally rare in this time.

The Chinese classics teem with references to Tan, Duke of Chou, who was adored by both Confucius and Mencius as the most enlightened statesman of the past. One day Confucius wondered aloud whether he was not suffering from some strange sickness, "for I have not dreamed, as I did in the past, that I saw the Duke of Chou." No other scholar or statesman recorded in history was such a paragon of virtue; and it was an article of faith among Chinese historians that the Duke of Chou charged the Chou dynasty with so much virtue and energy that it was able to endure for more than seven hundred years.

According to the family tradition the Chiangs were descended from Pei-ling, the third son of the Duke of Chou, who was given the fief of Chiang in what is now Honan. At some period before the founding of the Han dynasty the descendants of Pei-ling settled in the province of Chekiang.

A lonely and unhappy child will take comfort from the knowledge that he is descended from a great ancestor. His dreams and ambitions will revolve around the ghostly figures of the past continually reminding him that he has inherited their virtue and must fulfill a great destiny. It is all one to him that there are hundreds of thousands, and perhaps millions, of Chinese who can claim the same ancestor. In his eyes he alone has been chosen to fulfill the destiny, and he will live out his life in the shadow of the ancient past. Chiang Kai-shek genuinely believed that he was descended from the Duke of Chou, and this belief was to color many of his actions in later life, for he saw himself as the man chosen to revive and reinvigorate a nation given over to dissension and war, leading it out of darkness into light, establishing a government which would endure for centuries.

But the child who went off to the small village school at Koh-si was less concerned with his ancestry than with his own survival in a world grown strange and hostile. He had no happy memories of Koh-si and seems not to have liked his mother's relatives. He studied at the Ssu-yuan Tang, which means the Hall of Tracing Things to Their Source, and was miserably lonely, sighing for the bamboos of Chikow, the little creek that ran outside his mother's house, and the huge cliff which was known simply as Ten Thousand Feet. With his mother's help he had read through Mencius and the *Analects*. Now he studied the *Shu Ching*, the classic of history, and *The Book of Changes*. In the following year, when he was fifteen, he studied the *Tso Chuan*, the brilliant historical annals written by the blind scholar Tso Chiu-ming, and at sixteen he read the *Annals* of Ssu-ma Kuang. He was in fact following the traditional pattern of education which was being followed throughout China, learning the classics by rote, his days filled with reading and recitation and mindless repetition. The same books were read and studied in exactly the same way two thousand years earlier.

In the summer of 1903 he took the examination for entry into Fenglu School at Fenghua. It seems to have been a frightening experience, and he complained about the rigidity of the examinations. Here he learned a smattering of English and developed an interest in mathematics. There were more classics to be learned by heart, including the *Chou Li*, which was supposed to have been written by the Duke of Chou during his retirement from the regency, and there was the considerably more famous *Li Chi* with its endless dissertations on the proper rituals to be observed at court. He absorbed all these classics gracefully, and his passionate concern for propriety may perhaps be traced to his classical education.

For some reason he left the Fenglu School and attended a

private school in Ningpo run by a certain K'u Ching-liang, a scholar who possessed a formidable reputation for bringing the best out of his pupils. The school was called the Hall of the Golden Arrow. K'u Ching-liang made his pupils read two works which were not generally studied by schoolboys. They were *On the Art of War* by Sun Wu and the writings of Tseng Kuo-fan, the great Viceroy who had put down the Taiping Rebellion. From K'u Ching-liang, who had a special talent for discussing historical movements, the boy learned for the first time about the vast changes taking place in the world and the indignities which China was suffering at the hands of invaders. Ningpo was no village hidden among bamboo and pine groves, but a great bustling town, the port full of ships, merchandise flowing through the streets. Here he learned from the lips of his teacher about the Tung Meng Hui, the revolutionary organization directed by Dr. Sun Yat-sen. For three days K'u Ching-liang spoke about the coming revolution, and on the evening of the third day Kai-shek had made the decision which was to change the course of his life—he would become a revolutionary.

In Ningpo revolutionary pamphlets and books were already being distributed secretly. Terrible punishments were visited on people who were found in possession of these books, for the Empress Dowager still ruled from Peking and the police were efficient in discovering the obscure shops where the books were sold. "When I was eighteen," Chiang Kai-shek wrote later, "the books that chiefly impressed me were Tsou Yung's *The Revolutionary Army*, Wang Yang-ming's *On Teaching and Learning*—a book of conversations between Wang Yang-ming and his disciples—and a book called *Awaiting Safe Brightness* by Huang Chung-hsi, attacking the Emperor and praising the people. The first book threw light on questions of nationality and laid a solid foundation for my revolutionary ideas, the second expounded the theory of extending one's knowledge to the utmost and so laid the foundation for my studies, while the third imbued my mind with the principles of democracy."

Tsou Yung's *The Revolutionary Handbook* is rarely read today, but in its own time it was regarded as a work of quite extraordinary brilliance. In seven chapters the young revolutionary —he was only eighteen when he wrote the book in the spring of 1903—discussed the nature of the coming revolution, the indignities of slavery under the Manchus, the way in which he hoped to see Manchu power destroyed. It was the most violent and outspoken attack on the Manchus ever composed by a Chinese. He advocated the killing of the Manchu Emperor, the expulsion of all Manchus from the soil of China, and the establishment of a republic. He also advocated freedom of speech, freedom of thought, freedom of the press, and a fourth freedom, which he called "freedom to revolt." Finally, he advocated that the constitution of the new Chinese republic should be based solidly on the Constitution of the United States.

Tsou Yung was a Szechuanese, and he wrote with the characteristic fire and passion of a Szechuanese student. The Manchu government issued a warrant for his arrest, for they recognized the importance of the book and were determined to make an example of him. Not long after the publication of the book, on June 29, 1903, he was arrested in the International Settlement in Shanghai. Knowing that he would be immediately executed if he was handed over to the Manchu police, the authorities of the International Settlement refused to extradite him, and there followed a sensational lawsuit, the Empress Dowager claiming the right to punish her own subjects in Shanghai, the judges of the International Settlement claiming that she had no jurisdiction. The case was still undecided when Tsou Yung died in his Shanghai prison two years later.

For Chiang Kai-shek, as for many thousands of young Chinese, Tsou Yung's book was like a trumpet blast summoning the faithful to overthrow a tyranny. He had decided to become a revolutionary, but as yet he had no clear idea what role he would play in the revolution. With the dangerous book in his pocket he returned to Chikow to brood over his future.

PRIVATE SECOND CLASS

IN 1905 THERE OCCURRED an event which was strangely symbolical of the vast changes taking place in China. For centuries the West had been hammering at the gates. Now, in the remote town of Chufu, the birthplace of Confucius, a small delegation of elders under Duke Yen, the lineal descendant of Confucius in the seventy-sixth generation, met to decide the measures to be taken in view of the extraordinary flowering of western ideas on Chinese soil. The old ways had been found wanting. It was not enough to pay tribute to Heaven, to recite the classics, and to model oneself on the ancient sages. What was needed, according to Duke Yen, was the study of the ideas that were being introduced by the West. He proposed to send a memorial to the Empress Dowager, petitioning her to permit certain changes in the ancestral school at Chufu. He asked for permission to teach science, modern languages, political economy, and international law.

The school at Chufu had a great reputation throughout China. It was the center of Confucian studies, the seat of the cult, the place of pilgrimage. For centuries the school had resembled a vast dynamo, transmitting the power and energy of Confucian thought across China. Now the dynamo was gradually coming to a stop. The Empress Dowager gave her consent to the teaching of foreign ideas at the ancestral school. China was entering the modern age. It was the year of Japan's victory over Russia at Port Arthur, and the Chinese were well aware that they would have to follow the example of Japan in order to survive.

Even in Chikow these modern ideas were beginning to penetrate. Chiang Kai-shek had been thinking strenuously about his future, and after much brooding he had come to the conclusion that he wanted to be a soldier—a modern soldier, armed with the knowledge of modern strategy and tactics, new weapons, new military concepts. His mother wanted him to be a lawyer, for she had spent a large part of her life in litigation and she possessed a deep knowledge of lawyers' ways. But his mind was made up. He was able to convince her that there was nothing more honorable than a soldier's calling, and at the end of the spring term in 1906 he made his way to Japan, intending to enroll in a cadet school.

He made the journey in great poverty, his mother having sold some of the family possessions to pay for his expenses; an uncle promised dubious support if he did well. He knew no Japanese, and was hopelessly at sea in Tokyo. His attempts to enroll in a cadet school met with failure, for the Japanese showed not the least desire to make him a soldier. He had a few letters of introduction, mostly to Chinese residents in Tokyo, and through them he soon met a certain Chen Chi-mei, who at that precise moment—for Dr. Sun Yat-sen had just left for America—was in charge of the conspiratorial activities of the Tung Meng Hui. Chen Chi-mei was very high in Dr. Sun Yat-sen's counsels, and at this time he was probably second-in-command of the entire organization. He had a sharp mind, an incisive turn of speech, and a scholarly bearing. Born in Chekiang in the silk-manufacturing town of Wuchow, to a family of some wealth, he was one of those people who seem to possess the innate gift of authority and command. Chiang Kai-shek was so impressed by him that he attempted to model himself on his newfound friend. He was nineteen, Chen

Chi-mei was thirty. Between them there sprang up a friendship which was to last until Chen Chi-mei's death.

In China friendships between men often run very deep, and it is not unusual for men to become blood brothers, swearing an intense devotion to one another. Either at this time or some months later Chen Chi-mei and Chiang Kai-shek became blood brothers, swearing to be loyal to one another beyond death, promising to protect each other's families and to defend each other's honor and life. Such oaths are not given lightly, and they are more enduring than marriage bonds.

The meeting with Chen Chi-mei in the summer of 1906 was decisive. From that day Chiang Kai-shek became the willing servant of the revolution, dedicated like all the other members of the Tung Meng Hui to the overthrow of the Manchu dynasty. In a single day he had found a lifelong friend and a conspiratorial party to which he could devote all his energies.

Chen Chi-mei knew his way about Japan, and he knew that the Japanese military authorities did not permit the Chinese to enter the cadet school unless they had already passed through a Chinese military academy. He therefore suggested that Chiang Kai-shek return immediately to China and prepare himself for the competitive examination for the Paoting Military Academy, which had recently been founded by Yuan Shih-kai. Paoting was in north China, not far from Peking, and most of the candidates for the academy belonged to well-to-do northern families with connections at court. Chiang Kai-shek was one of the very few candidates who was wholly lacking in influence of any sort, but he did well enough at the entrance examination to convince the examiners that he would make a good officer. He was quiet, orderly, intelligent, and ruthlessly determined. He made a good impression on most of his teachers. There is a story that he fell afoul of a Japanese lecturer in hygiene who placed a cubic inch of earth on his desk and announced that it could support four hundred million microbes, adding that this inch of earth could be likened to China, which supported four hundred million people. Chiang Kai-shek was so incensed by the comparison that he loudly demanded whether Japan, with a population of fifty million people, could be

PRECEDING PAGE: *Chiang Kai-shek and his mother, 1905*

LEFT: *Cadet in Japanese Military College, 1909*

RIGHT: *Chiang Kai-shek in Shanghai, about 1913*

ABOVE: *The Emperor Kuang H'su*

RIGHT: *Yuan Shih-k'ai*

RIGHT: *Marshal Feng Yu-hsiang*

BELOW: *Marshal Chang Tso-lin*

BELOW RIGHT: *General Wu Pei-fu*

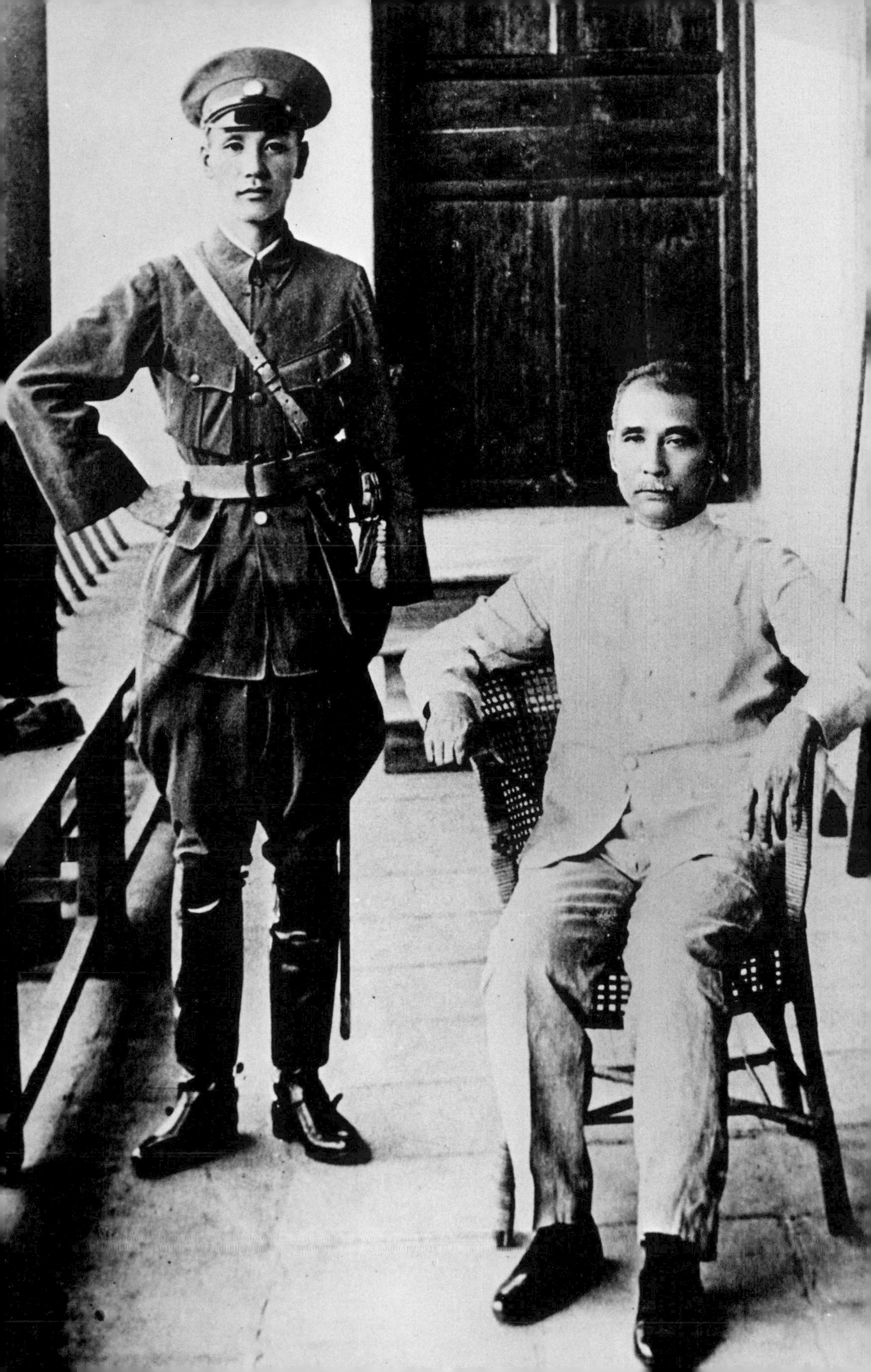

Chiang Kai-shek and Dr. Sun Yat-sen, 1924

Wedding photograph, December 1927

From right to left: Chiang Kai-shek, Madame Chiang, Madame Chang Hsueh-liang, Madame H. H. Kung, the "Young Marshal" Chang Hsueh-liang
Photograph taken in 1929

Official photograph, 1930

Chiang Kai-shek and Madame Chiang pay homage to Dr. Sun Yat-sen at the end of the war

Chiang Kai-shek, Roosevelt, Churchill, and Madame Chiang at Cairo Conference, November 1943

Mao Tse-tung and Chiang Kai-shek, September 1945

Dr. Leighton Stuart, Chiang Kai-shek, and General Marshall

LEFT: *General Chiang Ching-kuo*

Chiang Kai-shek and Madame Chiang on Sun-Moon Lake, Formosa

likened to a much smaller cube of earth. Taken aback, the Japanese lecturer is supposed to have said, "Then you must be a revolutionary?"

"I simply wanted to know whether the comparison was correct," Chiang Kai-shek replied. "You should not beg the issue by raising another question."

The Japanese lecturer was deeply offended and ran to the director of the military academy, demanding condign punishment for the pupil who dared to question him. Instead the pupil was given a mild reprimand.

The story, which is told by Chiang Kai-shek's official biographer, is almost certainly untrue. A Japanese lecturer who behaved in this fashion would have been given short shrift and sent back to Japan on the next boat. No Chinese would have tolerated such an insult, and the Japanese would have been lucky to escape physical assault. The story appears to have been invented to underscore the fervent nationalism of the future Generalissimo.

Of far greater importance was the fact that Chiang Kai-shek was more than holding his own among the pampered young officers at the military academy. His progress was rapid, and the instructors liked him. If he was not particularly brilliant, he was a dedicated student determined to show his superiors that he had the makings of a first-rate officer; and when the time came to select the candidates for further training in Japan, he was one of the few who were chosen. With four other students he sailed for Japan from Shanghai in the following year, to enter the Preparatory Military Academy in Tokyo.

The period of apprenticeship was over, and he was now a full-fledged officer. The Preparatory Military Academy was in fact an officers' training college under Chinese auspices, but with a Japanese staff. All the students were Chinese, but they lived according to Japanese ways. He was never a popular student, because he held himself aloof and had a biting tongue. Silent, reserved, avoiding the other students whenever possible, he was wholly absorbed in his studies.

He had a passion for hard work which never left him. From the Japanese he learned the advantages of silent meditation in the early morning, cleanliness, order, and frugality. At first he disliked Japanese food; the portions were so small, and he wearied of thin slices of uncooked fish. In time he came to discover unsuspected virtues in frugality and learned to enjoy his short commons. Life at the training college consisted of endless drills, endless lessons, and endless menial tasks faithfully accomplished. In an address to students delivered in 1930, he was careful to point out that these menial tasks served an educational purpose. He said, "When I studied in the military college in Japan, I scrubbed the floors every morning, poured the mess out of the spittoons, swept the latrines, and washed clothes. I believe that this kind of work should be done not only by the poor, but also by the rich. Do not be finicky: otherwise when you grow up you will find that you have accomplished nothing and you will be sad."

The young Chiang Kai-shek genuinely believed in the salutary benefits to be derived from cleaning out spittoons, just as he believed in the need for anonymity and humble service to the cause. Dr. Sun Yat-sen had returned to Japan after his money-raising campaign in America, and there were the usual clandestine meetings of his followers in Tokyo. The Japanese had no objection to these meetings, and Chiang Kai-shek appears to have attended them regularly. On one occasion Dr. Sun Yat-sen urged the Chinese revolutionaries to follow the example of the American revolutionaries. "The revolutionary should seek anonymity," he declared. "In the United States only one revolutionary became known—Washington. But besides Washington there were the innumerable unknown Washingtons, and we who are members of a revolutionary party should be nameless heroes like these." Chiang Kai-shek was deeply impressed. "After I had received this lesson from Dr. Sun Yat-sen," he wrote many years later, "I toiled hard at my work, caring nothing for my reputation or position, all my thoughts dedicated to my country and the revolutionary cause. My attention was wholly concentrated on my career. Because I preferred the taste of bitterness to sweetness, many obstacles were removed from my path."

Dr. Sun Yat-sen's brief study of the American Revolution led him into a number of errors, and he seems to have believed that

Washington exerted dictatorial powers over his followers. Since he knew only the name of Washington, he assumed there were no other revolutionary leaders. Chiang Kai-shek's fervent desire to embrace anonymity as a revolutionary derived from Dr. Sun Yat-sen's strange misconceptions about the nature of the American revolution; but it was not a desire which remained with him for very long. Even in those early days he thirsted for fame.

If life in the military college was hard, it was inconceivably harder in the regiment which he joined in 1909 as a private second class. It was felt that young officers should experience life in the ranks, and accordingly Private Chiang Kai-shek of the Thirteenth Field Artillery Regiment was made to undergo the grotesque and meaningless trials always reserved for privates. "The winter was very severe, but he always turned out promptly for early morning parade," wrote his official biographer admiringly. But this is to misunderstand the demands made on privates in the Japanese army. If he had failed to turn out promptly, there were punishments designed to make him regard early rising as the most important thing that ever happened to him. Ferocious and degrading punishments were meted out to late risers.

In retrospect Chiang Kai-shek was inclined to regard the days he spent as a private as among the happiest of his life. He remembered, too, the endless desolation of the Japanese landscape blanketed by heavy snow, and there were times when he found his servitude very nearly unbearable. The brutality of the officers, the harsh miseries of the soldiers, the sense of absolute abandonment to the cruelties of a foreign country—all this affected him deeply, and sometimes when he looked back on those days he would cry out with joy and anguish, joy because he had survived so much cruelty and known so great an exhilaration, and anguish because the wounds were still aching.

Again and again in his private conversations and in his speeches he would speak of that savage winter when he first wore the badge of absolute servitude. "The life was so hard that it is completely beyond the imagination of the youths of this country," he said in an address to cadets, and he went on to describe what it was like to be a private in Japan:

We all enlisted in winter with the rank of private second class —the time when most Japanese soldiers enter the army. The place where we enlisted was Takata, a village in the administration of Nugota on the island of Hokkaido. It was terribly cold, and every day there was heavy snow—the kind of snow you hardly see even in Mongolia. No matter how cold it was, or how heavily the snow was falling, we had to rise before five o'clock in the morning, and then we would have to take our basins to the wells and wash our faces in ice-cold water. In this field artillery group it was necessary for all the cadets to learn about horses. Immediately after we had washed, we were marched to the stables by our officers, and there we scrubbed down the horses—every joint and every muscle had to be rubbed down with straw, and this took about an hour. At the end of this time the horse was warm, and we ourselves were too warm to feel the cold—our bodies, hands, and feet all warm—and often we were perspiring. I regard this interlude of my life as important, for it was then that I learned not to fear danger and to take pleasure in bitterness.

After scrubbing the horses many things still remained to be done. We had to take them out through the snowfields to pasture, and then we had to return to our barracks for breakfast. In the evening we returned to the stables and rubbed the horses down again, exactly as we had done in the morning.

Now let me tell you something about food in a Japanese barracks. Those of you who have joined the army in China may not always find there is sufficient meat and vegetables, but there are always unlimited supplies of rice and you can eat as much as you want. But in Japan you are limited to a medium bowl of rice at each meal, and occasionally there is wheat. Sometimes you will find three pieces of salted turnip and a slice of salt fish, and on Sundays there will be a little meat, a little curd, and a few vegetables—but there was always a limit to the amount of rice.

Takata was a barren and impoverished place. Many of the soldiers came from the gentry, and there were even some from the nobility, but they were treated exactly like the rest. During the first two weeks after I entered the artillery group, I was continually hungry and could hardly work during the day. In the evening we were allowed to buy biscuits at the barracks, but they were very limited in quantity and we were allowed to buy only two or three pieces at a time. These biscuits were so hard that we would not have given them a second thought at home, but we ate them with tremendous enjoyment. You can grow accustomed to this kind of life. After two weeks the hunger left me, and in three weeks I no longer felt any need for the biscuits. Such was the kind of life I led.

I was a private second class. Above me there was a private first class, then a corporal, then a sergeant, then a sergeant-major, then a sergeant-major first class, and then there were officers. Those warrant officers and officers had complete control over us. Also, the older soldiers made life hard for the younger ones. We had to wash their clothes, brush their boots, and sometimes mend their bedclothes. The second-class privates received orders from the first-class privates, and if you did not obey them instantly, you were scolded and beaten, and it was quite common to see Japanese officers scolding and beating soldiers.

During this period Chiang Kai-shek especially enjoyed artillery drill, and he was devoted to heavy weapons. It was said that he came to know so much about the inner workings of cannon that he infuriated his instructor, who knew considerably less. The menial work was borne patiently because it gave him the opportunity to study the latest weapons, to mix with other soldiers, and to absorb both consciously and unconsciously the intricate machinery of war. He was not thinking of becoming a revolutionary but of becoming a good soldier.

Nevertheless, the thought of revolution still occupied a place in his mind. While studying at the military college in Tokyo, he took part in the formal inauguration of a small revolutionary society called the Cheng Cheng Society, meaning "Society of Heroes." For some reason the name was later changed to "Society of Builders of Walls." This revolutionary society was pathetically small and ineffective, and although a few other recruits were later permitted to become members, it chiefly consisted of the three founding members: Chiang Kai-shek, Chang Chun, and Huang Fu. Chang Chun and Huang Fu were both to become high officials in the Kuomintang government. The secret society had its own initiation rites, secret code words, and blood-curdling oaths, and the three founding members became sworn brothers. But in the hills of Takata there was no opportunity to practice revolution. The handful of Chinese were being watched closely by the Japanese and by agents of the Manchu government, and little news trickled in from China.

In the early months of 1911 the Tung Meng Hui was mobilizing its forces to stage an insurrection in Canton. On March 29, towards evening, a small group of revolutionaries, numbering about 130 men, attacked the Governor General's yamen. The yamen was captured and set on fire without difficulty, but the revolutionaries were no match for the garrison troops who hurried onto the scene a few minutes later, and some eighty-five revolutionaries were made prisoner or shot out of hand. Huang Hsing, the leader of the revolt, was wounded, but escaped miraculously. For a few days he hid in one of the villages south of Canton, and then he made his way secretly to Hongkong.

Although the insurrection failed, accomplishing nothing except the deaths of many young revolutionaries, legends flowered out of it. The gallantry of the rebels and the destruction of the yamen were remembered, and the fact that the insurrection was ill-conceived and badly planned was forgotten. The bodies of seventy-two of the rebels were buried on Yellow Flower Mound, which became a place of pilgrimage when the revolutionaries later succeded in overthrowing the Manchu dynasty. There had been a small skirmish followed by a massacre; such skirmishes and massacres had happened before. But in the eyes of the revolutionaries the defeat was the prelude to an inevitable triumph. In time so many legends accumulated around the insurrection that the truth was in danger of being forgotten. Thirty years later Chiang Kai-shek, delivering an address to the army and the people, quoted Dr. Sun Yat-sen as saying: "At Yellow Flower Mound three hundred men faced thirty thousand, pitting pistols and grenades against rifles and artillery." Not all these statements were accurate. The fighting did not take place at Yellow Flower Mound, three hundred men had not faced thirty thousand, the revolutionaries were armed with rifles rather than pistols, and the troops did not employ artillery. But there was no doubting the courage of the revolutionaries. They had made the first breach in the wall; others would come later, and the wall would fall down.

Chiang Kai-shek learned about these events many days later in a letter from Chen Chi-mei, who had left Tokyo in March and established himself in Hongkong. Chen Chi-mei said the failure of the Canton insurrection must not be regarded as decisive, for the revolutionary tide was rising. Chiang Kai-shek said later that he had offered to take part in the insurrection, but had been dissuaded by Chen Chi-mei on the ground that he could not speak Cantonese: he would be more useful when the revolution reached Chekiang and more especially Shanghai. Meanwhile he was ordered to hold himself in readiness for the next attack on the Manchu dynasty.

There is some mystery about Chiang Kai-shek's movements in the summer of 1911. According to some authorities he remained in Japan; according to others he made a secret journey to Shanghai to see Chen Chi-mei and was given the task of making a tour of inspection through Kiangsu and Chekiang, to provide ammunition to the secret societies and to prepare them for the uprising. He is said to have spent the summer months moving in disguise from one city to another, one village to another, wielding great powers as a revolutionary leader, returning to Japan in August, when his mission was completed. Chiang Kai-shek's official biographer does not mention the secret tour of inspection, and it is unlikely that the Japanese would have permitted him to take a prolonged leave of absence. He was still a private second class, and leaves of absence were not generally granted.

The uprising which was to bring about the downfall of the Manchu dynasty broke out on October 10 in Wuchang. On the morning of the previous day a bomb accidentally exploded in the revolutionary headquarters in the Hankow Russian Concession; the police raided the headquarters, captured several revolutionaries, and discovered a number of proclamations and revolutionary documents including the names of soldiers in the Manchu army who were secretly affiliated with the revolutionary parties. There were many revolutionary parties and they were not yet organized under a single leadership with a common program. Nevertheless it was necessary to act quickly. The soldiers whose names appeared on the lists knew they would be executed as soon as their identities were learned, and they came out in open rebellion on the evening of the next day. Huang Hsing was in Hongkong, and Dr. Sun Yat-sen was making a leisurely tour of the United States. The revolutionary soldiers amounted altogether to about two thousand, and there were at least fifteen thousand loyal troops defending Wuchang.

In later years Dr. Sun Yat-sen would say that "everything happened quite accidently, without plans and without anyone knowing what was happening." This was true, but resentment against the Manchus had been mounting for a century and the revolutionaries were well armed and had the courage of despair. They attacked the yamen at Wuchang, and the Manchus made the first of the strategic errors that demonstrated the decadence of the dynasty. Instead of fighting back, Jui Cheng, the governor-general of Hupeh, took refuge on a gunboat moored in the Yangtse river. Wuchang fell to the revolutionaries that same night. They needed a leader, and their choice fell on Colonel Li Yuan-hung, second in command of the government troops. He was a man of liberal sentiments and popular with the troops. When the revolutionaries burst into his bedroom, they found him hiding under his bed with only his boots visible. Asked to sign the manifesto calling upon the whole country to unite against the Manchus, he demurred and explained that he had no authority to sign such a document and begged them to wait until the morning, when he would be able to give the matter some reflection. They could not wait, forged his signature, and appointed him leader of the revolution. In this strange way the revolutionaries set out to conquer China.

Wuchang, Hanyang, and Hankow lie clustered together, forming a kind of triple city, and on the following day the revolutionaries captured Hanyang and Hankow. Hanyang was the most important of the three cities, for it contained the arsenal; soon the revolutionaries were well armed. The government forces counter-attacked, and for a while the fate of the three cities hung in the balance. But the news of the capture of the cities traveled quickly along the Yangtse. Changsha fell to the revolutionaries on October 22, and Kiukiang, the important port city in Kiangsi province, fell a day later. Chen Chi-mei's revolutionaries rose in Shanghai on November 4. All of south China was in revolt, while the north remained firmly in the hands of the Manchus.

As yet there were no leaders, no programs, no generally accepted revolutionary doctrines. Nearly three weeks passed before Huang Hsing was able to reach Hankow. In the Chinese phrase, it was a revolution made by "dragons without heads." As the weeks passed, the leadership was disputed by Huang Hsing and Li Yuan-hung. Finally it was decided that Huang Hsing should bear the title of Generalissimo, and Li Yuan-hung should be Vice-Generalissimo. Nearly two and a half months later Dr. Sun Yat-sen reached Shanghai.

Dr. Sun Yat-sen was to be known in later years as the Father of the Chinese Revolution. It was a title that he well deserved, for he was the most uncompromising advocate of a revolutionary uprising against the Manchu regime, but throughout the early weeks of the revolution his influence was never felt. The disasters that followed the first revolutionary upsurge might have been avoided if he had been closer to China.

Chen Chi-mei had been placed in charge of revolutionary activities in Shanghai. Soon after the uprising in Wuchang, he sent a coded telegram to Chiang Kai-shek, summoning him back to China. Together with his friend Chang Chun, Chiang Kai-shek then applied for forty-eight hours' leave from his regiment and made his way to Tokyo, where he was ordered to remain in hiding until passage to China could be arranged. The Japanese gendarmerie learned that he had overstayed his leave and went in search of him, but he had vanished without a trace.

On the night before he left his regiment, he attended a small private feast to celebrate the revolution in China. Not all the Chinese cadets in the regiment were invited, for some seven or eight of them were known to be convinced monarchists. It was a convivial meeting. Toasts were drunk in sake, and speeches were made in honor of the revolutionaries who had already conquered large areas of south China. Suddenly Chiang Kai-shek remembered that when a Japanese soldier goes into battle, he drinks pure water as a sign of his perfect submission to authority in preparation for death. Thereupon he threw the sake away and drank a cup of water. Later that night he left for Tokyo, and a few days later he sent his uniform and ceremonial dagger by registered mail to the military headquarters at Takata. In this way he hoped to prove to the Japanese authorities that he was not a deserter but a Chinese officer whose services were urgently needed elsewhere. At all costs he felt it necessary that his record remain unblemished.

With a hundred and twenty other Chinese revolutionaries he made his way to Nagasaki and took ship to Shanghai. He had hoped that the revolutionary wars would be over in a few weeks. He did not know, and could not guess, that the wars would continue for the rest of his life.

WHITE SUN IN A BLUE SKY

A REVOLUTION IS ALWAYS a battle of wills, and the revolutionaries soon discovered that they were confronted by a powerful adversary in the person of Yuan Shih-kai, a man of quick intelligence and an extraordinary capacity for intrigue. The son of an obscure farmer, he was adopted when very young by a general in the Manchu army, and grew up to become a pillar of the Manchu regime. At the age of twenty-six he was appointed Resident or Governor of Korea. Later he became commander-in-chief of the army, and was one of those who helped to depose the Emperor Kuang Hsu in 1898. Basking in the favor of the Empress Dowager, he acquired a position of dominant power which came to an end only with her death in 1908. Her successor, the Regent Prince Chun, acting on behalf of the boy Emperor Pu Yi, dismissed him from office with a polite note urging him to go on vacation for his health's sake. The Regent was the younger brother of the Emperor Kuang Hsu, and he had reason to believe that the Emperor had been murdered at Yuan Shih-kai's orders. Yuan Shih-kai went into retirement. He knew he had only to wait and he would be recalled to high office.

He was a small man, with a strange pallor and a commanding presence. He tended to fat, rejoiced in all the pleasures of life, and was completely without moral scruples. With his prematurely graying hair, wispy mustache, and small beady eyes, he looked like a shopkeeper. In fact he had the most astute brain in China, and knew exactly what he wanted. He wanted power, and was prepared to betray or murder anyone who stood in his way. When the revolution broke out in Wuchang, he was immediately recalled by the Regent, who hoped he would place his services at the disposition of the Manchu court. His aim was to establish his own unchallenged power by betraying both the Manchus and the revolutionaries, and ultimately to make himself emperor of China.

The revolution had failed. Although large areas of southern China were in the hands of the revolutionaries, the Manchu dynasty was not immediately overthrown. Yuan Shih-kai offered a truce, a long détente while the questions relating to the future government of China could be ironed out. The revolutionaries, knowing that they could not win China by force of arms, were compelled to submit to the man to whom the Imperial Family had bequeathed all its rights and authority. In the following months Yuan Shih-kai was able to consolidate his power in an atmosphere of intrigue and conspiracy.

Meanwhile the revolutionaries continued to wage a desultory war. Hankow and Hanyang were recaptured by the Imperial Army, but elsewhere the revolutionaries went on the offensive. Chen Chi-mei was planning the simultaneous capture of Shanghai and Hangchow, the capital of Chekiang province. It was abundantly necessary that these two cities, both occupying strategic positions, should be captured, and accordingly he decided to seize the arsenal at Shanghai and to send Chiang Kai-shek to conquer Hangchow. He was a man of great daring, and he thought he might win over the workers in the arsenal by suddenly appearing among them and demanding that they come out on the side of the revolution. The moment he appeared at the arsenal he was arrested. Trussed up like an animal, he was about to be carried off to a Manchu jail when the revolutionaries, learning of his fate, decided to attack the arsenal in the hope of being able to release him. Chen Chi-mei was saved, and the revolutionaries, armed with guns from the arsenal, had little difficulty in taking possession of Shanghai.

Chiang Kai-shek spent a week in Hangchow secretly organizing the revolt. At two o'clock in the morning of November 5 he led a small attacking party armed with bombs and pistols against the yamen. There was no dramatic battle. Some of the yamen guards had already declared for the revolution, and there was considerable confusion and a good deal of wild pistol fire. The guards surrendered, the provincial governor was captured, and the yamen was put to the flames. It was a small but important victory for the revolutionaries. Chiang Kai-shek had acquitted himself well, but people were more inclined to remember the daring of two young sisters armed with homemade bombs who led the attack on the yamen. The capture of Hangchow scarcely affected the course of the revolution; the capture of Shanghai was more important.

As Dr. Sun Yat-sen observed some years later, "It was not the revolt of Wuchang which saved the revolution, but the response of the provinces when Wuchang appeared to be in dire straits. The party members themselves realized this, and without any coordinated plan they voluntarily fought against the Manchus. Within a few months fifteen provinces declared their independence. The greatest response, and the greatest influence on the country, was exercised by Shanghai. When Hankow fell to the enemy, Chen Chi-mei captured Shanghai and brought it into the power of the revolutionaries. From Shanghai it was possible to launch an attack on Nanking, and when Hanyang was again lost, Nanking was captured by our party members to offset its fall, so promoting the revolutionary cause. Chen Chi-mei's revolt in Shanghai contributed more than any other to the success of the 1911 revolution."

Dr. Sun Yat-sen's estimate of revolutionary victories was not entirely accurate. Although Shanghai was the turning point, and its capture was far more valuable to the revolutionaries than the capture of Wuchang, nevertheless the revolution was not won or lost by the capture of cities; it was won or lost at the conference table. In the interminable conferences that followed, the revolutionaries were ill equipped. Yuan Shih-kai showed his contempt for them by continually out-maneuvering them.

When Dr. Sun Yat-sen arrived in Shanghai on Christmas Eve, it was generally assumed that he would immediately inaugurate a revolutionary government to rule over the areas of the south which had fallen into the hands of the revolutionaries. But in fact he did little more than issue proclamations and go through the motions of ruling. Even in his speech proclaiming the birth of the Chinese Republic, he seemed strangely hesitant. "The time has come for all the revolutionary armies to unite under a single commander," he said, "and all the provinces, which are governed in so many different ways, must be brought under a single central government." But he did not explain how this should be done, or how the armies should be financed, or why the Chinese people were expected to submit to a revolutionary leader who had spent so much of his life abroad that he knew very little about the problems of China. He organized a phantom government, procured a loan from Japan on the security of the ironworks at Hanyang, and settled down for what he thought would be a long-drawn-out struggle against the north. Meanwhile emissaries were constantly traveling between Peking and Nanking.

For reasons which have never been sufficiently explained, Dr. Sun Yat-sen abandoned the struggle almost before it had begun. On January 15, 1912, exactly fifteen days after being inaugurated as provisional president, he telegraphed to Yuan Shih-kai and offered him the presidency on condition that he formally accept the republic and secure the abdication of the boy Emperor. On the following day there was an attempt to assassinate Yuan Shih-kai as his carriage was turning into Morrison Street in Peking. The attempt failed, several innocent bystanders were killed, and Yuan Shih-kai came to regard his survival as a demonstrable sign of Heaven's favor. He began to see himself as the divinely appointed successor of the emperors.

Since the army was firmly under his control, and the Manchus possessed no effective weapons, and Dr. Sun Yat-sen was prepared to accept him as president of China, Yuan Shih-kai found himself in a position where he could exert a steady and powerful influence. When the Manchu princes were obstinate, he pointed out the fate which awaited them under the republic unless they placed themselves under his protection. Similarly, when the mother of the boy Emperor said she could not face the prospect of signing the instrument of abdication, thus bringing the three-hundred-year-old dynasty to an end, Yuan Shih-kai explained patiently that the Emperor would retain all his titles and privileges, he would still be in possession of his palaces, and nothing would change except that he would no longer be confronted with the awesome responsibilities of ruling a vast empire. Dr. Sun Yat-sen, too, was invited to seek the protection of the new dictator, who assumed the title of Plenipotentiary, "the man with full powers."

On February 12, 1912, in the great Hall for Cultivating the Mind in the Forbidden City, the boy Emperor and his mother ascended their thrones, and the instrument of abdication was read out to a small throng of courtiers and imperial ministers. In a broken voice which could scarcely be heard, the boy's mother read the words which had been dictated by Yuan Shih-kai. The message took the form of a valediction, a last farewell to a nation which would henceforth be ruled by commoners. The throne granted its powers to the people, and begged Yuan Shih-kai to consult the revolutionaries in the south for the purpose of forming a united republican government:

> From the preference of the people's heart, the will of Heaven is discernible. How could we oppose the desires of millions for the glory of one family? Therefore We, the Dowager Empress and the Emperor, hereby vest the sovereignty in the people. Let Yuan Shih-kai inaugurate with full powers a provisional republic and confer with the republicans as to the ways in which we can ensure peace to the empire, thus forming a great republic which will include the territories of the Manchus, Hans, Mongols, Mohammedans, and Tibetans. We, the Dowager Empress and the Emperor, will retire into a life of leisure, free from public duties, spending our years pleasantly and enjoying the courteous treatment accorded to us by the people, while watching with satisfaction the glorious establishment and consummation of the perfect government.

Such was the edict signed with the imperial seal, soon to be distributed in hundreds of thousands of copies over the length and breadth of China. The consummation of the perfect government, however, lay far in the future. The abdication of the boy Emperor was followed by the abdication of Dr. Sun Yat-sen, who telegraphed a long letter to Yuan Shih-kai in which he complained only that the new government could not properly accept its rights and privileges from the Manchus. He asked Yuan Shih-kai to meet him in Nanking, well knowing that the mouse can scarcely ask favors of the cat. Yuan Shih-kai found excellent reasons for postponing his visit to Nanking. When a delegation of Nanking ministers arrived in Peking to consult with him, he thoughtfully offered them the treatment previously reserved for royalty and then in a characteristic maneuver threatened them with violence by staging riots, from which they barely escaped with their lives. He had carefully weighed the innumerable telegrams which had reached him from the south, and found that they carried very little weight. On March 10 he proclaimed himself provisional president. Sun Yat-sen retired from the scene to devote his time, as he said, to "the reconstruction of the country in its social, industrial, and commercial aspects." He was especially interested in railroads. He still maintained an interest in political affairs, and from time to time he would emerge from obscurity to issue a call to order or a denunciation of the government, but he felt that his chief work had already been accomplished. In his view Yuan Shih-kai possessed the shrewdness and native intelligence to lead the country out of the doldrums. His party was represented in the National Assembly, and he hoped in this way to influence the course of events.

Many of Dr. Sun Yat-sen's followers were outraged by his surrender. The revolutionaries had sacrificed their lives to bring about a new government, but instead of an Emperor there was now a self-elected President with plenipotentiary powers ruling by edict. To combat the vast powers of the President, Dr. Sun Yat-sen labored to bring about an amalgamation of the existing revolutionary parties, and so it happened that in August the People's Progressive Party, the Union Republican Party, the Tung Meng Hui, and many other smaller groups were merged into a single party called the Kuomintang, which meant the National Popular Party. It was an amalgamation brought about in the hope of toppling Yuan Shih-kai from power, and since many diverse revolutionary interests were involved, the party was never stable and never acquired a clear-cut program. Born in diversity, it was to reflect the permanent contradictions of the Chinese revolutionary mind. There would come a time when anarchists, communists, egalitarians, the bourgeoisie, and the warlords would all find shelter under this capacious umbrella.

For Chiang Kai-shek the revolution was a disaster. The sacrifice of so many lives in order that Yuan Shih-kai should inherit the powers of the Emperor seemed to him an act of treachery. His hopes lay in a military victory over the north. To Chen Chi-mei he declared: "We have accomplished the easy task of overthrowing the dynasty, but there are hard times ahead. We must now take the responsibility of drilling troops at the right time and the right place, and we must create a general staff. As for the other matters, they can be done at our leisure." By "other matters" he clearly meant political affairs.

His hopes for advancement were not realized. The only post that could be offered to him was that of party secretary in a small town near Hangchow, and he spurned the offer. Convinced that the future of the revolution lay with the army, he threw himself into the study of the German language under the impression that the Germans were the greatest military nation on earth, superior even to the Japanese. With his newly acquired knowledge of German military theory, he wrote articles for *The Military Voice*, which were later collected and published under the title *Records of Self-Examination*, with a preliminary quotation from Mencius: "If, when I examine myself, I discover that my conduct is not upright, then surely I shall fear a poor man dressed in loose sackcloth. If, when I examine myself, I discover that my conduct is upright, then surely I shall go forward against thousands and tens of thousands." Fifty years later he would still repeat these words with approval.

An indication of the extent of Chiang Kai-shek's reading is given in his *Records of Self-Examination*, where he says that up to

1912 he had read the Five Classics, the Four Books, the Annals of the Warring States, the *Tso Chuan,* Sun Wu, the *Liu Tao* (Six Arts of War), the *Li Sao,* Chuang Tzu, Ssu-ma Kuang, Ssu-ma Chien, the writings of Yo Fei, Tseng Kuo-fan, Li Hung-chang, and the *San Kuo* (The Three Kingdoms), adding that he had also perused many military histories, geographies, and books on psychology, statistics, sociology, economics, and literature. As might be expected, the list of books is heavily weighted in favor of history and military memoirs, but it is significant that he included the mystical philosopher Chuang Tzu and the long poem, the *Li Sao,* which in heavily embroidered language describes the complaints of an upright prime minister who committed suicide because he fell into disfavor.

Records of Self-Examination was far more than an experiment in self-analysis. Chiang Kai-shek was a determined exponent of the role of the military, and many of the articles were disguised attempts to define the role of revolutionaries in the army. He also displayed a keen awareness of the military problems involving the defense of the Chinese mainland against an outside enemy, paying special attention to the vast and probably undefendable coastline. In these essays there appears for the first time his demand for military and political unity, which was to be repeated again and again when he came to power.

Having rejected the offer of a party post, he was without any effective influence. That winter he returned to Chikow to think out his problems afresh. He had no patience with half-measures, and he had long ago come to the conclusion that the revolution had failed because it had not gone far enough. He objected strongly to the merger of the revolutionary parties, on the grounds that it weakened rather than strengthened Dr. Sun Yat-sen's position, and in a despairing letter to Chen Chi-mei he expressed his distrust of the revolutionaries who now worked for their own profit rather than for the revolution. The gist of the letter was sent to Dr. Sun Yat-sen, who replied in the approved manner by sending a poetic scroll to the young soldier:

In safety and danger I shall put my trust in you.
Through bitterness and sweetness we shall face the future.

It was a consoling crumb from the table of the Father of the Revolution, but it had no special significance. Such scrolls were written in great numbers, usually being composed by a secretary. Chiang Kai-shek had no gift for dissimulation, and he was still in opposition to the party.

Meanwhile Yuan Shih-kai remained in power through his command of the army and a resourceful secret police. There was no effective opposition, for although the Kuomintang represented itself as the revolutionary party, there was a host of other parties that claimed the same distinction. Political parties were proliferating. Many of them were financed by Yuan Shih-kai, who was aware of the advantages of inventing political parties and ensuring their loyalty by a cautious distribution of favors. Yet the opposition to his policies was continually mounting. The Kuomintang was demanding equality of the sexes, obligatory military service, reforms in taxation and public finance, development of natural resources, and responsible cabinet government. The party had a wide following, and this was due less to the rare speeches of Dr. Sun Yat-sen than to the extraordinary ability of one of his young followers, Sung Chiao-jen, who led the Kuomintang party in the National Assembly. He had a gift for oratory and a severely practical mind; he knew exactly where he was going; and he was clearly marked for high political office. Yuan Shih-kai ordered his execution, and he was shot while about to take the train from the North Station in Shanghai. The gunman fled, and Sung Chiao-jen, mortally wounded, was taken to a nearby hospital where he died two days later, leaving a last ambiguous message to the man who had ordered his death: "I hope the President will rule our country with sincerity and justice and strive to protect the rights of the people. In so doing, he will help the Assembly to make a permanent constitution. If that can be done, my death will not have been in vain."

The murder of Sung Chiao-jen became a *cause célèbre*, for Yuan Shih-kai was forced to issue a warrant for the arrest of the murderer and the police had little difficulty in tracing the plot to the President's private office. The sensational trial opened in a court in the International Settlement on April 16, 1913, less than a month after the assassination. Telegrams from the President's confidential secretary to the murderer were discovered and offered in evidence. There was not the least doubt that Yuan Shih-kai was directly responsible for the assassination, but it was beyond the power of the judges of the International Settlement to punish him. The Kuomintang had lost its most effective leader, and there was no one to take his place. At the time of his death Sung Chiao-jen was only thirty-one years old.

Yuan Shih-kai was one of those irresponsible rulers who rejoice in dangerous expedients. Needing money, he raised a loan of £25,000,000 through an international consortium. The loan was secured on the salt revenues, and accordingly foreigners were placed in charge of the machinery of taxation. The negotiations were so hurried and secretive that it was generally believed that Yuan Shih-kai was filling his own pockets. It was also generally believed that the terms were so unfavorable to China that only an incompetent or corrupt finance minister could have approved them. The Kuomintang leaders in the National Assembly denounced the loan and passed a bill declaring it null and void. They then appealed to the provinces. Only three provincial governors supported them, and these were immediately dismissed from their posts by Yuan Shih-kai, who announced that he permitted no interference in his rule.

The assassination of Sung Chiao-jen and the so-called reconstruction loan played havoc with the country's affairs, and soon it became evident that a new and far more powerful effort was needed to bring about a revolution. On the morning of July 12 revolutionary groups all over south China sprang into action, declaring their independence from the Peking government. Nanking became the scene of wild fighting, as General Chang Hsun, one of Yuan Shih-kai's most trusted lieutenants, led his northern troops into the city to put an end to the revolution and to take what plunder was available. In Shanghai the revolutionaries were no more successful. Chen Chi-mei proclaimed a state of revolution. Chiang Kai-shek took charge of the renewed attack on the arsenal. The attack failed, for the garrison remained loyal to the northern government. The revolutionaries also had to contend with the gunboats which picked them out with searchlights at night, making them easy targets for the northern soldiers. The fighting went on sporadically for a week. On June 28 Chiang Kai-shek, who had advanced to a forward position close to the arsenal, found himself surrounded by enemy troops. He was captured and dragged off for interrogation, and might have been executed but for a lucky escape in the darkness. It was his closest brush with death. On the following day the revolutionaries retreated into the comparative safety of the International Settlement. The Shanghai uprising, like all the other small uprisings in south China, had failed. In later years Kuomintang historians would speak of the failure of the Second Revolution, but in fact there was no Second Revolution. Unprepared, ill-equipped, they had shown once more that they were no match for the regular soldiers in Yuan Shih-kai's standing army.

Chen Chi-mei and Chiang Kai-shek fled to Japan. They could take small comfort from their revolutionary experiences. It was almost as though there had been no revolution at all, for the power of Yuan Shih-kai extended over the whole length and breadth of China.

THE YOUNG REVOLUTIONARY

FOR A YEAR in Japan Chiang Kai-shek disappeared from sight. Like Dr. Sun Yat-sen, who was also in hiding in Japan, he was living underground. He was one of those obscure revolutionaries who live out their threadbare existence with the memory of continual defeats to remind them of their future victories. He lived by odd jobs, under an assumed name, in fear of arrest by the Japanese police, who still regarded him as a deserter from the Japanese army. In the small group surrounding Dr. Sun Yat-sen he was beginning to be marked out as a sober, hard-working revolutionary soldier, whose opinions on military revolutionary techniques were not to be dismissed lightly. It was remembered that he had displayed considerable skill during the attack on the Shanghai arsenal.

During this period of exile he came for the first time into close contact with Dr. Sun Yat-sen; and from being a man without any effective influence he gradually came to occupy a position of some responsibility within the party. In an address delivered in 1940 he spoke of those early days when he sat at the feet of the master:

> Now I regard the most fortunate thing of my life to have been obedient to the party and to have been one of Tsungli's revolutionary followers.* My happiest days were spent in rebuking the proud and exalting the weak, and sacrificing myself for the sake of others. At the age of nineteen I first joined the Tung Meng Hui. At the age of twenty-seven, after the campaign against Yuan Shih-kai broke out in 1913, I began to have individual talks with Tsungli. Before that time he had never granted me an interview or a private talk, nor did I ever go alone to see him. I behaved always like an ordinary member of the party, and I have continued to behave in this way for thirty years.

Chiang Kai-shek's verdict on himself is not entirely convincing: he did not always rebuke the proud or exalt the weak, nor did he always sacrifice himself for the sake of others. What is revealing is his statement that he was never alone in a room with Dr. Sun Yat-sen until 1913 and the implication that he was still regarded as a very junior member of the revolutionary party.

In order to improve himself and to rise higher in the revolutionary hierarchy, he lived according to a spartan regimen, dividing his day into watertight compartments—a part was spent in breathing exercises, a part in study, a part in exercise, a part in practical revolutionary work. There were secret meetings, coded messages, manifestos to be smuggled into China. Money had to be raised to finance a succession of small revolutionary conspiracies. The revolutionaries were kept busy, but the revolutionary flame on the mainland was burning low.

The truth was that the people were showing remarkably little enthusiasm for revolution. They wanted security and they were frightened of reforms—especially social reforms. Pigtails were coming back again. It was becoming fashionable to regard Yuan Shih-kai as the upholder of traditional virtues. The desire for a "strong man" who possessed the authority and power to unify the country was widespread. Yuan Shih-kai was receiving a constant stream of memorials urging him to act forcefully and decisively against the revolutionaries, and not all of these memorials were

* Tsungli means 'director general,' and was the title usually given to Dr. Sun Yat-sen.

written in the offices of his secretaries. Many, even among the peasantry, regarded him as the savior of his country, the inheritor of both the imperial and the revolutionary traditions.

The problem of the revolutionaries was to find the weakest spot in his armor. Some thought it was in Shanghai, where the presence of the International Settlement offered many advantages to revolutionaries who might want to escape from the prying eyes of the police. Accordingly, it was decided to send Chiang Kai-shek to Shanghai to investigate the possibilities of an uprising.

In the early summer of 1914 Chiang Kai-shek slipped into Shanghai. Yuan Shih-kai's police had been warned of his coming, and he was followed as soon as he landed. For a few days he was able to shake off the police, but when he went to call at the house of a well-known Kuomintang party member the police were tipped off. Chiang Kai-shek's friend was not at home, and he went away to call on some other friends. When he returned to the house, he found the police gathered at the door, waiting for him. He slipped away and made his way back to Tokyo, reporting that there was not the least prospect of an uprising.

A few weeks later he was sent on another mission, this time to Manchuria. Chen Chi-mei had long believed that the party suffered from an inherent defect: because it consisted largely of men from south China, they had always believed the revolution would begin in the south. But what about an uprising in Peking? Or if it was thought impractical to bring about a revolt in the capital, what about Manchuria? Chiang Kai-shek was sent to sound out the opinions of the handful of revolutionaries known to be living in Harbin and Tsitsihar. It was a dangerous journey, and there was the further difficulty that Chiang Kai-shek could not speak the northern Mandarin spoken in Manchuria. He reported that an uprising in Manchuria was even more unlikely than one in Shanghai. In July war broke out in Europe, and Chiang Kai-shek went to work on a lengthy memorandum concerning the prospects of the European war.

Chen Chi-mei was one of those men who thirst for action at all costs and whatever the risk. He decided to attempt another uprising in the Yangtse valley. Arriving in Shanghai, he organized a plot to assassinate Cheng Ju-sheng, who was Yuan Shih-kai's chief representative in the city. On November 10, 1914, there was a reception at the Japanese Consulate General in honor of the Emperor Taisho. It was decided to kill Cheng Ju-sheng when he was on his way to the reception. Accordingly, ten revolutionaries armed with pistols and bombs were posted between Cheng's official residence and the Japanese Consulate General and two more were posted on Garden Bridge inside the International Settlement. Cheng Ju-sheng had got wind of the plot and instead of making the whole journey by automobile he took a steam launch to the Bund, and then drove the very short distance to the Consulate General. However, he had to cross Garden Bridge, where the conspirators were waiting for him. The first bomb missed, the second damaged the car and brought it to a stop. Cheng Ju-sheng was unhurt. He got out of the car, and at that moment one of the conspirators shot him dead. It was a particularly meaningless assassination and reflected little credit on the revolutionaries.

In the following year the tempo of revolutionary violence increased. Chiang Kai-shek was summoned from Japan to assist Chen Chi-mei in a plot to take over the Chinese gunboats stationed off Shanghai. One gunboat, the "Shao Ho," was already commanded by a party member, and it was expected that the commanders of the other gunboats could be brought over to the side of the revolution. With the gunboats in their possession, the revolutionaries hoped to make a concerted attack on the arsenal, the police station at Nantao, and the power and telephone companies supplying Shanghai. Two hundred revolutionaries were to attack the police station, twenty more would attack the power and telephone companies, and the gunboats would shell the arsenal. The plans were carefully drawn up. Chiang Kai-shek, from his secret headquarters in the French Concession in Shanghai, was given overall command of the operation. The attempted uprising was a total failure, for the revolutionaries who attacked the Nantao police station and the power and telephone companies were beaten back, and as soon as the "Shao Ho" took up a position opposite the arsenal, it was promptly shelled by other gunboats loyal to Yuan Shih-kai. The revolutionaries took flight, but many were captured and executed out of hand.

There was something hopelessly impractical in these sporadic and ill-prepared attempts to overthrow the government in Peking. The heart seemed to have gone out of the revolutionaries, who acted with the impulse of despair, without any clear idea of the advantages to be gained by their raids and skirmishes. An even more disastrous raid took place in the spring of 1916. The fortress of Kiangyin, lying midway between Shanghai and Nanking, was attacked by a small picked force of revolutionaries on April 16. The fort fell, and some of the surrounding villages were occupied. In theory the capture of the fort gave the revolutionaries a base for control of the lower Yangtse; they could hold up half the trade of China and demand a ransom. In fact, the fort was difficult to hold, and five days later mutiny broke out among the revolutionary troops who realized that they would soon be at the mercy of an overwhelming force. At midnight on April 21 Chiang Kai-shek found himself alone in the fort except for two revolutionary soldiers who were begging him to go into hiding. Chiang Kai-shek later wrote a brief account of the debacle at Kiangyin: "In the fifth year of the Republic I launched an attack on the Kiangyin fort, but at a most dangerous juncture all the revolutionaries fled, leaving me alone in the fort."

A few weeks later Chen Chi-mei was assassinated. Some Japanese financiers had offered to make a loan to the Kuomintang party, and Chen Chi-mei was invited to a meeting in the International Settlement to put his signature on the final agreement. He did not know that the Peking government had contrived the plot and the Japanese financiers were in fact agents of the government. He was shot down in cold blood. Chiang Kai-shek was grief-stricken. He owed nearly everything to Chen Chi-mei, who had been his closest friend and his mentor in party affairs, his protector when things went badly, his admirer on the rare occasions when they went well. "Chen Chi-mei was everything to me," he wrote. "He taught me, encouraged me, loved me, supported me, remained with me at all times of safety and danger, in joy and in sorrow. We were like one mind with one soul." Chen Chi-mei died poor: only twenty Chinese dollars were found in his pocket at his death. It was all the money he had in the world.

It was the worst blow Chiang Kai-shek had ever received. His father had died when he was too young to feel the full weight of grief. Chen Chi-mei's death came at a time when there were altogether too many failures in the revolutionary organization. The loss was all the greater because he was one of those men who inspired confidence and trust, and there was no one else to take his place.

In loyalty to his dead friend Chiang Kai-shek decided to adopt Chen's two nephews as his own brothers—with curious effects on the course of Chinese history, for eventually the two nephews acquired vast powers within the Kuomintang. They became Chiang's most trusted advisers, ruling over the secret police, education, and propaganda with an iron hand, so that sometimes it seemed that they were the effective government of China.

But in 1916 no one could ever have expected that the Kuomintang would one day rule over China. Chiang Kai-shek was still living under an assumed name in Shanghai, making a poor living as a junior clerk in one of the small Chinese commodity exchanges. From time to time he would vanish from his usual haunts and take part in conspiratorial activities, but nothing came of them. Yuan Shih-kai died quietly in bed on June 6, 1916, and power passed into the hands of the provincial governors and warlords, who were even more determined to suppress any revolutionary uprisings. The revolution had come to a standstill.

They were years of heartbreak and indecision. In the autumn of 1916 Chiang Kai-shek visited Peking to observe the military situation, but learned nothing of value for the revolutionaries. Through the whole of 1917 he remained in Shanghai, working at the commodity exchange and occasionally preparing reports for the benefit of the Kuomintang high command. He wrote a report on "A Plan of Campaign Against the Northern Army" and "A Plan by Which the Yunnan and Kwangtung Armies Could Wage War Against Fukien and Chekiang," and these reports were then filed away and forgotten. Dr. Sun Yat-sen had lost hope of organizing a revolutionary uprising in the Yangtse valley, and increasingly his thoughts turned to his native Kwangtung. The National Assembly had been dissolved in the summer of 1916, and many of the Kuomintang party members had taken refuge in Canton. It was hoped that the revolution, so long delayed, would come about there. For nearly ten years Canton was to be the focal point of the revolutionaries.

In March 1918 Chiang Kai-shek was invited to assume a post in the Kwangtung army. It was not a very high post: he became simply one of the many military advisers attached to Dr. Sun Yat-sen's staff, under Chen Chiung-ming, the commander-in-chief of the Kwangtung army. Chen Chiung-ming was a man of many ambitions who had not yet decided whether to place his military knowledge at the service of the party or whether to carve out a small empire of his own. Inevitably there were quarrels, and Dr. Sun Yat-sen soon found himself in disagreement with his military advisers and especially with Chen Chiung-ming. At first Chiang Kai-shek kept apart from these quarrels, taking part in some successful forays into the neighboring province of Fukien. He trusted Chen Chiung-ming; they worked well together, and he still regarded the commander-in-chief of the Kwangtung army as a convinced revolutionary. Abruptly in the following year he abandoned his command of the second detachment of the Kwangtung revolutionary army and sailed for Japan. Meanwhile, Dr. Sun Yat-sen had retired to Shanghai once more, to ponder the changes of his revolutionary fortunes. Chiang Kai-shek had come to the conclusion that Chen Chiung-ming was a traitor to the party, intent only on his own ambitions. Dr. Sun Yat-sen preferred to believe for a little while longer that he was a loyal and obedient servant of the revolution.

The revolution was in danger of collapsing in futile misunderstandings and treacheries. There were constant comings and goings between Shanghai and Canton, and the Peking government seemed totally unconcerned about the upheavals in the south, believing that the revolutionaries were at loggerheads and would never be able to install a working government. Chiang Kai-shek spoke of the need for "firm and direct action," but the Kuomintang appeared to be dedicated to indirection and weakness.

One of Dr. Sun Yat-sen's most trusted colleagues, Chu Ta-fu, an experienced revolutionary, was acting as the liaison officer between Chen Chiung-ming and the Kuomintang headquarters in

Shanghai. On September 21, 1920, he was killed in battle, and Dr. Sun Yat-sen was heartbroken. A few days later he wrote to Chiang Kai-shek, expressing his grief, his continued faith in Chen Chiung-ming, and his doubts about whether Chiang Kai-shek had sufficient resilience and practical sense to take the place of the trusted and much beloved lieutenant. He wrote:

> *To my dear Elder Brother Chiang Kai-shek,*
>
> When my Elder Brother Chen Chiung-ming fought back to Canton he was using all his strength to serve our party and our country. We, on our part, are using all our strength to help him. With only one aim and of only one mind, our cooperation cannot be compared with any ordinary alliance. . . .
>
> The sudden and tragic death of Chu Ta-fu is a loss to me comparable to that of my right or left hand. When I look among the members of our party, I find very few who are experts in war and also loyal. Only you, my elder brother, are with us, you, whose courage and sincerity are equal to those of Chu Ta-fu, and your knowledge of war is even better than his. But you have a very fiery temper, and your hatred of mediocrity is excessive. And so it often leads to quarreling and difficulty in cooperating. As you are shouldering the great and heavy responsibility of our party, you should sacrifice your high ideals a little and try to compromise. This is merely for the sake of our party and has nothing to do with your personal principles. Would you, my elder brother, agree with this?

In this way, with a combination of gentle chiding and some praise, Dr. Sun Yat-sen showed that he was aware of Chiang Kai-shek's defects of character and hoped for a sharp improvement. What he feared was a certain rigidity, a harsh, uncompromising manner, an incapacity to listen to the other side. Once his mind was made up, Chiang Kai-shek was inflexible; and though inflexibility may be useful in a statesman, it is useless in a revolutionary. Dr. Sun Yat-sen saw the danger signals, but he could do little to change the character of his young disciple.

STORM AND STRESS

VERY OFTEN in the lives of young revolutionaries there comes a moment of intolerable anguish and despair, when everything that prompted them to take up a revolutionary career is suddenly in doubt. A revolutionary lives a dedicated life, and like the saints he often goes through a period when the world turns sour and arid. For the mystic, God hides in impenetrable darkness, no longer to be reached in those desperate days before the vision suddenly emerges; and so too for the revolutionary there comes a moment when the revolution no longer has any savor and he is tempted to abandon it altogether, to resume the ordinary everyday life of an ordinary person. Many revolutionaries fall by the wayside.

In the life of Chiang Kai-shek this period seems to have coincided with the news that his mother was dying, which came to him in the late spring of 1921, shortly after he had received the stinging rebuke from Dr. Sun Yat-sen. It was a period of helpless confusion. The moment he heard the news he hurried to her bedside. There had been ominous presages. He had dreamed of a mountain covered with snow, and because white is the color of mourning in China he felt sure the dream signified her coming death. For five weeks she lingered on in great suffering. Doctors were summoned, and priests waved incense. Chiang Kai-shek found himself helping to prepare potions from the Chinese pharmacopoeia instead of leading armies. She was very frail, and there was no doubt that she was dying. She died at eight o'clock in the morning of June 4, 1921. He had been very close to her. Only a few months before, at her urgent invitation, he had accompanied her on a pilgrimage to a Buddhist temple in the mountains of Chekiang, in the hope that her prayers would be answered. He had not altogether enjoyed the experience, for he complained of the vegetarian food and the length of the Buddhist ceremonies, saying that they would have been improved by considerable cutting. His mother had believed that the pilgrimage would improve her health; instead, it only made it worse. At her deathbed he was inconsolable.

In China when a son loses a parent he may go into retirement for many months, even for years. There is no effort to conceal the weight of grief. Sometimes he will simply stop working, abandon all his interests, and turn his back on the world. Many months or years later he will suddenly resume his life at the point where he left off.

A few days after his mother's death Chiang Kai-shek received a telegram from Dr. Sun Yat-sen, demanding his presence in Canton. He was in no hurry to obey. He needed a period of rest and *recueillement;* he was at odds with the party, and he felt that nothing would be gained if he returned immediately. June, July, and August passed, and it was not until September that he made his way to Canton where he found that the quarrels between Chen Chiung-ming and Dr. Sun Yat-sen had been patched up, but the party remained in a state of disorder and confusion. The Second Kwangtung Army was put in a state of readiness for a projected march to the north, and Chiang Kai-shek was given a position on the general staff. The Second Kwangtung Army consisted largely of mercenaries recruited locally; there was little opposition to their advance; and Wuchow and Kweilin were soon occupied. Dr. Sun Yat-sen made his headquarters in Kweilin, and debated whether to march on Hankow.

He remained for more than a month in Kweilin, uncertain of his aims and with a growing lack of confidence in the government he had installed in Canton. He dared not advance without the support of Chen Chiung-ming, who remained in Canton, and he had many doubts about the loyalty and effectiveness of his mercenary army. Kweilin was a pleasant sprawling city which lies in the shadow of strange volcanic mountains, and he was perfectly content to remain there while the political issues were being resolved.

Chiang Kai-shek was also contentedly enjoying his stay in Kweilin. He had fathered two sons by a peasant woman, and though he had separated from her, he was still fond of her, and he especially liked the younger son, who was called Wei-kuo. To this boy, who was then about eight years old, he wrote a letter from Kweilin describing his loneliness and the kind of life he was living:

Kweilin, January 28, 1922

Dear Wei-kuo,

Today I am in Kweilin, passing the New Year's Day according to the old calendar. When I recall the contentment of our family today, I feel sad that I cannot enjoy the pleasures of the fireside with you at home, and so all the more I think of your active behavior, which I never forget. Also I think of the loss of my dear mother, who no longer lives in this world and can no longer pass the New Year's Day with me at home. I have lost one more who has pity on me, and you also have lost one more who loved you. So in this life I shall never be able to enjoy again the pleasure of passing the New Year's Day with my mother at home, and I shall never again see my mother and fulfill my filial duty to her. When I think about this, I feel so sad, and I would like you to obey and reverence your mother and love your elder brother at home and be a model for others, so that you may not feel sad when you grow old, as your father feels now.

In Kweilin I am always passing the time happily with Dr. Sun Yat-sen. I stay at Pa Kuei Tang (Eight Cinnamon Hall), which is truly the most elegant and beautiful place in Kweilin. I have sat for several photographs with some of my friends here, and I shall send two to you as soon as they are printed. No matter how happy I feel here, I shall never forget the happiness of my family and my grief over my mother's death. I wonder whether you share these feelings.

This letter was written exactly two months after Chiang Kai-shek's formal separation from the mother of his two sons. In the past he had been accustomed to write long letters to his mother, but now there was no one to write to. He spoke of "the contentment of our family today," but he knew there was no family. A few weeks earlier he had written a curiously formal letter to his sons, saying that he did not know when he would ever see them again, but he expected them to behave with filial devotion to their mother, "so that in due course you will make yourselves worthy of your ancestors and thus reward the efforts of your grandmother, in this way helping me to obtain for her an eternal blessedness in heaven."

Such phrases, no doubt, belonged to the acceptable conventions of the time, but they reflected a deep anguish. Chiang Kai-shek was still inconsolable. Nor did he have any great faith in Dr. Sun Yat-sen's ability to escape from the impasse in which he found himself. In his view there could be no northern march, and there was little to be gained by returning to Canton, where Chen Chiung-ming was in effective control. On the plea that he must return to tend his mother's grave, he left Kweilin and returned to Shanghai. On the eve of his departure Dr. Sun Yat-sen said, "If you leave me now, all the significance of the things we have done together will be lost." But in fact they had done verry little together. Chiang Kai-shek felt that the revolution was entering a treacherous phase, and he had very little hope for the outcome.

The real reason for his sudden departure was well understood by Dr. Sun Yat-sen. Again and again Chiang Kai-shek had referred to his overwhelming distrust of Chen Chiung-ming. The seeds of this distrust had been planted long ago. Recently, during a visit to Canton, he had become more than ever convinced that Chen Chiung-ming was a traitor only waiting for an opportunity to display his treachery.

The incident that aroused his gravest suspicions took place at a dinner given in Chen Chiung-ming's headquarters. During the course of the dinner Chiang Kai-shek heard a certain Yeh Chu describe Dr. Sun Yat-sen as a "*Ta pao*," which means "great gun" and implies a man given to excessive boasting and incompetence in the management of affairs. Many people regarded Dr. Sun Yat-sen as a "*Ta pao*," but they would usually make sure that none of the Doctor's intimate friends was present when they used the words. Chiang Kai-shek was thunderstruck by the impropriety. Chen Chiung-ming evidently approved of the words, for he sat there quietly and made no attempt to rebuke the speaker. Chiang Kai-shek was so indignant that he asked Chen Chiung-ming to accompany him to another room and then asked him bluntly why he had permitted such a calumny. Did he not understand that it was the purest treachery to speak in this way? Was Yeh Chu to be permitted to attack the Father of the Republic with impunity? Chen answered with amused tolerance, very amiable and sophisticated, leaving no doubt at all that he too considered Dr. Sun Yat-sen a "*Ta pao*."

Chiang Kai-shek's suspicions, which had been aroused long before this incident, were now confirmed. He had not the slightest doubt that Chen Chiung-ming's true colors would soon be revealed. Then he learned that Dr. Sun Yat-sen had returned to Canton and was apparently on the best of terms with Chen Chiung-ming. Chiang Kai-shek waited for the moment when Dr. Sun Yat-sen would be stabbed in the back.

The moment came sooner than he expected. In the early hours of June 16, 1922, the presidential palace in the Kuanlin hills just outside Canton was surrounded by soldiers under the command of Yeh Chu. Guards were set along the road to prevent the escape of Dr. Sun Yat-sen. The plan was to murder him and then set the palace on fire; on no account must he be permitted to escape. Dr. Sun Yat-sen had been warned during the evening that there was a plot against his life, and in his usual fashion he had dismissed the warnings out of hand. But at three o'clock in the morning there was no longer any doubt that there had been an uprising and that his life was in danger. There was in fact a price of two hundred thousand Chinese dollars on his head. He slipped out of the palace in disguise with three others, mingled with the rebel troops, and gradually made his way to the gunboat "Yung Feng" anchored off Whampoa. There, for the moment, he was safe, for the naval forces with some few exceptions were loyal to him. The presidential palace had burned to the ground, and most of his papers and documents were reduced to ashes.

Chiang Kai-shek hurried from Shanghai to be close to Dr. Sun Yat-sen. He succeeded in reaching the "Yung Feng," and for the next fifty-six days he was virtually in command of the gunboat and the six other gunboats which remained loyal. On July 10 these gunboats sailed down the Pearl river to take up positions close to the enemy batteries at White Goose Pool. There was a confused battle, with the "Yung Feng" receiving six direct hits. While Dr. Sun Yat-sen remained in the hold, Chiang Kai-shek stood in the captain's cabin with his eyes fixed on the chronometer, for he had calculated that after the six direct hits the gunboat would remain afloat for only twenty minutes. But the danger passed, the gunboat proved to be seaworthy, and the battle ended in the usual revolutionary manner—a great number of innocent people were killed, but no one won. The gunboats went up and down the Pearl river, but the rebels were in command of the shores.

During this period Chiang Kai-shek found himself for the first time in intimate daily contact with Dr. Sun Yat-sen. Sometimes he would serve the doctor's meals, and on one occasion when there was no more food on the gunboat he was rowed ashore at night to forage for food in a friendly village. He swept the decks and polished the guns. He liked to make himself useful.

In retrospect, he was inclined to regard those days as among the happiest of his life. The opportunity to be close to the Father of the Republic never occurred again. The relationship between them was cordial and respectful, but not affectionate. Yet they suited each other perfectly, for they were like the two sides of a coin, at the furthest possible extremities from each other, facing in different directions, and seeing entirely different worlds. The older man's incredible feats of idealism remained meaningless to the young staff officer, who saw himself destined to occupy himself with military tactics and tables of organization, not with high policy. Bandages, guns, fodder, forage parties, scales of pay, uniforms—these were matters which never concerned the Father of the Republic, while for Chiang Kai-shek they were matters of grave concern. The revolution must be fed and clothed and given guns; it must be disciplined; it must be led. There must be people who knew how to direct and manage ships under gunfire, and there must be people to sweep the decks. Chiang Kai-shek attended to these practical matters and seemed mildly surprised that Dr. Sun Yat-sen knew so little about them.

In spite of their differences they worked in harmony together, and in later years Chiang Kai-shek would imagine that the days spent on the "Yung Feng" were dedicated to earnest discussions on the nature of the coming revolution, and that he became the devoted pupil of a devoted master. He spoke as though some special grace was granted to him during those hot summer days. In fact they spent those days in hideous discomfort, in continual fear of a sudden attack or of treachery, in the vague hope that the Second Kwangtung Army would come to their rescue and with the certain knowledge that they commanded nothing more than seven gunboats, which were not very much larger than rowboats.

On August 6 they learned that the Second Kwangtung Army had been roundly defeated by Chen Chiung-ming's forces, and all hope was lost. The time had come to abandon the "Yung Feng" and return to the comparative security of the International Settlement at Shanghai. Negotiations were opened with the British Consul in Canton and arrangements were made for transferring the fugitives to a British warship, which would take them to Hongkong. A fast mail steamer, the "S.S. Empress of Russia," brought them four days later to Shanghai.

In the eyes of Dr. Sun Yat-sen the revolution was not over; it had simply suffered a temporary reverse. Chiang Kai-shek took the defeat more keenly than Dr. Sun Yat-sen, and became ill. He went to a rest home near Ningpo to recuperate, remaining there until the middle of October. There he wrote a letter to his elder son, who had been left behind in Shanghai.

October 13, 1922

Dear Ching-kuo,

Tomorrow I leave Ningpo for Fukien, and I hope you are studying hard at Shanghai. So far I can see no progress in your calligraphy. You must get up early every morning and practice your calligraphy—one hundred words in rigid style and fifty words in cursive style—and you must learn to write accurately and quickly. I have heard that you have almost forgotten the Mencius you have read. Why so careless? Your Mencius must be reviewed, you must study the *Analects* after your teacher, Mr. Wang, has explained it, and you must keep studying until you have completely understood it. In Chinese, if you have a thorough knowledge of the Four Books and can recite the extracts from the *Tso Chuan*, Mencius, Chuang Tzu, and the *Li Sao*, you will be able to write your compositions with ease.

Chiang Kai-shek did not often write to his children, for he was preoccupied with his military studies. Sometimes it occurred to him that he should show them more affection, but a moment later he would remember that he had long ago dedicated himself to the revolution. In a revealing letter written about this time to his elder son, he identified himself with the ancient heroes, who were serenely determined to sacrifice everything for the country:

> When the father of Liu Peng, the first Emperor of the Han dynasty, was captured by Hsiang Yu, then Hsiang Yu threatened Liu Peng with his father's death unless he surrendered. Liu Peng replied that he would gladly drink a cup of soup made from his father's body after his father had been killed and boiled. This means that he cared less for his family than for his country. Struggling for the revolution, I have already forgotten my family, so that we can obtain freedom and independence for the people and their descendants.

Chiang Kai-shek had no qualms about comparing himself with the heroes, for he firmly believed in heroism as a way of life. Nevertheless, he did not always act heroically. Small armies proclaiming their loyalty to Dr. Sun Yat-sen still operated in south China, and when Dr. Sun Yat-sen ordered him to take up a command in the province of Fukien, he delayed, prevaricated, and offered one reason after another for refusing the order. He explained that there were traitors everywhere, he was unprepared, the small revolutionary army was inadequately equipped, he could not take a subordinate command. He paid a brief visit to Fukien, and then returned to the security of his native village. In January Kwangtung fell to the revolutionary army, and Dr. Sun Yat-sen began to make plans for returning to Canton. He wrote to Chiang Kai-shek, urging him to come at once. "We are in urgent need of your services," he wrote. "Please come as soon as possible, without delay. I have given you the post of chief of staff. We must never let a day pass without having you at the head of our military forces."

At first these blandishments had no effect, but a week later Dr. Sun Yat-sen sent a telegram in code, repeating that he was in urgent need of his services and begging him to set a date for his arrival in Canton. Reluctantly Chiang Kai-shek obeyed the summons. He had grave doubts about his usefulness in Canton, and in fact there was very little need of his services, for Kwangtung was unusually quiet and the northern march, so often contemplated by Dr. Sun Yat-sen, had been abandoned. It was decided that he would serve the Chinese revolution best by visiting and reporting on the Soviet Union, where a revolution of vast scope had been successfully accomplished. Dr. Sun Yat-sen was intrigued by the personality of Lenin and by a revolution which was so much more successful than his own.

Before leaving for Moscow, Chiang Kai-shek sought out Lenin's chief representative in China, a Dutch Communist called Hendryk Sneevliet, known to the Chinese as Maring. The meeting took place in Shanghai in August 1923. Maring had visited Dr. Sun Yat-sen in Kweilin and knew a good deal about the Kuomintang party, which at one time he had hoped to bring into the Communist fold. One day he asked Dr. Sun Yat-sen to describe his revolutionary movement. The doctor had a very simple reply. "We derive," he said, "in direct line of descent from King Wen, King Wu, and Confucius." Maring could make nothing of the reply and reported to Moscow that Dr. Sun Yat-sen's revolutionary principles were ultimately based on nationalism.

Chiang Kai-shek's task was to prepare an itinerary, to choose his traveling companions, and to get letters of introduction in the Soviet Union. Maring apparently knew everyone of importance, and provided a large number of letters of introduction. Altogether

Chiang Kai-shek spent three months in the Soviet Union. Lenin was too ill to receive him, but he met Trotsky, who gave him the somewhat nebulous advice: "Patience and action are the two essential factors for a revolutionary party, and the one complements the other." Chiang Kai-shek had more than a fair share of patience and he was a devotee of action; he scarcely needed to be told that these were important attributes in a revolutionary. He met Chicherin, the Commissar for Foreign Affairs, who explained at some length that Outer Mongolia feared China and was therefore more disposed to being ruled by the Soviet Union, a statement which was not calculated to commend itself to a young Chinese nationalist. There was a long conversation with Ianis Rudzutak, now forgotten but in those days a powerful figure in the Bolshevik hierarchy. Rudzutak embarked on a long description of the emergence of the Russian Communist Party to power; it was a speech he had made many times before, and he delivered it with all the heavy-handed loquaciousness of a provincial schoolmaster. Chiang Kai-shek was not impressed. He was more impressed by visits to the Red Army headquarters and military schools in Moscow, where the cadets were so strictly disciplined that they resembled machines. But in Petrograd the atmosphere was charged with a more ominous electricity. He was taken to see the island fortress of Kronstadt, where an uprising against the Bolsheviks had been suppressed with ferocious brutality only two years before. "We could see that the revolt left deep scars," Chiang Kai-shek noted in his diary.

The visit to the Soviet Union enthralled him, but it also exasperated him. He was uncomfortable among the Russians, who were continually urging him to join the Communist Party. He would reply that this was a matter he would have to discuss at length with Dr. Sun Yat-sen, but the polite answer was greeted with incomprehension by his hosts. One day, viewing the bloody relics exhibited in the Museum of the Revolution in Moscow, he expressed his dominant feeling about the Russian revolution: "It terrifies one's eyes and soul, but it is inspiring!"

On October 10, 1923, he delivered a lecture on the Chinese revolution—the date had been chosen deliberately, for it was the twelfth anniversary of the revolution. Afterward he was shown the letters which Dr. Sun Yat-sen had written to Lenin and Trotsky, and in the Chinese fashion he wept when he met with favorable references to himself. Though the Russian officials were cordial and went out of their way to show him respect, he was well aware that they were not in agreement among themselves. "From my observations and from my conversations," he wrote later, "I readily perceived that fierce struggles were going on not only in Russia generally but also among the Communists themselves. I became convinced that Soviet political institutions were instruments of tyranny and terror, and basically incompatible with the Kuomintang's political ideals."

Nevertheless, he was impressed by the party's iron control of the nation. Some six hundred thousand party members ruled a nation of 130 million. The smooth-running, well-oiled, splendidly manipulated machine of the Soviet empire fascinated him. He attempted to learn Russian, but gave it up after a few short lessons, and then attempted to read Marx's *Das Kapital*, but could make little headway. Later he was to maintain that Marxism was contrary to the spirit of China. The longer he remained in Russia, the more convinced he became that the Soviets had designs on China.

He held fast to this opinion, even though Trotsky went out of his way to emphasize that the Soviet revolution was not exportable, pointing out that Soviet attempts to encourage revolution in Poland and Germany had ended in failure. Why, then, should the Chinese fear Soviet influence in China? On the contrary, they should welcome it, for the Soviets alone among world powers were prepared to aid the Chinese revolutionaries with weapons and economic assistance. Trotsky's air of sweet reasonableness was unconvincing. Chiang Kai-shek was convinced that the Soviet leaders were merely continuing the Tsarist policy of imperialist expansion against China.

He returned to China in December, worn out by an exhausting journey which had begun in August. All through the autumn and early winter he had watched processions, visited museums, talked to dignitaries, and all the while he had been deeply aware that Lenin was dying and that the battle for the succession was about to begin. It was a time of détente, when no real decisions were being made. The opposing forces were grouping for the coming struggle. Only one thing was certain: the Russian Communists were enlarging their field of operations in China.

When Chiang Kai-shek reported his findings to Dr. Sun Yat-sen in Canton at the end of the year, he described the monolithic nature of the Communist Party machinery and suggested that the Kuomintang should be organized on the same principles. At the same time he emphasized that the aims of the Kuomintang were profoundly at variance with the aims of the Russian Communist Party. Then, having made his report, he took a leave of absence, and shortly after the New Year he returned to a secluded temple near his native village.

His report to Dr. Sun Yat-sen was substantially the same as a memorandum he drew up the following March for the benefit of the Kuomintang Central Standing Committee:

> There is another thing I wish to tell you frankly. It is the question of the Russian Communist Party. A distinction should be made between realities and theories. We must not ignore realities just because we happen to believe in certain theory or theories. According to my observation, the Russian Communist Party can really cooperate with it for long. It is the Communists' only ten per cent of what the Russians had to say. That was really an understatement because, in view of the exclusive trust you seemed to place in the Russians, I did not want to upset you too much. It is significant that only members of the Communist International, as distinct from those of the Russian Communist Party, defer to Dr. Sun, while the Chinese Communists in Russia always speak of him slightingly and with suspicion.
>
> The Russian Communist Party, in its dealings with China, has only one aim, namely, to turn the Chinese Communist Party into an instrument for its own use. It does not believe that our Party can really cooperate with it for long. It is the Communists' policy to convert the Northeast Provinces, Mongolia, Sinkiang, and Tibet into parts of a Sovietized domain. It may even harbor sinister designs on China's other provinces.
>
> Success is absolutely impossible if one should depend en-

> tirely on the help of others. It will be the height of folly for us to surrender all self-respect and abjectly to idolize others in the hope that they would carry out "the will of Heaven" altruistically. Their brand of internationalism and world revolution is only Tsarism by other names, the better to confuse and confound the outside world.

As the years went by, he would see very little reason to change his opinion of the Soviet Union. He had talked to the most powerful people in the Soviet hierarchy, discussed the future of China with Trotsky, and refused tempting offers to become the standard-bearer of Communism in China, and he had returned to his homeland with a foul taste in his mouth and the knowledge that he had been among enemies.

What particularly rankled and annoyed him was that the Russians had no conception of China as a nation which had heroically engaged upon a course of revolution. In their eyes there was only one kind of revolution—the Communist revolution. All other revolutions must bow to their will. Anyone who questioned the rightness of the Communist revolution was anathema. The dogmatism of the Russian intellectuals appalled him; and his own dogmatism, founded on Confucius and Mencius, became all the stronger as he observed the Communist claims to dominate the entire revolutionary scene.

There were other things that disturbed him: they told lies, they rewrote history, they possessed a strange capacity to believe their lies and their rewritten history. They showed very little knowledge of China or the workings of the Chinese mind, and they seemed to be impervious to the idea that the Chinese were intensely nationalistic and determined to be the masters of their own country. In his report to Dr. Sun Yat-sen he emphasized their vast territorial ambitions and their capacity for intrigue, their use of misleading slogans and their absolute ruthlessness. He was puzzled and saddened when he learned that Dr. Sun Yat-sen, far from accepting his conclusions, dismissed them out of hand.

According to the general custom, a report submitted to Dr. Sun Yat-sen would be returned with annotations in his hand. He would ask questions, seek for clarifications, argue on the margin of the manuscript. But nothing of the kind happened. The doctor simply read the manuscript and shelved it, and there was not even a message of thanks. He had come to the conclusion that Chiang Kai-shek had less authority to speak about Russia than the Russian advisers who were flocking to the headquarters of the Kuomintang.

At this time Chiang Kai-shek was in no position to dispute with Dr. Sun Yat-sen. His judgments on the Communists were carefully reasoned, and he was convinced of their accuracy, but no one would listen to them. He succeeded in having a brief talk with the doctor, but nothing came of it. He went to all the members of the Executive Committee in turn, but they were busy with their own affairs. To Liao Chung-kai, whose sympathies with the Communists were well known, and whose influence on Dr. Sun Yat-sen was such that the management of party affairs had fallen increasingly in his hands, Chiang Kai-shek spoke at some length, but to no avail. Yet he thought he detected a gleam of understanding in Liao Chung-kai's eyes, and some time later he wrote a long letter in which he repeated his conclusions:

> From what I have observed the Russian Communist party has absolutely no sincerity. As I have told you earlier, the words of the Russians are only thirty per cent dependable. Even that is an overstatement.
>
> The sole objective of the Russian Communist party is to communize China under its protective wing. I can never believe our party and the Communist party could successfully cooperate from the beginning to the end. With regard to her policy in China, Russia wants to bring Manchuria, Mongolia, the Moslem and Tibetan dependencies into the orbit of the Soviet Union. As regards China proper, I am not convinced that Russia does not want to grab it too. It would be against logic if we should give up our spirit of self-reliance in favor of dependence on others. Are our people, plagued by such an inferiority complex, willing to let aliens rule us and then worship them like gods?
>
> The internationalism and the idea of the world revolution which the Russians propagate is actually not different from the ideas of imperialism preached by the Tsars. The only difference is that the Russians are clever enough to change slogans for the

> purpose of bewildering the public. It pains me to say that my report was not given even the slightest attention. I feel ashamed of myself for having lost both confidence and pride.
>
> But I wish to add here that while I was in Russia, my activities, I believe, should have been no theme for slander. Nor did I do anything which would bring discredit on the party. But on the subject of our arbitrary association with the Communist party, I have ventured to speak my mind to Dr. Sun Yat-sen. As a loyal subordinate, I felt it was my duty to make my views known to my superior.

For having made his views known, he had fallen into disfavor. The consequences, as he knew, might have been fatal to his ambitions, for there was no one close to Dr. Sun Yat-sen who would speak up for him. In a mood of self-examination he decided to retrieve the manuscript and study it in order to learn whether he had made any errors of judgment, only to discover that it had vanished. He suspected that the Communists had taken hold of it, but it is just as likely that Dr. Sun Yat-sen, who was careless with documents, had simply thrown it away.

From this unsettling experience he drew a conventional lesson. Henceforth he would devote himself strictly to military affairs.

CLIMBING TO POWER

ALTHOUGH HE HAD very little real knowledge of fighting, Chiang Kai-shek had a profound belief in the military arm of the revolution. He had fought in a few disastrous skirmishes, in which he had displayed neither conspicuous bravery nor the capacity to direct a brilliant plan of campaign, but he had acquired the reputation of a capable theoretician and a dogged proponent of revolutionary militarism. What he had seen of the Red Army and the military colleges in Petrograd and Moscow only whetted his appetite for a well-trained revolutionary army. On this subject he had already written many essays, and during the visit to the Soviet Union he took copious notes on the organization of the training schools. He was an "organization man," with a special predilection for discipline, tables of organization, and correct procedure, and he sometimes spoke yearningly of the day when he would be able to train young Chinese officers in the art of revolutionary warfare.

The opportunity came shortly after his return from Russia in a letter written by Dr. Sun Yat-sen from Canton. The letter was addressed to Chiang Kai-shek when he was still recuperating at

Chikow from his long journey. Dr. Sun Yat-sen wrote on January 29, 1924:

> The military academy has been opened for you to take charge of. Preparations are afoot, and we shall find means of raising funds. From considerable distances some hundreds of military officers and cadets have come already, mostly because they admire the choice of the superintendent of the school. You should not disappoint them. I urge you to come without delay.

Chiang Kai-shek was in no mood to obey the order, for it was clear from the letter that there was only the prospect of a military academy and that nothing had been done. February and March were spent in seclusion; in April he traveled to Shanghai; and it was not until May that he reported to Canton, to take charge of the academy. By this time funds had been appropriated, a site had been chosen at Whampoa, and there were already about three thousand applicants. Some five hundred were selected, and the academy officially opened its doors on June 16, 1924, with Dr. Sun Yat-sen presiding over the inaugural ceremonies.

From the beginning it was intended that the academy should offer short, intensive courses, not a complete, many-sided curriculum. Money was always a problem; the teaching staff sometimes quarreled among themselves; the students were often more revolutionary than the teachers. "We had almost no money," Chiang Kai-shek complained later, "and sometimes we did not know how we would be able to pay for our food." Yet he loved the academy ardently, and the schoolmaster in him rose to the occasion. He delighted in officiating at the weddings of the cadets, and he was fond of addressing the students at great length on the subject of their common revolutionary brotherhood. "We should share our afflictions together, share our lives together, share our deaths together, and our hearts should remain here forever." Such mystical sermons were uttered with complete conviction. He was realizing his dreams, and it pleased him to make the cadets live according to his own spartan rituals. Since he was regarded as vaguely leftist—he had been to Russia, could speak a few words of Russian, and was on fairly intimate terms with a Russian military adviser known as Galen—he had very little difficulty in keeping the peace between the Kuomintang and the Communist cadets. Dr. Sun Yat-sen was in a permissive mood, and he permitted the young Communists to enter the military academy so long as they swore an oath of loyalty to the Kuomintang.

Galen, whose real name was Vasily Konstantinovich Blücher, was not the only Soviet citizen in the service of the Kuomintang. Mikhail Borodin, a swarthy and heavily mustached political adviser, was also beginning to exercise a profound influence on the movement. Borodin later vanished into obscurity as the editor of an English newspaper in Moscow, and Marshal Blücher was executed by order of Stalin during the 1937 purges.

Gradually the Kuomintang was being infiltrated by so many Communist members that it was beginning to lose its original character. Sometimes Dr. Sun Yat-sen would throw the weight of his influence on the side of the Communists, and just as abruptly he would withdraw it.

Danger came from the right as well as from the left. The merchants of Canton had organized a Merchants' Volunteer Corps, a private army designed to safeguard them from the exactions of mercenary armies. The corps had grown in size and influence, and was believed to be in league with Chen Chiung-ming's armies, which were still occupying parts of Kwangtung; it was also supported by foreign banks and regarded favorably by the consuls of foreign powers. When Dr. Sun Yat-sen learned that a Norwegian steamer was bringing nine thousand machine guns to Canton, to be given to the Merchants' Volunteer Corps, he issued a peremptory order that the ship be boarded and the guns confiscated. The Merchants' Volunteer Corps demanded the return of the guns and threatened a general strike. The customs commissioner protested, and various foreign consuls also threatened retaliatory action. Dr. Sun Yat-sen held firm, and the nine thousand machine guns became part of the armament of his revolutionary army.

The Merchants' Volunteer Corps was determined to have revenge. The occasion came on October 10, the anniversary of the revolution, when a procession of students and workmen marched through the streets. They were fired upon by the corps, and about eighty were killed. The Whampoa cadets were then called into action. There were five days of fierce street fighting. There was no further trouble from the Merchants' Volunteer Corps.

It was a year of treachery and tumult, of increasing Soviet pressure, of strikes, raids, and uprisings. China was at the mercy of many armies. Hu Han-min and Wang Ching-wei, once Dr. Sun's intimates, were already rebelling against his leadership. The Soviets were pumping more advisers into Canton. Dr. Sun Yat-sen seemed to be falling into the arms of the Communists. He wrote about this time:

> The Revolutionary Committee must come into existence immediately to deal with various extraordinary affairs. It does not matter if Hu Han-min and Wang Ching-wei refuse to join. Today our revolution must follow the example of Russia, but Hu no longer believes this and definitely refuses to accede to it—this is good. His participation would only be a hindrance. Neither is Wang Ching-wei a revolutionary of the Russian school, and so it does not suit him to join us. Henceforth our revolution can never succeed unless we take the Russian revolution as our model, and, as I said, it is unlikely that Hu Han-min and Wang Ching-wei will see fit to follow us. Moreover, these two gentlemen are strong in the idea of maintaining the status quo, but they are not strong in solving new problems. The present situation is neither alive nor dead. It is easy for them to preserve such a situation, but it is not easy for them to develop it along new lines. So they will do those things they are capable of doing, and that too is good; otherwise nothing would ever be accomplished.
>
> So let Hu Han-min and Wang Ching-wei preserve their status quo until it verges on collapse, and we shall be compelled, whether we succeed or fail, to 'cut the entangled hemp with a sharp knife.' The Revolutionary Committee is prepared to resort to this measure, and it does not behoove Wang Ching-wei and Hu Han-min to behave likewise. We must do what we are strong enough to do.

The letter was addressed to Chiang Kai-shek, but it was not calculated to please so much as to alarm. In a mood of tortured frustration, with his back to the wall, Dr. Sun Yat-sen was attempting to explain why he was cutting off his right hand to spite the left. With its hesitations and threats, its insistence on an undefined Russian system to be imitated, and its curious winding repetitions, the letter suggests that he was at the end of his resources. What part of the Russian system was to be held up as a model? Its state socialism? Its efficiency? Nothing is explained, and because there was no final explanation the Kuomintang was to remain divided throughout its existence. Dr. Sun Yat-sen was old and ill. It was observed that while he was delivering those vague lectures which came to be known as "The Three Principles of the People," his hand was continually pressing against his body—his liver was already being eaten up by cancer. He suffered from occasional dizzy spells, and there were inexplicable attacks of blindness. "I am old," he said at the First National Congress of the Kuomintang in January 1924, "and cannot live very much longer in the world. Afterward I shall have to entrust to you, my comrades, this orphan child the Kuomintang." Nearly a year had passed since he made the speech, and he was now busy on his last determined effort to unite the country. Once more he would march against the usurpers in the north.

By the end of October plans for the northern march were again in full swing. Chiang Kai-shek was clearly out of favor, for he was given no important command. In July he was appointed to command a battery at Chengchow, then he was made a member of the Military Affairs Commission, and still later he was given the post of head of the Military Training Preparatory Committee. They were not positions of any great importance, but he had his own followers in the Whampoa military academy and he could wait his time.

Although Dr. Sun Yat-sen spoke at great length and very often about the northern expedition, he had no very great belief in the efficacy of arms, and when there were ways of avoiding military engagements he usually took them. He had seen the revolutionary successes of 1911 vanish in smoke, and the Kuomintang had suffered more than its fair share of military reverses. At this juncture, when all preparations were made, when the northern expedition was about to begin, the ammunition purchased, the soldiers in uniform, there occurred one of those strange alterations, part tragic, part comic, on which the fate of China so often depends. With almost incredible temerity, Tuan Chih-jui, who had assumed the role of "provisional chief executive functioning as the President of the Republic," sent an official invitation to Dr. Sun Yat-sen to confer with him in Peking, recently captured by the army of the "Christian General" Feng Yu-hsiang. Having some faith in Feng Yu-hsiang and little in Tuan Chih-jui, Dr. Sun Yat-sen had decided to abandon the march and go to Peking.

Before leaving Canton in a government cruiser, he paid a last visit to the Whampoa military academy.

"I know very well that the visit to Peking is quite dangerous," he told Chiang Kai-shek, "but I have to go for the sake of the revolution. I must struggle to save the country and the people. So really there is no danger. I am now fifty-nine years old, I am nearing death, and in this way I shall feel at ease when I die."

Chiang Kai-shek had not expected him to speak in these lugubrious tones.

"You shouldn't speak in this way," he said. "There is no question of your dying."

"I am telling you what is on my mind," Dr. Sun Yat-sen answered simply. "But now, when I see the spirit of the Whampoa academy, then I know that my revolutionary aims will continue, and when I die, my soul will be at ease. Two or three years ago I would not have been able to die. These cadets will fulfill my aims."

In this way Chiang Kai-shek reported his last conversation with Dr. Sun Yat-sen, and though there may have been some minor embellishments there is not the least doubt that they spoke their farewells in the classic Chinese manner.

Dr. Sun Yat-sen left Canton on November 12, 1924, and made his way by slow stages to Peking. For a few days he settled in his apartment at 29 rue Molière in the International Settlement in Shanghai, and later he paid a brief visit to Japan, where he called upon the Japanese people to assist China in a spirit of benevolence. Already he looked old and wraithlike, his face deeply lined and chalk white, and the sea journey from Kobe to Tientsin did nothing to improve his health, for it took place in the depth of winter, the sea stormy and icy winds blowing. He was on the verge of collapse when he reached Peking. Doctors were summoned from the Peking Union Medical Hospital; cancer of the liver had been suspected in the past, but he had always refused to accept the provisional diagnosis; now it was confirmed. The doctors operated on him, but it was too late. He lingered on for a few weeks in the house of Dr. Wellington Koo, too weak to speak. He was leaving his revolutionary movement without any effective leadership.

While Dr. Sun Yat-sen was hovering between life and death in Peking, the Kwangtung rebels began to mass their forces against the Kuomintang. A quadrumvirate, consisting of Hu Han-min, Wang Ching-wei, Liao Chung-kai, and Chiang Kai-shek, had taken control of the pathetically small forces loyal to the Kuomintang. Liao Chung-kai, a small thin man with a powerful and penetrating intelligence, had taken up a position on the extreme left, while Hu Han-min occupied a position on the extreme right. Chiang Kai-shek was regarded as belonging to the middle, and Wang Ching-wei, always brilliant and erratic, occupied a position of his own. The quadrumvirate was divided, and without any program of its own. When Chen Chiung-ming attacked, Chiang Kai-shek found himself for the first time in command of a substantial army. On the eve of the battle he addressed his troops:

> Our Generalissimo, Dr. Sun Yat-sen, is now lying seriously ill in Peking, and he has not yet recovered. His disease is so serious that it is possible he is beyond recovery. Why is he stricken with this disease? Because for scores of years he has dedicated himself to the revolution, without any armies to put his plans into effect, and so he got cancer.
>
> Now we, who are the most reliable troops in the army of the Generalissimo, knowing that he is stricken with a mortal sickness and that the destiny of the country is at stake and the people are suffering—we are the ones who must struggle on bitterly to save the country and the people, and in so doing we may be able to cure the Generalissimo, who is already beyond all medical aid.

It was a speech which must have appealed to the soldiers, for they fought well and destroyed the army of Chen Chiung-ming, who finally escaped to Hongkong. The soldiers would have found nothing at all disconcerting in the idea that cancer was caused by intolerable frustrations and that a man beyond medical aid might be cured by news of victories. But not even the news of victories could cure Dr. Sun Yat-sen now.

During the last month of his life he could scarcely speak and nearly all his bodily functions had fallen in abeyance. Terribly bloated and unrecognizable, he seemed to survive by a series of daily miracles. On the afternoon of February 24 the nurse reported that he was sinking rapidly, and a family council was summoned. In a weak voice, speaking slowly and enunciating with difficulty, he announced his pessimistic conclusion to his revolutionary dreams.

"I see that you are in real danger," he said. "After my death, our enemies will either weaken or destroy you. And if you escape from danger, you will still be weakened, so why should I say anything?"

As he lay dying, Dr. Sun Yat-sen was filled with despair. He saw no hope for the revolution and believed that the party he had brought into being was doomed to destruction, and therefore he had no last message, no testament, no blessing, to give to the people. It was necessary, however, that a last message should somehow be extracted from him, and accordingly Wang Ching-wei, who had hurried to Peking when he learned that the doctor was dying, wrote a message intended to convey the dying revolutionary's deepest convictions about the revolution and to give encouragement to his followers. He read out the words slowly, and Dr. Sun Yat-sen gave his assent to them, even though they did not conform to his own ideas. This document, which came to be known as Dr. Sun Yat-sen's Testament, read:

> I have devoted forty years to the work of the National Revolution with the aim of securing for China a position of freedom and independence. After forty years of experience I am profoundly convinced that in order to achieve this aim, we must call upon the masses of the people and unite with those peoples of the world who will treat us on terms of equality and who will struggle together with us.

> At present the revolution is not yet completed. All my comrades should work unceasingly according to the "General Principles of Reconstruction," the "Outline of Reconstruction," the "Three Principles of the People" written by me, and the declaration issued by the First National Congress of the Kuomintang, until this aim is achieved. The convocation of the People's Convention and the abolition of the unequal treaties that I have advocated recently must be carried out with the least possible delay. This is what I wished to call your attention to.

In this strangely arid document there was only one memorable phrase: "At present the revolution is not yet completed." There were many who believed that the revolution had not yet begun, for instead of revolution there had been a series of ineffectual battles and skirmishes lasting for more than thirteen years, with China at the mercy of warlords and wandering armies, and no party or person strong enough to unite the country. For the dying doctor there was only the realization that his revolutionary ideals had ended in abject failure. He lingered on until March 12. On the night before his death he was heard to murmur the words: "Peace—struggle—save—save—China."

Dying, he left no successors. The quadrumvirate in Canton continued to rule a small area of south China for a few months, at loggerheads among themselves. On August 20, as he was walking up the stairs of the Kuomintang headquarters in Canton, Liao Chung-kai was shot dead by an assassin, who was mortally wounded. Suspicion fell on Hu I-sheng, the brother of Hu Han-min, and for the benefit of the party it was agreed that Hu Han-min should take a long vacation in the Soviet Union. In this way the representatives of the extreme left and right wing of the Kuomintang were removed from the scene, leaving Wang Ching-wei and Chiang Kai-shek in disputed control of the party.

While Wang Ching-wei busied himself with theoretical affairs and sometimes gave the impression that he was only waiting for the moment when he would assume the mantle of Dr. Sun Yat-sen, Chiang Kai-shek took charge of the army, led his troops against the rebels who still infested Kwangtung, and for the first time he was able to score a clean-cut victory. In September he suppressed a revolt in Swatow, and in the following month he brought artillery up to Waichow and bombarded the city. With the capture of Waichow after thirty hours of vicious street-fighting, he could claim that the main rebel forces had been wiped out, and no more rebellions could be expected for many months.

Then for the first time since the 1911 revolution Kwangtung was unified by force, with every town and hamlet flying the banner of the Kuomintang. Chiang Kai-shek returned to Canton in triumph. He had succeeded where everyone else had failed, and with Kwangtung as a base he began to prepare for the long march to the north.

PUNITIVE EXPEDITION

"CHINA'S EXISTENCE or ruin depends on whether we can launch the northern expedition," wrote Dr. Sun Yat-sen in 1917. "If we succeed in marching north, then the revolution will be victorious and China will long survive."

The march to the north had become the obsession of the Kuomintang revolutionaries, who failed to realize that it was perfectly possible for an army to move across China without in any way affecting the destiny of the country, for the army would not necessarily take possession of the country; it would simply move from one town to another, losing itself in the vastness of the landscape. Since Dr. Sun Yat-sen had insisted on the march, it had become an article of faith that the march was desirable, necessary and justified by history. Gradually there came into existence a body of doctrine which emphasized the importance of the march: salvation would come only when the revolutionary army had carved a passage across China and reached Peking. The long march acquired a mystique. If it took place, then in some mysterious way all China would be united under the Kuomintang.

Shortly before his death Dr. Sun Yat-sen attempted to launch his northern expedition; the attempt ended in failure. Chiang Kai-shek was determined to succeed where the Tsungli failed. He could scarcely hope for immediate success—the distances were too great, the warlords were too powerful, and Canton, in spite of its wealth and revolutionary fervor, was not an ideal base for launching the northern expedition. Not everyone in Canton thought the march would succeed; there were many who thought it unnecessary and undesirable. Some believed that the proper course of action would be to strengthen the revolution within the province before embarking on a venture which could not hope for success. To crush the warlords they needed overwhelming military force, and the Kuomintang had only a small army. They needed great financial resources, and the Kuomintang had only a bankrupt treasury. They needed a well-constructed social program which would appeal to the people of the towns and the villages, and the Kuomintang had only the sketchy outlines of a program based on Dr. Sun Yat-sen's lecture notes. Nevertheless, Chiang Kai-shek was determined to proceed with the northern expedition. He hoped to destroy the warlords who stood in his path, and even if he failed to destroy them, there was always the hope that the expedition would assume the form of a symbolic act of conquest. He realized that the Kuomintang would remain insecure as long as it remained in Kwangtung. It must at all costs burst out of its provincial boundaries.

There existed, of course, other means for bringing about the desired revolution. There had been no northern expedition in 1911, and the revolution which brought about the overthrow of the Manchu dynasty was not conceived in military terms. Instead, there were spontaneous uprisings by the people of twenty cities against their overlords. With only a little fuel provided by the Kuomintang, the fire had swept across China. But the time for spontaneous uprisings was now over, for there was no clearly defined enemy. If the Kuomintang was to come to power, either there must come about a symbolic act which would resound throughout China or the party must acquire the physical strength to destroy all the other military powers. Chiang Kai-shek was a soldier, and he thought of the revolution largely in military terms.

The secret history of the political moves in Canton during this period is still unknown and may never be known. All that is certain is that the split between the Communists and the Kuomintang was widening. There were undercurrents of revolt, strikes, intrigues, sudden alarms and excursions. Early in February Borodin left Canton and made his way to Mongolia, where he discussed the prospects of the revolution with Feng Yu-hsiang, who was then about to make a prolonged visit to the Soviet Union. Borodin returned to Canton in August, only to discover that Chiang Kai-shek's power had vastly increased in the interval. From being the garrison commander of Canton he had become the undisputed ruler of the province, in control of the political and military machinery and in possession of an effective secret service. It was this secret service, hastily organized, which was to rout the Communists in Canton. Henceforward the Kuomintang was to be armed with an efficient, unscrupulous, and totally dedicated secret police working in the shadows and gradually infiltrating the whole body of China. In time the secret police became a separate arm of the government, and there were some who said that China was ruled not by Chiang Kai-shek but by the chief of his secret police.

The need for a secret police force had become evident in March when Li Chih-lung, the commander of the gunboat "Chung Shan," brought his ship close to Canton and invited Chiang Kai-shek to pay a ceremonial visit. There was nothing in the least unusual in such an invitation. Li Chih-lung was a graduate of the Whampoa military academy, and Chiang had a special fondness for his graduates. At midnight on March 20 a secret agent brought the news that Li Chih-lung intended to murder Chiang soon after he had stepped on board the gunboat. Convinced that there was a plot to murder him, and that the Communists would attempt to take over Canton, Chiang acted quickly. Martial law was declared, there were widespread arrests, Li was dismissed from his command and placed under arrest, and the headquarters of the Russian delegation was placed under guard. The Communists ordered a strike, and the workers obeyed the order. Chiang arrested the leaders. For three days Canton was under martial law, and the secret agents took command of the city. At the military academy about a hundred strike leaders, sailors, and naval officers were given drumhead courts-martial, and those who were considered most dangerous were executed. The Communists spoke of a "reign of terror"; Chiang Kai-shek said he had been forced to take "a certain amount of disciplinary action." The truth was somewhere between the two. There was a small reign of terror, and Chiang Kai-shek welcomed the opportunity to reduce the power of the Communists. He knew he had exceeded his authority, and later offered to submit himself to punishment by the Political Council of the Kuomintang, an offer that was rejected.

It was a time for reorganization, and in the eyes of Chiang Kai-shek it was especially necessary to remove the Communists from positions of authority. The Communists were ordered to provide full lists of their membership to the Kuomintang authorities, and these lists were then delivered to the secret police for appropriate action. An obscure former librarian of Peking University, Mao Tse-tung, was dismissed from his post as head of the propaganda section of the Kuomintang. In every possible way Chiang Kai-shek was attempting to circumscribe the power of the Communists.

These disciplinary actions had become necessary because the preparations for the northern expedition were in full swing. Chiang Kai-shek was obsessed by the need to safeguard the rear. Dr. Sun Yat-sen had rightly or wrongly insisted on the expedition to the north; his followers, seeing China splitting up into vast colonies owned by warlords, could only obey. Borodin and the Russian military advisers had been opposed to the expedition, saying that it was ill timed and that the Kuomintang possessed neither the strength nor the solidarity to succeed in its main purpose. It was sensible advice, but revolutions are not waged sensibly. Chiang Kai-shek was convinced that the northern expedition would succeed—he refused the suggestion that the Kuomintang troops should be taken by sea to the north of Marshal Wu Pei-fu's forces, saying that he did not possess enough ships nor were there any safe places for disembarking his troops—and he planned the campaign with the knowledge that the rear might still be imperiled. All he could do for the moment was to inspire fear in the hearts of the Communists, hinting at the kind of treatment they might expect if they rose against him. It was partly faith, partly necessity, partly knowledge that his opponents, though powerful, had few fundamental beliefs of their own. There is a sense in which the expedition to the north was an act of bravado, an almost fanatical attempt to weld the country together in the face of its traditional centrifugal tendency.

His enemies were the Communists and the armies of the three major warlords and their innumerable satellites. They were strange bedfellows. The warlords were well equipped with weapons and ammunition. If they combined their forces, they could muster an army five times greater than any the Kuomintang could put into the field. They possessed the most important railroads, the main fortifications, ships, telegraph services, customs revenues, nearly all the large industrial cities. There were no bases in the north belonging to the Kuomintang. According to the plan, the northern expedition would sheer through the country like a knife until Peking was occupied and the opposing generals were in flight.

Less than two months after the "Chung Shan" incident Chiang Kai-shek was appointed commander-in-chief of the revolutionary army by proclamation of the Central Executive Committee of the Kuomintang. He was formally inaugurated at nine o'clock in the morning of July 9, 1926, when he swore an oath which is impressive because it underlines the purely military character of the northern expedition:

> The existence or ruin of the party and the country, the success or failure of the Three Principles, the welfare or misery of the people, the glory or disgrace of our comrades—all these depend upon the success of this campaign. The rank and file of the whole army and those who follow us should be of one mind, they should maintain strict discipline, they should obey orders and spare no sacrifice in the performance of their duties, and all of us should show our mettle in the accomplishment of this mission.

> In the name of Heaven we swear to weed out the warlords in Fengtien and Shantung, to accomplish the national revolution, to practice the Three Principles of the People, to exert ourselves to save China, never to fall short of the expectations of the masses nor to disappoint the spirits of the Tsungli and of the officers and soldiers and dead comrades in Heaven.

This oath was composed by Chiang Kai-shek, and reads very much like the speeches he delivered to the young cadets at the military academy. At the oath-taking ceremony Dr. Sun Fo carried the portrait of his father beneath the waving blue flag of the Republic, and there was the solemn presentation of the seal of the revolutionary government.

Chiang Kai-shek's troops amounted to about a hundred thousand men divided among seven army corps. Almost immediately an eighth army corps, commanded by the Hunanese general Tang Sheng-chih, became available, the commander having quarreled with Chao Hung-ti, the warlord or *tutuh* of Hunan. Nearly all the officers were trained at the Whampoa military academy, and were carefully chosen by Chiang Kai-shek himself. Though each army corps was small, it made up for its deficiencies in weapons and effective troops by the strictest discipline. Orders were given that if a company of soldiers retreated, the head of the company was to be summarily shot. The punishment for any soldier caught stealing was death. No excuses for officers who failed in their duty would be allowed. If, for example, the commander of an army corps died in line of battle and his divisional commanders thereupon retreated, they were all to be shot. Similarly, if the divisional commanders stood their ground and were killed in line of battle, those below them in rank would be summarily shot if they retreated. Discipline, which is always harsh in the Chinese army, became harsher, stricter, more implacable.

This harsh discipline, however, was necessary. Chinese armies resemble the heavy elements: they are unstable and tend to disintegrate. The leaders of the revolutionary army were determined that no soldiers would be bought over by the enemy. They insisted that everything taken from the peasants should be paid for. They invented slogans to appeal to the people: "We do not fear death, we do not want money, we love our country." There were also other slogans which depended on the political atmosphere of the moment, like "Down with Wu Pei-fu," and "Leave Chang Tso-lin alone." It was not difficult to leave Chang Tso-lin alone, for his armies were almost beyond reach in the north.

Changsha was occupied on July 13 by an army which had already reached the province of Hunan. This army, under Tang Sheng-chih, simply drove up the Hsiang river from the south. Another and more powerful army under the command of Li Tsung-jen moved out of Kweilin and made its way to Hunan. Chiang Kai-shek had feared bloody battles in Hunan, the province which produces the best soldiers and the most hardened revolutionaries, but so far the victories were bloodless. He remained in Canton, still obsessed by the need to protect the rear. Before he left Canton he met the foreign correspondents. He was hardly known to them, and they were puzzled by the spectacle of this slight man who looked hardly more than a boy, with a gold ring in his ear and a reputation for hard drinking. Asked for his autobiography, he answered curtly, "I am a native of Chekiang, I was educated in the Paoting Military Academy and Japan, and since then I have followed Dr. Sun Yat-sen in the cause of the revolution."

Many days passed before he felt that it would be safe to leave Canton. There were interminable conferences and interminable delays. He was still feeling his way, and in no mood to embark on hasty decisions when at any moment there might be another Communist uprising in Canton. The Cantonese were surprisingly quiescent. It seemed too good to be true. All the Communists had been eliminated from the military commands; the Kuomintang army had borrowed various Communist techniques. Political commissars were attached to the headquarters of each army corps, and they went to great lengths to stir up revolutionary enthusiasm among the peasants. In the early days of the march a kind of social revolution seemed always on the point of coming to birth: the people hoped desperately for the end of the reign of the warlords, but they were still dubious about the social revolution contemplated by the Kuomintang. Most of the Kuomintang soldiers came from the southern provinces of Kiangsi, Hunan, and Kwangtung: they were southerners about to fight the northerners; and they wanted nothing better.

Chiang Kai-shek reached Changsha on August 12. Here he proposed to make the final dispositions of his army. Against him were ranged six supreme commanders and six armies. Some of them could be bribed off, some were too far in the north to matter for the moment, but not one of them was known to be in favor of Dr. Sun Yat-sen's Three Principles, and all of them could be expected to fight. There was Chang Tso-lin, the old opium-smoking warlord of Manchuria, with great powers over the province of Hopei. There was the quiet, scholarly Wu Pei-fu, a devoted Buddhist, a man of great charm and energy, ruling over vast areas of Hopei, Honan, Shensi, Szechuan, Hupeh, and Hunan—the immediate enemy. He was a good soldier, brave and cunning, and he despised foreigners so much that he refused at any time to take refuge in the foreign concessions. He had assumed the title of commander-in-chief of the North Allied Army, which in firepower and reserves was the strongest in China. There was Sun Chuang-fang with his Five Provinces Allied Army, who ruled over large parts of Kiangsu, Chekiang, Fukien, Anhwei, and Kiangsi. There was the strange "Dogmeat General," Chang Chung-chang, who possessed innumerable White Russian concubines, in Shantung. The "Dogmeat General," with his appalling sadism, belonged to another age. People spoke of his "three negatives"—he did not know how much money he had, how many women he had, or how many children he had. He was not worthy of Chiang Kai-shek's steel, and the officers of the Kuomintang army regarded him with the slightly hesitant respect that one has for a mangy dog with sharp teeth. There was Yen Hsi-shan, the "model governor" of Shansi, who might be bought over or induced to join the Kuomintang out of patriotism, since he was a man who was thought to be genuinely concerned for the future of China. Finally there was Feng Yu-hsiang, the "Christian general," with his Kuominchun or National Army in the northern provinces of Suiyuan, Chahar, and parts of Hopei, who had left for Moscow mysteriously, but might at any moment return. Like Wu Pei-fu he was a man of great charm and ability, and beloved by his troops. His temper was mercurial, and no one could ever guess which way he might spring.

The largest and most disciplined army, and therefore the most dangerous, belonged to Wu Pei-fu, who was also the commander who possessed the greatest contempt for the revolutionaries. Chiang Kai-shek regarded him quite rightly as a man deeply rooted in the pre-revolutionary period, dangerous precisely because he had a powerful following. In generalship and ability he was a match for any of the Kuomintang army commanders.

Two days after he arrived in Changsha, Chiang Kai-shek issued a proclamation to the nation, in which he outlined some of the reasons which led him to embark on the northern expedition.

> The revolutionary army is about to wage a decisive campaign against the followers of Wu Pei-fu, the leader of the Peiyang party, in Hankow and Wuchang. The battle is to determine the fate of the militarists and to decide the issue whether the militarists shall remain or whether the Chinese people shall recover their independence and liberty. It is a struggle between the people and the militarists, between the revolutionaries and the reactionaries, between the Three Principles of the People and imperialism.
>
> Entrusted with the duty of carrying out the northern expedition advocated by Dr. Sun Yat-sen, I am now concentrating my armies in Changsha and Yochow. As a revolutionary I am fighting for the people. Very soon our army will arrive at Wuchang and Hankow. I hope the people will give it all assistance, and simultaneously arise and try to save the country. The object of the expedition is the same as that announced by Dr. Sun Yat-sen in November 1924 when he went to Peking at the invitation of Tuan Chi-jui and Chang Tso-lin. The object was to hold a People's Convention and to give birth to a unified government based on the Three Principles of the People and to abolish the unequal treaties, so that the people may be enabled to lay the foundation for liberty and independence.

Inevitably there were simplifications in the proclamation, some of them deliberate. The purpose of the northern expedition was not quite so clear as Chiang Kai-shek made out. The revolutionary army was making a bid for public support against Wu Pei-fu—the less important generals in the southeast and east were expected to wait their turn before being conquered. It was hoped that Chang Tso-lin in the north would remain quiet, and it was confidently expected that Feng Yu-hsiang would do nothing to assist Wu Pei-fu, for they were enemies of long standing. It was decided to attack Wuchang and Hankow at once. They were important cities, with large mining and steel production, but there was also a symbolic reason for attacking them. It was in these cities that the revolt against the Manchus had broken out fifteen years before.

The fourth, seventh, and eighth army corps, forming the central column, were ordered to move up to the attack. The right wing, composed of the second and third army corps, was ordered to attack Yu-hsien, while the ninth and tenth army corps forming the left wing were to move up when they were ready. All these armies were gradually enlarged with conscripts gathered on the march. Farmers were employed as guides, as muleteers, as spies and secret agents. It was not yet a popular movement, but it was continually gaining strength.

On August 8 Tang Sheng-chih's eighth army corps had crossed the Milo river—the famous river in which the great poet Chu Yuan was drowned and where there was to be more furious fighting during the Japanese war. Meanwhile the fourth army corps was battering Pingchiang in a prolonged contest with Wu Pei-fu's vanguard; the battle lasted for eleven days. These battles were bloody. The small towns of northern Hunan were continually changing hands. Wu Pei-fu was ordering the execution of his commanders when they retreated, and retreating regiments were decimated—one man in ten was shot dead, as an example to others. Yochow fell to the revolutionaries on August 22. Wu Pei-fu was in Hankow. Realizing the danger, he immediately took personal charge. There followed the long, costly, and bitterly disputed battle of Tingszekiao, which changed hands three times in a week. On August 29 it fell for the last time. Three days later the revolutionaries were outside the gates of Wuchang. Then Henyang fell, and at noon on September 7 the first revolutionaries marched through the gates of Hankow.

The first stage of the northern expedition was now over. The conquest of Wuchang and Hankow was the traditional starting point for the conquest of all China south of the Yangtse river. It had been a grim and murderous campaign, with no quarter given. Few prisoners were taken; the advancing armies massacred at their leisure; no effort was made to convert captured soldiers. There was a significant bitterness in these brief and bloody battles, and this bitterness was to leave its traces on future events. From now on there would be an end to discussion, and any commander who found himself in the hands of the enemy could expect to be summarily executed. The commanders and soldiers knew that the battles being fought in small and obscure villages would be decisive for the future of China.

Wu Pei-fu was a good general, but though he had fought twice in the past through Hunan, his intelligence system was imperfect and the loyalty of his troops was often dubious. The intelligence system of the revolutionaries was excellent; the farmers were on their side, and they denied to the northern enemy their knowledge of the unmapped paths over the mountains. It was a strange war. Scaling ladders were employed in the assault on Wuchang; villages were captured by peasants armed with pitchforks; bombing airplanes were used for the first time, with tremendous effect. It was a war of ambushes, night marches, sudden attacks on sleeping villages. For most of the time Chiang Kai-shek kept in the background, but at important moments he would leave his railroad car and visit the front lines. He was completely fearless, and seemed to believe that no enemy bullet would dare to strike him. Twice he threatened to commit suicide if his soldiers failed to capture towns by a certain time. The ruse was successful; the towns were captured; and Chiang Kai-shek, wearing sandals and a cotton gown, returned from the front line to his telephones. It was observed that the telephones of the revolutionary army worked far better than those of the enemy.

In a country as vast as China battles are won when towns are captured and lines of communication are maintained. The second proviso may sometimes be more important than the first. Chiang Kai-shek thought he had stamped out all opposition in the rear. He had not paid sufficient attention to his neighbors, who were likely to march into Kwangtung once the Kuomintang army had marched out of the province. This, indeed, is what happened. General Chao Yin-jen, the military governor of Fukien, saw his opportunity. He marched into Kwangtung from the east, and would probably have succeeded in occupying the province if General Ho Ying-chin, later to become minister of war in the Kuomintang government, had not led his troops by forced marches into Fukien. Fuchow was occupied on December 18. In February still another province was added to the roster of fallen provinces, for Hangchow was captured late in the month and a few days later the whole province of Chekiang fell into Kuomintang hands. The capture of Chekiang gave special pleasure to Chiang Kai-shek, who could now make a ceremonial visit to his birthplace. Five provinces were flying the blue and white flag of the Kuomintang.

The fighting might have ended with the capture of the five southern provinces, but the initial momentum of the armies was not yet exhausted. The sixth and seventh army corps took the province of Anhwei, and Nanking was taken on March 24. For some reason which has never been made clear the Kuomintang troops who entered the city were given license to attack foreigners; missionaries and consular officials were killed; some women were raped; looting went on for several days. What came to be known as the "Nanking incident" caused consternation among foreigners throughout China. There was a widespread belief that the Kuomintang, heady with victory, deliberately provoked the incident in order to warn the foreigners that the time of the unequal treaties and the international settlements was coming to an end. In China xenophobia is easily aroused, and the behavior of the Kuomintang troops was not entirely unexpected. In the tense situation foreign governments rushed reinforcements to guard the International Settlement in Shanghai.

During the following weeks Chiang Kai-shek offered his own explanation of the "Nanking incident." He explained that the murder of the foreigners in Nanking was ordered by the political commissar of the sixth army corps, a Communist called Lin Tsu-han, who took his orders from Borodin. The purpose of the plot was to discredit Chiang Kai-shek in the eyes of foreigners. It was a self-regarding explanation, and not altogether convincing. Lin Tsu-han slipped away, but others were arrested, tried, and summarily shot. Documents were found by the secret police, implicating the Communists in the plot. Chiang Kai-shek assumed full responsibility for the incident and published a proclamation setting out his views on the foreigners who chose to live in China:

> It is the settled policy of the revolutionary government not to use force or mass violence in any form to effect a change in the status of the foreign settlements. That has been repeatedly stated by the responsible Revolutionist authorities, and I am here to repeat that the Revolutionists will use only peaceful methods, namely negotiations.
>
> The aims and aspirations of the Revolutionist movement in foreign affairs are to secure international equality. We wish to be equal among the family of nations. This is clearly stated in Dr. Sun Yat-sen's will.
>
> Any nation which is prepared and willing to treat us as an equal is our friend, and we are willing and anxious to work with it and associate ourselves with it even though it is a nation which has previously oppressed us.

Chiang Kai-shek's statement did little to allay the fears of foreigners: too many veiled threats were included within it. The division of China into satrapies had served their interest, and the emergence of a powerful single party possessing a formidable army, and with a clear-cut program for sweeping away the old feudal China, was likely to fill the compradores in the International Settlement at Shanghai with apprehension. Chiang Kai-shek's task was to use the special privileges of the International Settlement to the advantage of the Kuomintang party. The Chinese Communists, who were well entrenched in the Shanghai labor movement, were determined to prevent him. In the feverish atmosphere of the time it did not need a great deal of perspicacity to realize that Shanghai would soon become a battleground between the Communists and the right wing of the Kuomintang. Chiang Kai-shek decided to forestall a Communist coup.

In his official biography Chiang Kai-shek dismissed these

events in a short paragraph, saying that with the assistance of Pai Chung-hsi he sent regular soldiers to disarm the guerrillas and armed laborers of Chapei, shot those who resisted, and declared a state of martial law. He would have us believe that there was a brief and salutary mopping-up campaign, of no particular importance. In fact, the Kuomintang coup in Shanghai assumed the dimensions of a major battle.

At four o'clock in the morning of April 12 troops armed with machine guns spread through the working-class quarters of Shanghai, and attacked the labor organizations defended by armed Communist pickets. The Communists were taken off guard, but fought back. All over Chapei, Nantao, Woosung, and Pootung there were early morning battles around factories, guild houses, and labor offices. The decision had been taken ten days before at a conference held at the Kuomintang headquarters in Shanghai, and there was time to prepare a coherent plan of attack and to summon the assistance of the secret societies. The attack took the form of a combined operation, the military working in close liaison with the Green and Red Societies, the two underworld gangs, successors of the Triads, which were the real rulers of Shanghai's Chinese quarter. Both Dr. Sun Yat-sen and Chiang Kai-shek are believed to have been members of the Green Society, which was closely connected with the Kuomintang from its origins.

The fighting was over within twenty-four hours, but sporadic killings continued through the following weeks, as the Kuomintang agents rounded up the Communists who escaped from the net. Chou En-lai, then a relatively obscure member of the Chinese Communist party, was one of those who escaped by a hairbreadth. He was captured by Kuomintang soldiers at the Huchow Guild in Chapei, but the Kuomintang lieutenant in charge was content to leave the captives in the guild house while he awaited the arrival of the underworld gangs; during the interval Chou En-lai slipped out of the house. Disguised as a woman, he remained in Shanghai for some weeks, carefully observing the defeat of the Communists and compiling a full report on the Kuomintang repressions.

Foreigners were stunned by the calculated violence of the Kuomintang troops. There were no trials. The workers were shot immediately if they were thought to be in sympathy with the Communists. About five hundred were herded into the local prisons; and most of them were shot or thrown into the furnaces of locomotives before the day was over.

Chiang Kai-shek's triumph in Shanghai was complete. The Communist movement was crushed, the leaders either dead or in full flight or hiding. In the following days similar measures were taken in Ningpo, Foochow, Amoy, Swatow, and Canton. Chiang Kai-shek was determined to obliterate communism from the map of China. In this he failed, and his failure was largely due to the fact that communism is a body of ideas which becomes more fervent and authoritative the more violently it is attacked. The blood of the dead Communists fertilized the faith.

When Chiang Kai-shek turned his attention to the northern expedition, he saw that there was an overwhelming need to consolidate his gains. It was not that he had any desire to abandon the expedition; it was simply that the expedition had changed its nature in the course of the long campaign which brought him from Canton to Shanghai. He needed to regroup his army, to refashion the political structure of the party, and to map out a strategy for the future. He also needed large sums of money, and he demanded and received a gift of three million dollars from the Shanghai compradores. The Communists claimed that this was blood money paid for the execution of so many Communist leaders, but this is to misjudge Chiang Kai-shek's motives. He had no more liking for the compradores than he had for the Communists, and he demanded the money for the same reason that the Communists, if they had succeeded in taking over Shanghai, would have demanded it. A revolutionary movement, and a revolutionary army, need money.

Meanwhile the northern warlords were behaving predictably. Wu Pei-fu had withdrawn his army to Honan after issuing a statement that the fall of Hankow was due to treachery, a statement which was at least partly true. For some time he dallied with thoughts of a coalition with Chang Tso-lin, but when the Manchurian warlord crossed the Yellow river, Wu Pei-fu had no alternative but to attack him. It was his last battle. The Mukden forces took Chengchow, and Wu Pei-fu abandoned his army and fled with a small bodyguard to Loyang in Honan, and when Honan fell to the armies of Feng Yu-hsiang, Wu Pei-fu fled to a Buddhist monastery in Szechuan. Chang Tso-lin, regarding himself as the protector of China against the Kuomintang, organized a "National Pacification Army," with himself as commander-in-chief, and the "Dogmeat General" as one of his deputy commanders.

These alterations in the balance of power in the north favored Chiang Kai-shek, who could confidently look forward to the time when the northern warlords would exterminate each other. Wherever he looked, he saw his efforts crowned with success. He had dealt—or thought he had dealt—a mortal blow to the Communists. In nine months his armies had swept through eight provinces—Kwangtung, Fukien, Hunan, Hopei, Anhwei, Kiangsi, Kiangsu, and Chekiang—and he had received the allegiance of the two outlying southwestern provinces of Szechuan and Kweichow. He was the master of nearly all the territory south of the Yangtse river. He had established himself as a strategist of extraordinary daring, relentless in the pursuit of his enemies, possessing unsuspected gifts of diplomacy. His name was on everyone's lips, and he was more loved and more feared than anyone else in China.

It might have been thought that the victories of his armies would consolidate his political strength within the Kuomintang party. In fact, the party was widely split among factions, and there were many members of the government who detested the young commander-in-chief, accusing him of pride and obstinacy and an overwhelming desire for self-aggrandizement. They claimed that his motives were essentially personal, that he desired to become the sole ruler of China, and that he was indifferent to the needs of the people. Factions were being brought together in the hope that they could combine with sufficient strength to defeat him. From time to time they would succeed in removing him from power by relieving him of his official duties, but he remained powerful through the strength of his legend and his hold on the army. Yet he knew that his victories were illusory, and at any moment China would once more become "a tray of shifting sand." Though Chang Tso-lin was far in the north and Wu Pei-fu had surrendered to

Buddhism and the "Dogmeat General" could no longer be taken seriously, it was still possible that the Kuomintang armies would dissolve into the landscape, emerging once again as the private armies of self-seeking warlords. Victory was as illusory as unity, a word that he was always repeating. To achieve a real victory, it was necessary that he triumph over the Kuomintang itself. For the next ten years he was at war with his own party. Not until the Japanese attacked China did he achieve the position of unassailable leadership which he desired.

WAR WITHIN A WAR

IN THEORY and perhaps in practice Chiang Kai-shek was inclined to regard military power as dangerous unless it was subservient to political control. Once in 1925, when he resigned from the command of the first army corps, he announced that he had come to this decision because he had no desire to become a militarist. Nothing was more likely than that an army corps commander would develop into a militarist, attempting to evade control by the politicians. He had come to the conclusion that the victories of armies are always rewarding, but rarely rewarding in the things that are most desired.

When he looked back over his nine months of victories, Chiang Kai-shek could congratulate himself on a succession of clean-cut thrusts. In the early stages at least there had been a revolutionary fervor among the troops; the people on the whole rejoiced in the army's successes. The warlords were in a state of disarray. There had been warlords like Chang Chin-yao—Wu Pei-fu had said of him in disgust that his fatty remains would serve to fertilize half an acre of Chinese earth—who taxed the peasants for seven years in advance and planted opium on all the red hills of Hunan. All this would soon be over, the peasants thought, gazing at the revolutionary soldiers who paid for everything they bought and did everything in their power to bring the peasants over to their side. It was the time before the corrupt officials and the financiers laid siege to cities.

The good reputation of the army was a good augury for the future. They had occupied the south at far less cost than had been expected—Chiang Kai-shek had counted on an expenditure of fifty million Chinese yuan, and had succeeded with only eighteen million. They had outwitted and outfought their enemies, and Chiang Kai-shek could congratulate himself on his generalship. At such a time he could almost be excused for regarding himself as the destined savior of China. When someone remarked that power was going to his head, he said bitterly:

> Is it that these mischief-makers are trying to lower others' estimates of me? An old proverb runs: 'There is no difficulty in finding words if one wants to pile sins on one another.' These rumor-mongers are so bent on opposing the leaders of the Nationalist Movement that they are acting in an insensate manner. They cannot understand that if the movement fails, China cannot get freedom and equality. It is my earnest wish to make success possible, and though I may be single-handed, I will still fight—I am prepared to be treated like Yueh Fei.* I care not for the present. I aspire to be a personality in history, about whom posterity will talk, and I sincerely hope that you will help me.

In such a mood, seeing himself as a figure in history, Chiang Kai-shek identified himself with the movement which would bring about the salvation of China. Unlike Dr. Sun Yat-sen he was not remarkable for his humility. The Father of the Republic never aspired to be "a personality in history, about whom posterity will talk." He had other aims, and chief among them was that of ending the suffering of the people.

Yet there were reasons for this almost incredible pride. His

* Yueh Fei (1102–1141 A.D.), one of the most famous Chinese generals, fought brilliantly during the last years of the Sung dynasty, and was arrested and executed at the orders of a treacherous prime minister.

successes had changed the map of China. Almost alone, and against the desires of a great number of party members, he had welded the army together and precipitated the northern expedition; and while he was the one military leader of distinction in the Kuomintang, he was still far from being dictator. He was subject to the politicians. It was no fault of his that just at the moment when he was exerting vast military power, his political power was diminishing.

After the northern expeditionary force occupied Hankow in November, it was decided to transfer the government to this city, making it the new capital. The actual transfer of the government was made in two stages. By accident or design the left-wing group arrived in Hankow before the others. So it came about that Dr. Sun Fo, T.V. Soong, Eugene Chen, Madame Sun Yat-sen, and Borodin arrived before the rest of the government, which remained in Nanchang in the south. T.V. Soong urged the Nanchang members to come to Hankow. They refused for reasons which are still mysterious, and their refusal was to cost the party dearly. The split between the two wings of the party grew. Separation confirmed the growing distrust, vastly increased the tensions, and made compromise virtually impossible. The attitudes of the Communists hardened. Mao Tse-tung, only recently deprived of his powers in the Ministry of Information, abruptly vanished from Canton and made his way to Hunan, where he attempted to bring about a communist insurrection. He could scarcely have foretold that he would become the dictator of China, and Chiang Kai-shek could scarcely have foretold that he would squander the energies of his best armies attempting to put down communist insurrections. The break between the Communists and the Kuomintang was already complete, although Borodin and the left-wing members of the Kuomintang still retained their political power.

The times were out of joint. It was as though history was determined that China should remain disunited, and that there should be incessant quarrels within the one party which might have been able to unite China. The soldiers who fought during the northern expedition had regarded themselves as a popular army, with powers to socialize the land and form farmers' unions, women's unions, unions of coolies and shop workers, tenant farmers and rice-huskers. In many cases this was done, and during the winter of 1926–1927 important experiments in socialization were carried out. Chiang Kai-shek, who showed very little interest in social reform, assailed these experiments, saying that they were inspired by the Communists; he demanded that the socialization of land should cease. On March 10 a meeting of the Third Plenary Session of the Central Executive Committee of the Kuomintang reduced Chiang Kai-shek to the rank of army commander, with no seat in the government. The meeting was held at Hankow, and was attended largely by the left-wing members of the government. The office of commander-in-chief of the revolutionary army was abolished. In its place there was set up a National Military Council consisting of nine commissioners, five chosen from the ranks of the Kuomintang and four from generals on the active list. Chiang Kai-shek did not attend the Plenary Session.

The true history of the ensuing events may never be known, for too many people have given conflicting testimonies. What is known for certain is that on April 6, 1927, Chinese soldiers and police on the instructions of Chang Tso-lin raided the palatial Soviet embassy in Peking and made a thorough search. The diplomatic corps in Peking apparently approved of the search, for the well-informed London *Times* reported that the diplomatic corps raised objections only to the excessive zeal displayed by the Chinese, who "exceeded the authority contained in the warrant of search granted by the Diplomatic Body." The search was illegal by international law, since foreign embassies enjoy diplomatic immunity, but according to Chang Tso-lin it was necessary to practice illegality in order to oppose illegality. A vast number of incriminating documents were discovered. Seventeen Chinese found on the premises were strangled, and fifteen Soviet officials were placed under arrest. Most of the documents published by Chang Tso-lin were authentic, and among them was a plan for the communist takeover of China written by Borodin. On the following day the Soviet consulate in Shanghai was surrounded by Chinese police and White Russian soldiers, and Soviet offices in the International Settlement were raided. Chang Tso-lin and Chiang Kai-shek had apparently agreed upon a common plan to destroy Soviet influence in China.

The terror which began in Peking spread down the Yangtse valley. It was a time of intrigue, of sustained excitement and continuous violence. None of the three contestants—Chang Tso-lin and the left and right wings of the Kuomintang—showed themselves to advantage. Six days after the arrests and murders in the Soviet embassy in Peking, Chiang Kai-shek launched his attack on the armed workers of Shanghai. In Canton orders were given that Communists report to the police within ten days; if they failed to report, they would be arrested and shot; if they reported, they were also arrested and shot. So it went on—the dismal catalog of sins committed and crimes unrepented, friend turning against friend, civil war flaming up, subsiding, flaming up again, the rule of the assassin and the gunman, with no end in sight. The right wing regarded the presence of Borodin in Hankow as an intolerable provocation. The Hankow government regarded Chiang Kai-shek's assumption of military and dictatorial power as an illegal abuse of authority. The historian cannot grant favors. The murders were indefensible.

Meanwhile there were continual conferences and attempts to bring about a compromise government, but they came to nothing. Wang Ching-wei returned from France, and for a time it was thought that he would act as mediator between the two wings of the Kuomintang party. Chang Tso-lin had published to the world a document written by Borodin which said, "Wang Ching-wei has ambition but no definite aim. He can be used." It was an accurate assessment, and Chiang Kai-shek for once agreed with Borodin, while attempting to use Wang Ching-wei for his own purposes. In Hankow Wang Ching-wei did everything in his power to have Borodin expelled from the Central Executive Committee on the grounds that it was intolerable that a foreigner should exercise power in China. In this he was successful, for in the middle of July Borodin was removed from all his official functions. With his passing some at least of the wounds of the party were healed. Less than a month later, realizing that his own presence was an obstacle to any settlement, Chiang Kai-shek resigned from all his offices.

It was not, however, a complete break with the Kuomintang government, and it was observed that he was in continual contact with advisers and military officials. He could be even more powerful when he was out of office. On August 13, the day after he arrived in Shanghai, he issued a statement saying that the cause of the split was the preponderance of power claimed by the left wing of the party, and he denied that Dr. Sun Yat-sen had ever encouraged the Communists. "China has no room for the coexistence of Communism and the Kuomintang," Dr. Sun Yat-sen had said. "We must admit the Communists, but we must also convert them, and the Three Principles of the People will serve as a melting pot." The Communists claimed that Dr. Sun Yat-sen had never envisaged a one-party state and had never shown the least desire to destroy the Communists. There could be no agreement between the factions: they remembered only the phrases which pleased them. Irked by the condemnation of the Hankow government, Chiang Kai-shek asked for condign punishment for whatever sins he had committed, called upon the soldiers in Hunan, Hupeh, and Kiangsi to continue the drive to the north, complained bitterly against the dissensions within the party and insisted that the Communists must be purged. It was an astute move, but it was largely dictated by events. By resigning, he was removing himself from both wings of the party.

Sixteen years later, writing in *China's Destiny*, he recalled the dissensions within the party and confessed that there were mysteries he had been unable to solve:

> During this period we should call sadly to mind the words of the Father of the Republic in his opening speech at the First National Congress of the Kuomintang. I shall repeat his words: 'The first thing that requires our attention is our previous lack of solidarity within the party, which arose not because there were powerful enemies destroying us from without, but because we destroyed ourselves from within, and so the united strength of the party was scattered and the revolution failed.' That is to say: if there is no trouble within, then there can be no trouble from without. If this is true of a nation, it is also true of a party. But unfortunately at this moment of life and death in the revolution

there occurred a split in the national revolutionary army, and the heavy mission entrusted to us by the Father of the Republic and the great tasks which the whole nation was striving to accomplish almost failed. It is heartbreaking to relate the history of these things.

Two things caused the split in the ranks of the Kuomintang—the intrigues carried on by Wang Ching-wei and those carried on by the Communists during the fifteenth and sixteenth years of the Chinese Republic. The Kuomintang could not accept the policies of the Communists. I do not want to repeat the story here, but even up to the present time I have been unable to understand all the secret details of their complicity. Whether it was Wang Ching-wei who made use of the Communists or the Communists who made use of the man Wang Ching-wei, or whether they mutually used each other is not clear. What is clear is that they regarded the national revolution as a bourgeois revolution and were prepared to attempt a social revolution of the proletariat.

All this is made abundantly clear by the Communist party leaders such as Chen Tu-chiu. Under the slogan of "class conflict" they made tools of the farmers and laborers, and brought production to a standstill. They called upon youth to despise and abandon the traditional virtues of the nation, and even to take courtesy, righteousness, carefulness, and conscientiousness as synonyms for obstinacy, while filial piety, brotherliness, loyalty, and fidelity were regarded as wrong-dealing. The situation was almost past hoping for.

Again and again during his meditations, and in the pages of his journals, Chiang Kai-shek would return to those angry days when the split widened and for the first time he saw the full extent of the chasm. The Kuomintang was dedicated to one kind of revolution, the Communists to another, and there could be no compromise between them. It was not only that there could be no compromise, but that each was vowed to the annihilation of the other. The small seed would grow into a vast poisonous tree, and innumerable Chinese would die under its shade.

THE MARCH TO THE NORTH

HAVING RESIGNED from all his offices, Chiang Kai-shek turned his attention to Japan, which he had not visited since the days when he was a private second class in the field artillery. He had maintained close ties with Japanese friends, and continued to have a healthy respect for the industry and civilization of the Japanese people. He was under no delusions about the danger which Japan represented to a renascent China, and he intended to probe the intentions of the Japanese militarists. There were other reasons—private reasons—for a visit to Japan. He was suffering from a peculiarly painful form of lumbago, which might be improved by attending the Japanese sulfur springs, and there was the question of his impending marriage, a matter of some delicacy. Above all, he had arrived at one of those periods in life when it was necessary to meditate and ponder carefully the next move in the game.

There was no question of going with a large retinue. His companion was General Chang Chun, who had served in the same Japanese field artillery unit with him.

In the photographs taken just before his departure he looks ill and worn; photographs taken in Japan show him to have miraculously regained his health. The heavy weight of responsibility had not completely left him, for he still regarded himself as the commander-in-chief of the Kuomintang army, and he knew that the revolution would continue the moment he returned. He held the destiny of China in his hands, and he was perfectly aware of it. He was in no hurry to reach Tokyo. On October 13, 1927, having passed through Kobe, he came to the Imperial Hotel in Tokyo late in the afternoon, rested, and in the evening telephoned his old divisional commander, General Gaishi Nagoaka. The text of the telephone message has survived: "Is the divisional commander in? Yes, please come soon. I have lumbago, and so you must excuse me from coming to visit you. I suggest that we go to the hot springs and take a bath. Is it possible for Regimental Commander Himatsu to come with you?"

It is difficult to understand why these words have been recorded when so much of greater value to Chinese history has been left unrecorded. But they show that Chiang Kai-shek was still deeply impressed by the officers who ruled over the small artillery group sixteen years before, and that he was in a mood for serious military discussions with the Japanese. It was remembered that he was particularly respectful to General Nagoaka, and was always careful to address him by his full title. When they returned from the springs some days later, Commander Himatsu called on him, and they drank toasts and wrote scrolls to one another. Chiang Kai-shek wrote, "Not to fall short of the education given by the teacher."

It was a pleasant interlude in a peaceful country, far from the civil wars. He called on various people, including Baron Giishi Tanaka, the author of the Tanaka Memorial. Tanaka asked him why it was still necessary to continue the northward punitive expedition, and suggested that it would be sufficient to set up a government in Nanking. Chiang Kai-shek answered, "The revolutionary forces can never be stopped. China must be united, and two governments cannot be allowed to exist in China, otherwise there will never be any stability in the country, or in the east." Baron Tanaka had excellent reasons for wanting to know Chiang Kai-shek's intentions, for since the spring of that year he had been both prime minister and minister for foreign affairs.

Chiang Kai-shek went on to spend ten days in the house of a Japanese millionaire, where there were more political discussions, and then traveled to Hakone and Nikko. Telegrams followed him, but when he returned to China it was not to resume his command: it was to get married.

Passing through Kobe, Chiang Kai-shek spent a few hours in the house of Mrs. Soong, the widow of Charles Soong. This formidable woman, the matriarch who presided over the Soong dynasty, held fast to her Methodist beliefs and felt no particular sympathy for Chiang Kai-shek, whom she regarded as a heathen. Her second daughter, Ching-ling, had married Dr. Sun Yat-sen, and her third daughter, Mei-ling, was determined to marry Chiang Kai-shek. Mei-ling was beautiful, obstinate, and proud; she had wanted to marry the General for many years, and the time had come to put an end to many uncertainties. Mrs. Soong knew that Chiang Kai-shek was the father of two children. She knew also that he had many concubines. There could be no compromise between her Christian beliefs and his paganism, and she would give her blessing to the marriage only if he espoused Christianity, and sent the concubines away. The concubines presented no problem, and he was perfectly prepared to consider the advantages of Christianity. When he arrived in Kobe, he found Mei-ling at her mother's side. The old matriarch was insistent that her future son-in-law must be converted to Christianity before she could even remotely consider the marriage, and Chiang Kai-shek gave indications that he was only waiting for an opportunity to be converted. When he left the house in Kobe, Mei-ling had the satisfaction of knowing that the marriage would take place before the end of the year.

The wedding, which took place in Shanghai on December 1, 1927, was divided into two parts. First there was the religious ceremony in the Soong's Seymour Road house, with Dr. David Yui, the local secretary of the Young Men's Christian Association, officiating. This was followed by the civil marriage in the ballroom of the Majestic Hotel. It was an exhausting ceremony, with some thirteen hundred guests in attendance, interminable speeches, an atmosphere as far removed as possible from the military camp. Above the rostrum hung the portrait of Dr. Sun Yat-sen. The bride was given away by her brother, T. V. Soong, and she entered the ballroom to the strains of "Here Comes the Bride." The *North-China Herald* dutifully reported: "The bride looked very charming in a beautiful gown of silver and white georgette, draped slightly at one side and caught with a spray of orange blossoms. She wore also a little wreath of orange buds over her veil of beautiful rare lace, and carried a bouquet of palest pink carnations tied with white and silver ribbons." Mei-ling Soong had been educated at the Wesleyan College for Women in Macon, Georgia, and had graduated from Wellesley, and every effort was made to combine the marriage customs of America and China.

Afterward came the official wedding photograph, with the bride sitting demurely on an ornamental plush-covered chair, while her husband leans forward over the back of the chair with a pair of kid gloves in his hands. In this photograph, wearing a formal tail-coat and stiff collar, surrounded by potted ferns in silver vases, he looks weary beyond words.

He had reason to be weary, for it was one of those protracted ceremonies which seem to be designed to punish rather than to give pleasure. There were speeches by Tsai Yuan-pei, president of Peking University, and by Tan Yen-kai, who had been chairman of the Central Executive Committee when Chiang Kai-shek led his forces northward from Canton. There was the solemn exchange of ceremonial scrolls. There were bows to the portrait of Dr. Sun Yat-sen, to the guests, and to relatives. Finally, there was a tea party. The honeymoon was spent at Hangchow, the capital of Chekiang province, with its famous lake and elaborate pagodas. The honeymoon was soon interrupted by visits from generals and high officials, for the northern march was about to be resumed.

The marriage between the twenty-five year old Mei-ling Soong and the forty-one year old commander-in-chief of the Kuomintang armies was to have a curious influence on the course of the Chinese revolution. A certain puritanism, derived from the Methodists and from the Young Men's Christian Association, was henceforth to color the Three Principles of the People; Christian missionaries were to receive favored positions; the dynamics of Christianity were to be harnessed once more, as in the time of the Taipings, to the revolution. With the ardor of a convert Chiang Kai-shek diligently read the Bible and sought in it revelations of God's purpose toward himself and toward China.

He who had always been obstinate became more obstinate; and his intolerance fed on the more intolerant chapters of the Bible. The daily readings under the tutelage of his wife and Christian missionaries had the effect of confirming his belief in his mission, and it seems never to have occurred to him that he was removing himself further and further from an understanding of the real forces that moved the Chinese people. He was to enter the most fateful years of his career armed with a Bible and with a wife who had spent the greater part of her life in America and within the foreign concession in Shanghai.

Mei-ling Soong was a young woman possessed of formidable ambition and relentless devotion to her family. In those years she was still plump, girlish, and unformed; the fashionable Madame Chiang did not emerge until the thirties. She was nine years old when she first went to school in America, and more than half her life had been spent abroad. She adopted western dress, spoke English in preference to Chinese, and had the tastes and predilections of a woman from one of the southern states of America. She was so much the product of two cultures, and so little inclined to follow traditional Chinese ways, that her father sometimes wondered whether he had done right in giving his youngest daughter an American education, and he warned a friend who was contemplating sending his daughter to America to think twice before committing himself. "They are so restless," he said. "When they come back they want everything changed, and they don't understand our ways."

But in fact Mei-ling Soong possessed an instinctive knowledge of politics and she knew exactly what was demanded of her as the wife of the most powerful person in China. While the wives of most of the Kuomintang leaders sought the security of Shanghai, she remained by her husband's side in Nanking, the Kuomintang capital. Her task, as she saw it, was to organize the moral forces of the revolution. Chiang Kai-shek's task was more complicated. He had to organize an army strong enough to destroy any combination of the armies of the northern warlords.

Three months were spent in preparing the ground for the northern march. On January 4, 1928, when he resumed his position as commander-in-chief of the National Revolutionary Army—the post had been held in abeyance during his long absence—he began to reorganize and expand the army until he had created what was probably the largest, best equipped, and most skillfully trained military force that had ever existed on Chinese soil. Altogether more than seven hundred thousand troops were at his disposal, while the warlords who opposed the northern march could scarcely muster half that number. Both Feng Yu-hsiang and Yen Hsi-shan had come out on the side of the Kuomintang, although with grave misgivings. The problem was to weld this vast army into a coherent and politically reliable unit obedient to his commands, capable of striking out into north China with a minimum of delay. Altogether sixty separate army groups were involved, and it was necessary to draw up a battle plan of extreme complexity.

Superficially, the plan appeared to be simple. The first army corps, which included all the troops under the effective control of Nanking, was to be under the command of Chiang Kai-shek. Its task was to thrust powerfully along the Tientsin-Pukow railway, and into eastern Shantung. The second army corps, comprising all the troops under the command of Feng Yu-hsiang, was poised in northern Honan for a push along the Peking-Hankow railway, and then eastward into western Shantung. The third army corps consisted of Yen Hsi-shan's troops, which were ordered to enter Chihli by three separate routes in an encircling movement which would effectively cut off the forces defending Peking. The fourth army corps, under Li Tsung-jen, would keep order in the rear and serve as a reserve corps if needed. A considerable part of this corps was accordingly sent into Hunan and Hupeh to suppress the Communist uprisings. Then it was withdrawn and thrown into the battle for the railways. Chiang Kai-shek set up his headquarters at Hsuchow, and gave orders for the general attack on April 9.

The war followed the general disorderly pattern of Chinese civil wars except in one respect: it was completely successful. Feng Yu-hsiang's cavalry drove into northern Honan without encountering much opposition, and if he had desired to act independently Feng could have captured Peking without any difficulty. Yen Hsi-shan occupied the strategic city of Kalgan on May 25, and a week later Marshal Chang Tso-lin abandoned Peking to return to his base in Manchuria. The war was virtually over by the beginning of June.

Meanwhile a new and unexpected element had entered the scene. The Japanese, who had landed troops in Shantung early in 1927, only to withdraw them on the advance of Sun Chuang-feng's forces, had now returned in greater strength. Some fifty thousand Japanese forces straddled the Kiaochow-Tsinan railway, determined to protect Japanese "interests" in Shantung. There were occasional clashes and skirmishes with Chinese troops, and several hundred Chinese soldiers were killed. The Japanese occupied Tsinan, took over the telegraph and post offices, put up sandbags in the streets, and gave every appearance of preparing to contend for the province of Shantung against four revolutionary armies.

Chiang Kai-shek was puzzled by this new development, and took care not to become too deeply involved. What became known as the "Tsinan incident" was in fact a concerted effort by the Japanese to delay the northern march and to deflect the course of the Kuomintang army. In occupying Tsinan the Japanese had acted with the same merciless brutality they were later to show during the sack of Nanking, and they were demonstrating that they were deeply involved in maintaining their own special position in defense of their puppets. Chiang Kai-shek deliberately avoided a direct clash with the Japanese, and bypassed the city. In *China's Destiny*, written many years later, he explained how the Japanese maneuvers, which were obviously intended to bring the northern march to an abrupt halt, only succeeded in aiding the unification of China:

> After the Tsinan incident, I warned the rank and file of the whole army: "In order to avenge this insult against the nation,

> in order to wipe out the national humiliation, in order to set China free from imperialist oppression and to give her real independence and freedom, we must today bear the insult patiently, we must "sleep on straw and taste gall, prepare for ten years, discipline ourselves for ten years," * as our forefathers have done, and then I believe that our losses can be regained and our national disgrace wiped out. If we can do this, I do not think it will be a difficult task to achieve freedom and equality among the nations." For the whole national revolutionary army, from the commander-in-chief down to the rank and file, there is only one lesson to be drawn from the Tsinan incident, and that is the lesson that we must wipe out this disgrace. For the last fifteen years our generals and soldiers have not let a day pass without thinking of this.

He was still more explicit in a memorial speech given on the first anniversary of the incident to the Whampoa cadets training in Nanking:

> Let us remember that if the Japanese had not brought about the Tsinan incident, we would not have captured Peking. We fear the foreigners' hypocrisy, but not the violence of their oppression. The more violently and cruelly they oppress us, the more quickly the revolution will succeed. I firmly believe this. I myself felt the humiliation, and I will never let a day pass without remembering it.
>
> Since we have suffered such insults, we should remember well that in order to avenge the insult, we have no alternative than to obey the Kuomintang's commands. We should move forward or draw back according to instructions from the Kuomintang. I have sent a telegram to the Central Party Headquarters ordering that no proclamations should be posted, no slogans be written, no processions be allowed to march, no holidays be granted on this day of national humiliation. On the contrary our brothers should do two more hours' work on this day. We should never let our vengeful feelings be known, otherwise we will never be able to fight against the enemy. Let us hide our desire for revenge, and never let it be seen. Let us store it in our

* In the *Spring and Autumn Annals* it is recorded that K'u Chien, King of Yueh, after his defeat by the King of Wu, "slept on straw and tasted gall" every day until he recovered his kingdom.

> minds, let us work together to avenge the insult, and let us attempt to lead the Chinese nation toward the goal of freedom and independence. I believe China can never be conquered by Japan.

What was clear was that the disaster at Tsinan was subtly transformed into a moral victory, and the rage which swept over China was of a kind to make the revolutionary army confident of victory. The folly of the Japanese was only too evident, but what was also evident was that their folly might be interminably repeated.

The armies were still marching north. One by one the key points on the Peking-Hankow railway were taken. The Yellow river was crossed in force, and the cities of Nanyuan, Tingchow, Chuyang, and Tangtsien were all taken. A decisive battle at Fangshunchiao and the occupation of Paoting led to Marshal Chang Tso-lin's offer to withdraw behind the Great Wall. The offer was made publicly, but the Kuomintang command sent no reply, and indeed their most effective weapon was a studied silence. On June 1, as "Generalissimo of the Northern Military Government," the old Marshal gave his last reception to the diplomatic corps in Peking. On the afternoon of June 3, 1928, he boarded a special train for Fengtien. During the night he complained of feeling unwell and said to one of his staff that he thought he had been poisoned by the Japanese. At half-past five in the morning, while the train was running at full speed, a bomb laid by Japanese soldiers in a viaduct exploded and the warlord died a few minutes later. The Manchurian provinces he had ruled for so many years became the property of his son, Chang Hsueh-liang, who now became known as the "Young Marshal."

There was some mystery attached to Chang Tso-lin's death. Although it was certain that the Japanese had planted the bomb, it was not clear why they should have acted at that precise moment, or what they hoped to gain by the murder. When the warlord was buried at Mukden, the Japanese sent a special envoy bearing a wreath of flowers made of hammered silver—a mysterious tribute to the man who had often served their interests and just as often opposed them. One theory seemed to explain the mystery.

According to this theory Chang Tso-lin had sought Japanese help when in the winter of 1925 his best general, Kuo Sun-ling, went over to join the forces of Feng Yu-hsiang. He was desperate, and prepared to make any promises in return for immediate assistance. The Japanese, in return for equipment and soldiers, extracted the promise that when he was once more in full power he would subscribe to the Twenty-one Demands. It was said that he made the promise although he had no intention of carrying it out. With the defeat of his armies, he had become useless to the Japanese, who murdered him as an example to other warlords who might not keep their promises. The Japanese then offered the same terms to the "Young Marshal."

Chang Hsueh-liang was in no mood to accept the Japanese terms. "I know nothing of my father's debts," he said. "I only know my responsibility to preserve our territorial integrity and have no right to agree to your commands. If the debts are real, you must ask the National Government to pay them. I am a Chinese. I love China as the Japanese love Japan. I believe that Chinese should not fight Chinese. All Chinese should share life and death together. My position and life may be sacrificed, but my confidence remains unshaken." Such at any rate were the terms of his rejection as they were communicated to the Kuomintang leaders. Later in the year, after protracted negotiations, the "Young Marshal" agreed to go over to the Kuomintang. The blue and white flag flew over Mukden, and the northern expedition was completed.

Meanwhile Chiang Kai-shek had entered Peking, and the name of the city was changed to Peiping, meaning "northern peace," thus expressing the hope that the years of civil war had come to an end. The new capital of China would be Nanking, with its central position on the Yangtse river. There was excellent authority for establishing a new capital, for Nanking had been a former capital of the Ming emperors. By design Peking, so long associated with the Manchus, was to become nothing more than a provincial city.

Among the first tasks of the commander-in-chief was to make his official report to the founder of the Kuomintang party, Dr. Sun

Yat-sen, whose body reposed in the Temple of the Blue Cloud in the Western Hills just outside of Peking. In such a way a victorious general might pay his respects to a dead emperor, knowing that the emperor could not hear the words spoken in reverence, but aware that immemorial custom demanded just such an act of fealty. Dr. Sun Yat-sen had himself offered a report to the last Ming emperors in Nanking, and the Chinese would have regarded the Generalissimo as lacking in piety if he had not made an offering at the tomb of the dead leader. Accordingly Chiang Kai-shek, Feng Yu-hsiang, Yen Hsi-shan, and Li Tsung-jen walked up the pine-clad hills and paid solemn tribute to Dr. Sun Yat-sen.

It was a moving occasion, and Feng Yu-hsiang in his memoirs has described how Chiang Kai-shek wept beside the tomb:

> When he prayed before the altar of Tsungli, he wept so bitterly that he could not even hold up his head, and the bystanders could not but be filled with indescribable thoughts of grief. The atmosphere was grave and solemn. Chiang Kai-shek wept for a long time, and at last, like someone who goes up to a filial son and begs him to stop weeping after a parent's death, I went up to him and begged him to cease. But it was a long time before he stopped weeping.

But, having wept, Chiang Kai-shek still had his duty to perform, and he began to read out in his high-pitched voice a memorial in which he expressed the real situation of the country as he saw it. There were ominous underscorings, and occasionally the memorial took the form of a manifesto addressed to the living rather than to the dead. The memorial was obviously drawn up by him, and by him alone. It read:

> (1) We shall expound the Three Principles in order to put an end to widespread heresies, and we shall exert our utmost to strengthen ourselves and to seek equality among the family of nations.
>
> (2) If the comrades within the party do not unite affectionately and strive in common for reconstruction, how shall we put an end to reactionary ambitions and bear the heavy responsibility of saving the country?

(3) We shall work hard for the spiritual and material reconstruction of the new capital, and thoroughly destroy a thousand years of traditional thinking so that we can begin again our country's destiny.

(4) In order to have a successful revolution, we must first revolutionize our minds—such was the advice of Dr. Sun Yat-sen, and we must faithfully obey it.

(5) In the psychological, material, political, and social reconstruction of the country, and for the welfare of the people, and for equality among the family of nations, we must take heed of the common struggle of the whole body of our comrades and our countrymen.

(6) We shall fix the number of soldiers in the army, and retain or diminish them in such a way that the army may be strengthened.

(7) We shall bring the whole nation to the realization that civil war is shameful, and we must devote ourselves to national defense.

(8) We must faithfully put into operation Dr. Sun Yat-sen's policy of ruling the state through the party so that China may have its systematic reconstruction.

These were the words of a conqueror only too well aware that almost insurmountable difficulties lay ahead. When he spoke of widespread heresies, he was indicating not only the existence of the troublesome Communist enclaves set up in the border regions of Hunan and Kwangsi but also the dissident factions within the Kuomintang party. There was a right wing and a left wing; there were military leaders still in control of provinces giving lip service to the Kuomintang but otherwise acting as though the Central Government scarcely had any existence. Feng Yu-hsiang had not disbanded his armies, and he still controlled large areas of Shantung, Honan, Shensi, Kansu, Chinghai, and Ninghsia. Yen Hsi-shan controlled Shansi, Hopei, Chahar, and Suiyuan. Chang Hsueh-liang had inherited his father's command over Manchuria. The provinces of Kwangtung, Kwangsi, Hunan, and Hupeh were under the control of a small group of powerful warlords known as the Kwangsi generals. The orders of the Kuomintang were obeyed or disobeyed according to the whims of generals, and there were some who regarded the northern march as more symbolic than real. Inevitably the Kuomintang government found itself in a perpetual quandary, not knowing whether to attack the generals who professed loyalty, or whether to believe the people's professions of faith, or where to begin the struggle which clearly had to be fought on so many fronts that no one could possibly fight them simultaneously. The Kuomintang government had not changed in essentials since the days when it ruled over only a small area of Kwangtung, with Canton itself occupied by the enemy. It had no program which appealed to the peasants, the working classes, or the soldiers; its strength came from its revolutionary fervor, but people were weary of revolution and the revolutionaries were now only a small minority. China, which Chiang Kai-shek had hoped to unite by the northern march, now split apart into its component divisions.

"The success of the northern punitive expedition is the most tragic and the most heroic page in the history of the Chinese nation," Chiang Kai-shek wrote in *China's Destiny*. But this was to underestimate the innumerable tragedies of the Chinese people. At a conservative estimate three-quarters of a million died during the northern march; far more had died during the Taiping Rebellion. But the Taiping Rebellion had scarcely affected the monolithic unity of the Chinese empire; the wound healed over, and the empire endured. But the civil wars fought by the Kuomintang and by the warlords were of another order; the wounds were infected with poison, and continued to bleed. In the end there was to be so much bloodletting, so much weariness, so much bitterness, so much dislocation and disappointment, so many broken families, so much hunger and starvation, that the people seemed to be genuinely indifferent to the government, and wanted only to be left alone.

If at this period a younger and more appealing figure, possessing the imagination which would kindle a fierce enthusiasm among the people, had emerged, then the situation might have been saved. But in the Kuomintang government there were only the familiar figures of the aging revolutionaries who had taken part in the 1911 revolution, asserting their right to rule by descent from Dr. Sun Yat-sen. Chiang Kai-shek was a stern schoolmaster, sober and well-meaning, but he had lost the power to kindle any enthusiasm. Remote and strangely inaccessible, devoted to the army and the cultivation of a somber didacticism, he seemed to have lost touch with the people; and though he was constantly employing the word "revolution," he had lost touch with the revolution.

The failure of the Kuomintang revolution lay in the fact that it was never revolutionary enough.

THE FIGHT GOES ON

LONG AGO CONFUCIUS had insisted on the "rectification of names," meaning that the appropriate words should be pronounced and that they should possess the proper meaning for the occasion. In something of this spirit the new government had changed the name of Peking to Peiping, and the province of Chihli, so long associated with northern military factions, was changed to Hopei, meaning "north of the river." But Confucius had never suggested that the names of cities were subject to change, or that the changing of a name could bring about a change in the real nature of the object. What was necessary was that the terms of government should be exact, without any possible alteration in meaning; and there were many terms in the "Three Principles of the People" and in the speeches of Dr. Sun Yat-sen that eluded definition. Dr. Sun Yat-sen never made clear what he meant by "democracy," or "freedom," or "unification." Was it to be unification under a single dominant party acting with dictatorial power? Or did it mean simply that there should be a central government responsible to all the provincial governments? How should the provincial governments be managed? To what extent would democratic elections be permitted?

Since none of these questions were answered, the new government in Nanking was in a position to make its own rules. It ruled by decree and by military force, and it had no roots among the people. In theory China was united; in fact the government was incapable of exerting its influence beyond the reach of its armies. In the winter of 1928, with Manchuria obeying the orders of the Central Government in Nanking, and with Kuomintang officials in positions of power in all the provinces, Chiang Kai-shek could congratulate himself that he had brought about the unification of the country, but when the Third National Congress opened in the spring there was almost nothing to show for it—the country had been split apart again into its original components.

In a chastened mood Chiang Kai-shek spoke to the delegates at the congress:

> After the northern punitive expedition China was in name united under the National Government, and in name the local military authorities obeyed the orders of the Central Government. But in name only. In fact things went by contraries. It was the local authorities who controlled finance, bought weapons, secretly increased the number of their soldiers and did as they pleased. The Central Government had no power over them. Furthermore, they were in a position to threaten the Central Government. During the four years since the death of Tsungli, the "orphan" has undergone a good deal of affliction, and it is indeed fortunate that the poor child is not dead. All comrades must exert themselves so that the "orphan" may grow up and not fall short of Tsungli's expectations.

It is clear from such passages that Chiang Kai-shek was perfectly aware that the country was in grave danger, and that the provinces were continually tending to slip away from the control of the Central Government. This centrifugal tendency was not new; it had existed under the Ching dynasty, where the authority of the emperor was never absolute; he succeeded in ruling the country only by the use of an elaborate system of checks and balances, through which the provincial authorities were brought to heel. Chiang Kai-shek could admit quite candidly that the Central Government had no power over the local authorities, but he continued to rule as though he possessed this power. So there arose, especially within the bureaucracy, an elaborate system of fictions which permitted the government to pretend it was ruling when in fact it was not ruling. The Kuomintang government appointed mayors over towns which already possessed mayors; it appointed generals to armies which had long ago been disbanded; it pretended to exact taxes from districts which were no longer under its authority. The fictions proliferated, and all were dangerous.

Chiang Kai-shek hoped the "orphan" would grow up, but it was not growing up. Instead, it was being torn apart by warlords whose power, far from decreasing, seemed to derive strength from the northern expedition, for many of them had made temporary alliances with the Kuomintang. The Communists, too, were establishing their own satrapies. The most important of these were the "Soviet border districts" in the north of Kiangsi and Hunan, but there were already scattered groups of Communist-directed armies in at least eight provinces. They were important not for their numbers, which were still small—in 1930 Kuomintang officials would admit that there were only sixty-six thousand Communists under arms—but because they were rapidly proliferating and represented a permanent threat to the existence of the Central Government. With the proper strategies the warlords could be expected to submit to the Central Government. Where necessary, they could be bought over. But no one was under the illusion that the Communists could be bought over. Although the Chinese Communists had not yet shown their strength, there was already a growing realization that they represented a greater potential threat than the warlords. The Kuomintang had no carefully considered social program. By socializing the land, by remitting taxes, and by liquidating the landlords, the Chinese Communists were in a position to show that their social programs brought about immediate advantages to the peasants; the Kuomintang could offer no immediate advantages to the peasants, who formed the greater part of the population.

Chiang Kai-shek was among the first to recognize the dangerous adventures of the Chinese Communists. He never minimized the threat, and fought against them with all the resources at his command—armies, saboteurs, block houses, German military advisers, money. He failed to understand that the Chinese peasants wanted to own the land and to rid themselves of their landlords, and were not in the least interested in maintaining the Kuomintang in power.

At the First National Congress of the Kuomintang in 1924, Dr. Sun Yat-sen's principle of the "people's livelihood" was adopted by a vast majority of the party members. There was a ringing declaration that "those who till the land shall have the right to the land." But the declaration never possessed the force of law, and the laws for the "equalization" and utilization of the land remained in abeyance. Chiang Kai-shek had no interest in land reform, and the landlords remained in full possession of their privileges.

What chiefly interested Chiang Kai-shek, to the exclusion of all other problems, was national unity, and he was inclined to regard this problem as so important that it vastly outweighed all others. At all costs the nation must be brought under a single government with a single standing army under a central command. It was therefore necessary to abandon the complex system of alliances with provincial warlords, to incorporate their armies in the army of the Central Government, and to reduce the warlords to impotence.

A first step in this direction was taken at the beginning of 1927 at a meeting of the national army reorganization committee, which passed a resolution that the army should be reduced to 715,000 soldiers, while the expenditure of the ministry of war should be reduced to $192,000,000. According to T. V. Soong, the minister of finance in the Nanking government at the time, the country was actually supporting two million soldiers at a cost of $642,000,000. These figures referred only to the army of the Central Government, and are given in Chinese dollars; they represented nevertheless a wholly preponderant amount of the revenue of the Central Government, and show that the crippling expenses of civil war were continually threatening to reduce the government to bankruptcy. The immediate fiscal task facing the government was to slash military expenditure. In fact, the civil wars continued and the expenditure increased.

There was no end to the wars. The Kwangsi generals revolted, and most of south China was in flames. In a series of quick thrusts the Generalissimo was able to put out the flames, but the campaigns were scarcely over before a new danger threatened from the north. On May 13, 1929, Feng Yu-hsiang held a military conference at his headquarters in Honan and sent telegrams to the Central Government charging it with a long list of crimes against the state. A countermanifesto, issued by the Generalissimo and signed by the five presidents of the Yuans, failed to have any effect. Once more Central Government armies were sent north on a punitive expedition. Feng Yu-hsiang, faced with drought and shortage of supplies, retreated westward, thus avoiding a battle. But the ferment was rising. In September new revolts broke out in Kwangtung and Kwangsi. There were mutinies in Changchow and Shanghai. By February of the following year matters were far worse, for in Peking Wang Ching-wei was threatening a march to the south with Yen Hsi-shan as commander-in-chief and Feng Yu-hsiang and Chang Hsueh-liang as the vice-commanders. At the last moment Chang Hsueh-liang refused to take part in the march, then Yen Hsi-shan declared he would go abroad, only to decide to join forces with Feng Yu-hsiang a few weeks later. They sent an ultimatum to the Central Government. Once more the north and the south were at war.

So the wars went on, implacable and absurd, like nearly all the Chinese wars, which had surely demonstrated by this time that nothing could be solved by war. The war swept through Shantung, Honan, and Anhwei. There was sharp fighting along the Lunghai railroad with the Central Government troops using bombing planes and heavy artillery. The government forces were numerically superior and better equipped, but they were mortally weary and inclined to disengage at the first opportunity. Han Fu-chu was compelled to retreat from Shantung with Yen Hsi-shan's forces coming close on his heels, Li Tsung-jen marched out of Kwangsi and captured Changsha, even reaching as far as Yochow, where he was finally repulsed. Wang Ching-wei organized a new national government in Taiyuan, Shansi, claiming to rule China from the edge of the desert. When the Central Government forces succeeded in taking the Peking-Hankow railroad, Feng Yu-hsiang and Yen Hsi-shan withdrew to Hopei, and for a while they vanished into the wilderness.

The miserable catalog of battles throughout this year promised no hope for the future. To the outsider it was as though ten large and brightly colored boxes stood on a stage, and out of one box there would spring a general who was immediately clubbed by another general springing out of another box. The boxes move about, the generals appear in different uniforms, and sometimes three or four generals spring out of the same box. It was a year of shame, of vast expenditure of effort and human lives, with nothing gained. The spectacle of the Chinese destroying themselves was vastly amusing to the Japanese Imperial General Staff.

The comedy of punitive expeditions was resumed in May 1931, when Wang Ching-wei, having abandoned Taiyuan, decided to set up another national government in Kwangtung. He threatened to send a northern expedition against Nanking. No expedition followed the threats sent by telegram, though the resources of Kwangtung might have made such an expedition possible. Historically, Canton was the generator of revolutions, the feeding ground of rebellion. Yet the revolt petered out. By this time men had realized only too well that the problem of governing China was almost insuperable. No one man, no one party was strong enough to command the allegiance of the population. The wars came to a brief end because the people were weary beyond all weariness. But in men's hearts and minds, in the raging conflict of opinions, in the poverty and dissatisfactions of the time, in sullenness and anger and trepidition, the wars continued.

There was a growing belief that only a massive attack by Japan would unify the country; and there were some who believed that when Japan attacked, she would find China in such a state of disintegration that she would merely have to pick up the pieces.

MUKDEN

IN HIS MONDAY morning speeches Chiang Kai-shek often repeated a phrase which his listeners knew by heart. "If the United States could fight for nine years for its independence, then China too can fight for many years for its independence." The United States was a model to be followed. But the Chinese had been fighting since 1911, and they were already weary of the struggle. Their enemies were their own kinsmen, and the ghastly spectacle of interminable civil wars was not one to fill them with compassion. A kind of sullen rage was eating away at the springs of action. China was being destroyed from within. Soon it would be destroyed from outside.

Japan had been making preparations for the conquest of China for a long time. Baron Tanaka's memorial to the Emperor, urging the colonization of all of Asia, was dated the summer of 1927, but the idea had been fermenting since the defeat of Tsarist Russia at Port Arthur in 1905. "In order to conquer China, we must first conquer Manchuria and Mongolia," he wrote, adding almost as an afterthought that the conquest of China opened the door to the conquest of the world. It was an enticing prospect, and the memorialist, writing in those dry tones which conceal an inner excitement, was not bound by logic. The simplicity of the plan commended itself to the Japanese, who admire simplicity in all things.

Now, all over Japan, there were people who openly relished the prospect of seeing China colonized as the first step toward a world colonial empire. "Before we set forward against America," wrote General Hondo, Japanese military commander in Manchuria, to his Minister of War six weeks before the invasion, "our troops must take up a decisive position in China, occupy the far eastern territories of the Soviet Union, and secure these countries for ourselves." In such simple terms did the Japanese militarists view the coming war. Simplicity had become epidemic.

The Chinese are an older and more settled people than the Japanese, and have fewer illusions. Although he was often excessively rigid and unimaginative, Chiang Kai-shek possessed many virtues denied to the Japanese. He was patient, pliant, rooted in an ancient world. He had a passion for old saws, pithy sayings, and fables, and he had a special liking for Aesop's Fables. There were two which particularly recommended themselves to him. In the fable known as "The Hare and the Tortoise," the tortoise reaches the winning post long before the hare, who was so full of contempt for his adversary that he lay down to sleep, imagining he would have time enough to win the race when he awoke. The other fable was called "The Dog and the Reflection." The dog crosses a bridge over a stream with a piece of meat in his mouth. Seeing his own reflection in the water, and thinking it another dog with meat in his mouth, the dog snaps at his reflection, hoping to acquire more meat. Chiang Kai-shek liked to relate these fables because they illustrated his preoccupations. He had no doubt that the Chinese tortoise would eventually win the race and that the Japanese dog would lose the meat.

1931 was a year of unprecedented disasters. In May large reinforcements were sent to Kiangsi to put down a Communist uprising, and in the same month the Yangtse river flooded its banks and fifty million farmers were rendered homeless. Later, the Kwangtung "National Government" raised an army against Nanking and in September advanced into Hunan. General Shih Yu-san revolted in Hopei—a revolt which was sternly suppressed by the "Young Marshal," Chang Hsueh-liang, who drove down from Manchuria. On September 18, with the nation on the brink of civil war, the Japanese saw their opportunity and invaded Manchuria.

They had many pretexts, and invented others. The Chinese had blown up a section of the South Manchurian Railway, and they were determined to punish the culprits. Japanese troops were already in Manchuria, policing the railroad. They claimed that Manchuria was in a state of disorder, and had been abandoned by the "Young Marshal." Some said he was recuperating from typhoid fever in a Peking hospital, others that he was pursuing a young lady called Butterfly Wu. There was also the mysterious Nakamura affair. On June 9 a certain Colonel Rikitaro Nakamura of the Japanese general staff began a tour of inspection through Liaoling province, disappearing from sight at the town of Saonan. The Japanese made a thorough search for the officer, finally concluding that he had been murdered by Manchurians. To punish the culprits they destroyed the railroad between Mukden and Hwangkutun, shelled the Peitaying barracks, and seized Mukden. Forty-eight hours later they had taken the whole of southern Manchuria and disarmed more than a hundred thousand Chinese soldiers.

It was the driving edge of the wedge. Anti-Japanese feeling was running high. The students came out with slogans attacking the "Young Marshal," Chiang Kai-shek, and the Japanese impartially. "Rather a broken jade than an unbroken tile" was one such slogan. "Punish Chang Hsueh-liang!" and "Boycott Japanese goods!" were others. More dangerous to Chiang Kai-shek, who felt that the time for resistance had not yet come, was the slogan "Oppose the policy of nonresistance." Painted on banners, these slogans and many others attacking the Japanese were carried by processions of students through the streets of Nanking and Peking. The Japanese press was whipped into a fury by reports of these processions; it was felt in Japan that the Chinese were lacking in gratitude for the great honor which had been paid to them by the Japanese soldiers in Manchuria. Why should a nation protest when the advantages of Japanese civilization were being bestowed on them? The Chinese students were almost insane with anger and frustration. They went on strike, drilled in their school compounds, and taught themselves military tactics. They commandeered trains in order to lay their petitions before the government. Dr. C.T. Wang, the mild and inoffensive minister of foreign affairs, was manhandled by the students, who very nearly succeeded in destroying the central party headquarters in Nanking. For a while it appeared that the country was being governed by bands of screaming students. They claimed that the government was criminally negligent, and they demanded the resignation of the leading government officers. It was reliably reported that when a delegation of students arrived in Nanking by special train, Chiang Kai-shek told them in confidence, "I give you my word that within three years we shall have beaten the Japanese to their knees. Believe me, go back to your schools and study hard—this is the only way we can save the country." The students thought there were better ways to save the country, and demanded weapons.

The government was so badly shaken by the Manchurian disaster that it seemed to have grown numb. Chiang Kai-shek was convinced that the time for attacking the Japanese had not yet come, but how to explain his conviction to clamoring students? He asked them to return to school and study, but study would not bring back the lost provinces. A succession of foreign ministers took office—Wellington Koo, Eugene Chen, Lo Wen-keng—but they had no influence on the course of events. The Kuomintang was losing its dynamism. Only a year before, Chiang Kai-shek had admitted with unwonted candor that the revolution had failed:

> We who brought about the revolution have come to be regarded as a privileged class. The people cherish toward us the same hatred they had for the Manchus. It is impossible to find a single Kuomintang headquarters which really administers to the welfare of the people: all are stigmatized for corruption, bribery, scrambling for power.

Chiang Kai-shek spoke so rarely in this way that the words came as a shock, as though he had admitted that his cause was lost. But the cause was even more in danger when he refused to act against the Japanese.

In fact, he could not act. To declare war against the Japanese at this time was to invite a general massacre. China was in no position to make any effective resistance. The clamor of the students arose from a deeply felt frustration, but there was scarcely anything he could do to make their frustration more endurable; and he arrested the more vociferous students. Whatever prestige he had gained seemed irrevocably lost: he had not foreseen the disaster, he had done nothing to prevent it, and he was henceforward to be described as the man who refused to fight when the whole country was willing to fight. It was not a pleasant description, and it evidently irked him. From time to time he would make ineffectual gestures toward the students and young officers, who asked why he alone seemed determined not to oppose Japanese aggression. At one of the Monday morning memorial services at the Central Military Academy, he declared that the responsibility for declaring war against Japan was not one that he could assume, for it would lead to the destruction of China. He said:

> About the anti-Japanese affair, if I wished to win the support of the whole nation, it would be quite easy—I would only have to declare war against Japan. Then the whole nation would praise me and extol me to the skies. Then why do I not do so? Why, on the contrary, am I suspected of "nonresistance" ? I do not fear death, but I cannot let the life of the country be lost, nor leave the nation at stake. I must think in terms of the future. I cannot sacrifice China for the sake of my own personal reputation. Even if China should forever be wiped out of existence or if it should take scores of hundreds of years to regenerate her after she had fallen into ruins, still we have the possibility of preventing her from falling into ruins, and surely we should take advantage of the possibility?

There were some who felt he knew the Japanese too well, their ruthlessness and the fantastic scope of their plans for world domination, and had long ago come to the conclusion that China would be saved only when some other power was embroiled. There were others who were aware of his natural impatience, and were surprised that he should be so calm at a time of such turmoil. Still others thought he might be preparing a trap for the Japanese, some secret and mysterious stratagem which would drive them out of China. "If we do not want to fight," wrote Sun Wu, "there are ways to prevent the enemy from engaging us. All we need is to throw something odd and unaccountable in his way." There were many who believed that Chiang Kai-shek was preparing to throw something odd and unaccountable in the way of the Japanese.

Yet he knew he was out of favor, and when he resigned all his offices in December under pressure from the government, he seems to have welcomed the enforced retirement, as though he felt that it relieved him from responsibility. He would bide his time. The Japanese were clearly determined upon the conquest of China, and would soon attack again. Then he would be recalled, and once more he would be compelled to take command of the army.

The Japanese attacked much sooner than expected. On January 28, 1932, a Japanese warship shelled Nanking and Japanese troops marched on Wusung and Shanghai. Three divisions of the Nineteenth Route Army, fighting in Shanghai, repulsed the first wave of Japanese invaders. "The coming war will be a struggle for the domination of the world," the Japanese press announced early in January, adding with disarming simplicity that "the conflict in Manchuria was merely the curtain-raiser." The simple prophecies were coming true: Chinese children were being tossed on Japanese bayonets in the bloody, tortuous sidestreets of Chapei. In Manchuria the Japanese had decided to inaugurate a new vassal state, called Manchukuo, "Manchu kingdom," under the vassal emperor, Henry Pu-yi, who in his childhood had been emperor of China. The principle of the "rectification of names" was invoked, and Changchun, the capital of Manchuria, became known as Sinking, meaning "new capital." Everything in Manchukuo was to be new and unfamiliar.

In despair the country recalled the only man who could deal with an impossible situation. Chiang Kai-shek resumed the post of Generalissimo, while the venerable Lin Sen was appointed chairman of the National Government and Wang Ching-wei became president of the Executive Yuan—a post in theory equivalent to premier. The seat of government was moved to Loyang, but later in the year the government returned to Nanking. It had been a brief war: a Japanese show of force, an attempt to frighten the Chinese into giving way to their demands. Chiang Kai-shek, realizing that the Japanese had no intention at this time of moving along the Yangtse valley, turned his attention to the Communists with the slogan "Internal security must precede foreign aggression."

The Japanese were digesting their Manchurian conquests. While the Generalissimo was dedicated to breaking the power of the Communists, the Japanese were concerned with the problem of absorbing China piecemeal. They were taking their time. This time they waited a year, and took Jehol, whose governor, T'ang Yuling, known as "Big Tiger" from his tiger head, tiger teeth, and tiger mouth, had been the sworn brother of the "Old Marshal," Chang Tso-lin. This did not prevent him from being an incompetent military commander. The "Young Marshal" Chang Hsuehliang failed to be of assistancc, and in April he sent in his resignation and sailed for Italy, to learn more about the government of nations from the lips of Mussolini. With Jehol occupied, the Chinese government was compelled to sign the humiliating treaty which came to be known as the Taku Agreement, named after the Taku forts near Tientsin, where the treaty was signed. The provisions of the treaty were so onerous that they were kept secret from the nation. The Japanese established a boundary line ten miles north of Peking; above this line no Chinese troops could be stationed. The Japanese were permitted to use airplanes to inspect the withdrawal of the Chinese troops, and there would be "noncombat zones" between the Japanese and the Chinese south of the line, who in theory were withdrawn behind the Great Wall. Beyond this wall the Japanese enjoyed undisputed authority. The silkworm was beginning to swallow the whale. The whale was already in the silkworm's mouth, and the silkworm would not be content until it had swallowed it whole.

Humiliation was piled on humiliation. The government acted

with exquisite caution, punishing the newspapers which hinted at the treaty and the students who clamored against it. The "odd and unaccountable" things which were being offered to Japan according to the wisdom of Sun Wu were pieces of China's bleeding flesh.

The Chinese found it increasingly difficult to tolerate the humiliation. There were riots in the army, which were sternly suppressed. In the winter of 1933 there was open rebellion from the least expected quarter. The Nineteenth Route Army, which had fought so valiantly in Shanghai, had been ordered to Fukien; there its most capable military commanders, Chen Ming-shu and Tsai Ting-kai, decided that the time had come to revolt against the government and set up a "Chinese Republic People's Revolutionary Government." The new government lasted less than two months. The rebellion was stamped out in the latter part of January 1934, a few weeks before the Generalissimo inaugurated his "New Life Movement," which was intended to invigorate the dying spirit of the Chinese.

Many odd things had happened, but this was perhaps the oddest of all. The source of the New Life Movement did not lie, as many might reasonably have supposed, in Dante's *Vita Nuova*, but in the doctrines of the Methodist church with its belief in original sin, general redemption, repentance, justification by faith, the witness of the Holy Spirit, and Christian perfection. Among these heterogeneous doctrinal foundations there may be detected a considerable element of Calvinism.

The historian Edward Gibbon once observed that history moves by the chance impetus of incalculables. That a form of religion introduced into the United States by a few pious emigrants from Ireland in 1766 should have so influenced the leader of the Chinese nation on the eve of a great war that he should yearn to see all China embracing the religion, or at least those elements of it which could be translated into Chinese, would seem at first sight unimaginable. Nevertheless, the New Life Movement was rooted in Methodism, and the Generalissimo meant exactly what he said when he declared that he expected everyone in China to follow the tenets of the new movement. The majority of the Chinese were Buddhists, Taoists, or Confucians; sometimes there could be found Chinese who believed in all three religions. The new movement shocked the Buddhists by its irrelevance, the Taoists by its self-righteousness, the Confucians by its categorical imperatives, which were somewhat more strict than those announced by Confucius. Yet the movement was well-intentioned, and did some good. Inaugurated on February 19, 1934, at Nanchang, in Kiangsi, where the eight principles were publicly proclaimed at a solemn ceremony, the New Life Movement reflected the preoccupations of the Generalissimo and became an arm of the government.

The eight principles, which were soon written up on hundreds of thousands of Chinese walls, began ominously:

(1) Regard yesterday as a period of death, today as a period of life. Let us rid ourselves of old abuses and build up a new nation.

(2) Let us accept the heavy responsibilities of reviving the nation.

(3) We must observe rules and have faith, honesty, and shame.

(4) Our clothing, eating, living, and traveling must be orderly, simple, plain, and clean.

(5) We must willingly face hardships. We must strive for frugality.

(6) We must have adequate knowledge and moral integrity as citizens.

(7) Our actions must be courageous and rapid.

(8) We must act on our promises, or even act without promising.

Quick-witted Chinese students had no difficulty inventing ironic counterparts to the eight principles, which were sometimes contradictory and strangely put together. "Regard yesterday as a period of death" seemed to indicate the total abandonment of the past, yet all the speeches made by the official spokesmen of the movement referred to China's ancient traditions. "We must observe rules" was a sweeping injunction which did not sufficiently clarify which rules were to be observed. The Chinese are passionately addicted to balanced phrases, and nearly all the eight principles involved a cautious balance of virtues, which were intended to reinforce each other. So knowledge and integrity, courage and rapidity of action, endurance and frugality were presented as desirable virtues, and little was said about the existence of vices. Yet, in its intentions, the New Life Movement was chiefly concerned with the eradication of vice. It came into being as a weapon which would cleanse and purify a people who, in the eyes of the Generalissimo, had abandoned themselves to complacency and moral degradation.

The origins of the New Life Movement lay deep in the Generalissimo's psyche. When he was asked whether there was any single incident which was responsible for his decision to introduce the New Life Movement, he always answered that the decision sprang out of an incident he had seen on a street in early February 1934. He was in his automobile, returning to his headquarters in Nanchang, when he saw a schoolboy behaving "in an unbecoming manner" in the street, and it occurred to him that unwholesome personal habits were having a deleterious effect on the Chinese character, especially among the young. Exactly what the boy had been doing was not explained, but left to the imagination. At the inaugural meeting of the New Life Movement a few days later, he told a slightly different story. At Kienow, a town in Fukien, he had seen a boy less than ten years old smoking in the street. Incensed by the child's depravity, he had summoned the boy's parents and upbraided them for permitting such behavior. The dressing-down apparently had some effect, for there was a conspicuous decline in cigarette smoking by children in Kienow thereafter. Both stories related to boys, and in both stories he pictured himself as a man returning from the front lines weighed down by a sense of moral responsibility.

The New Life Movement, though hastily organized, was the fruit of long pondering and heart-searching. Although Methodism played a dominant role, other elements could be detected. His mother had inculcated in him a passionate inclination toward a life of purity and virtue. His military training in Japan had developed in him a strict devotion to duty. His German military advisers had described to him how Germany, once humiliated by the

Treaty of Versailles, had succeeded in abrogating nearly all the conditions imposed on her by the victors. In fifteen years Germany had risen from the ashes, and under Hitler she was well on the way to assuming a proud place among the nations. All this had been accomplished, according to the advisers, as a result of the Spartan discipline of German youth and the manifest virtue of the Führer. The Germans no longer paid war indemnities, and the Führer felt no need to abase himself before the leaders of other nations. The New Life Movement was partly modeled on the Hitler Jugend.

When the New Life Movement encouraged the cleaning of the streets and the opening of playgrounds, schools, and hospitals, and discouraged spitting, gambling, prostitution, and opium-smoking, it was fulfilling a long felt need. When it dictated the length of skirts and prohibited cigarette smoking and the wearing of rouge, it was attempting the impossible. As a moralist, Chiang Kai-shek suffered from the disadvantage that his own morals were not above reproach. His puritanical approach to life was pragmatical, and very devious. He was concerned to eradicate vice and to enforce discipline, and he seems to have believed that by eradicating vice, discipline would naturally follow. In a pamphlet published later in the year, he wrote of the four virtues—*li,* meaning obedience to regulations; *i,* meaning right conduct; *lien,* meaning honesty; and *chih,* meaning integrity. Then he continued:

> By observing the four virtues, it is hoped that rudeness and vulgarity will be got rid of, and that the life of our people will be refined in accordance with cultural and artistic standards.
>
> By observing these virtues, it is hoped that beggary and robbery will be removed, that officials will be honest and patriotic, that corruption will cease, and that people will pursue more productive enterprises. . . . We have to make people work harder and spend less, and the officials must be honest. . . .
>
> By observing these virtues, it is hoped that social and official discord will be remedied, and that people will become more military-minded. If a country cannot defend itself, it has every chance of losing its existence. We have to preserve order, emphasize organization, responsibility, and discipline, and be ready to die for the country at any moment.

The New Life Movement attracted youths dedicated to cleanliness and virtue; it also attracted youths who were anxious for promotion in the ranks of the government. The physical manifestations of the movement were the toothbrush, the tight buttoned collar, the slightly glazed eyes of the youth waiting for an order to obey. Nevertheless, the advantages probably outweighed the disadvantages. There was less litter in the streets, and wherever the Generalissimo or a high Kuomintang official appeared, there was a feverish rush to clean up a city in case there should be an inspection tour. The Generalissimo would pounce on a scrap of paper lying on the roadside, and he would threaten punishment whenever he found someone, particularly a boy, who was dressed in a slovenly way. At the mass meeting held at Nanchang to celebrate the launching of the New Life Movement on a national scale, the Generalissimo was annoyed by a photographer who was running about in an effort to take as many photographs as possible from different angles. The Generalissimo liked being photographed, but this photographer was carelessly dressed, slovenly and unkempt. From the platform the Generalissimo ordered the man to be brought forward so that everyone could see this abject specimen of humanity, who lacked the virtues of orderliness and cleanliness. "Observe," said the Generalissimo, "that he has a modern machine in his hand, but otherwise there is nothing modern about him—he belongs to the old decadent China, and has no place in the new China." The wretched photographer was compelled to serve as a model of the antiquated past. The story is told by the Generalissimo's official biographer, who comments, "The inborn kindliness of the Generalissimo is well known, and he can have taken no pleasure in the incident, but as an orator he could hardly fail to appreciate the dramatic possibilities of extending the finger of rebuke to a 'terrible example' so opportunely at hand."

A week later there came a torchlight procession through the streets of Nanchang, with banners inscribed with the slogans of the new movement. "Don't spit," "Avoid wine, women and gambling," "Kill flies and rats," "Politeness and obedience smooth the way"—these slogans, painted on white cloth, were held high above the processions, which included the inevitable dragons. Thereafter similar processions were held in most of the towns of unoccupied China.

About this time the Generalissimo began to apply himself seriously to wiping out the habit of smoking opium. All government officials were warned that they must break themselves of the habit within three years, or face the consequences. In the following year the punishment was spelled out in considerable detail: public officials who refused to break themselves of the habit would be executed. The same punishment would be visited on the manufacturers and sellers of narcotics. There were a few spectacular public executions, but the habit persisted.

The Generalissimo appears to have been perfectly aware that the much publicized New Life Movement and the edicts against opium-smoking scarcely touched the heart of the problem. What was needed was a large-scale economic and social reconstruction of the country. The people cried out for change, but there was no change. From time to time he would speak of the program of economic reconstruction which he would introduce once the Communist danger had been averted, but although he summoned a convocation of governors and generals to discuss the plan, nothing came of it. The feudal landlords, the compradores, the governors, and the Kuomintang officials held all the power, and there was nothing left for the people.

Meanwhile Communist power was growing, for they alone were presenting plans for wide-scale social reform which would benefit the peasants and the lower middle classes. Armed Communists were solidly entrenched in Kiangsi; and although the Generalissimo with the help of his secretaries had prepared a long monograph showing how the Manchu emperors had successfully dealt with bandits and insurgents, the monograph failed to explain how to deal with the Communists. They lived in mountain hideouts, above the mists, with machine guns posted along the forest paths, in a province so badly governed that the peasants flocked to them. Chiang Kai-shek's armies had attempted to destroy them, using bombing planes and blockhouses. German military advisers were given the responsibility for devising strategies which would bring about the destruction of armies as invisible as air. There had been some minor successes. A few Communist leaders were caught and executed; in return the Communists caught and executed a few Kuomintang officers. In eastern Kiangsi so many blockhouses were erected that they came to resemble the Great Wall. The Pieh Tung Tui, or Special Movement Force, consisting largely of officers, was organized to enforce the blockade and to attempt to win over the peasants. The Pieh Tung Tui was given wide powers and acted independently of the army, being directly responsible to the Generalissimo. It was in fact a separate army, and the peasants caught between the Communist troops, the national army, and the Pieh Tung Tui, could only pray for the day when the three yokes would not press so heavily on their shoulders.

In October 1934 a Communist army under Mao Tse-tung broke through the encircling net of Kuomintang troops and began the long march which was to add a new legend to Chinese history. Through eight thousand miles of inhospitable land, the small army battled, gathered recruits, destroyed title deeds, passing through sixty-two towns and cities, fighting the armies of ten warlords and occupying parts of seven provinces. The army had no carefully wrought plan, and did not know where it was going, changing its program day by day according to circumstance. For a while it thought it might settle in Szechuan, but the Kuomintang troops were hot on its trail, and it turned aside into the mountainous province of Kweichow. Sometimes the troops saw a small airplane flying high above them. Inside the airplane the Generalissimo was watching the march of the straggling army.

The leader of the army was educated at the Normal School in Changsha, and for a brief while he had been an assistant librarian at Peking University. He was a sick man during the greater part of the long march. Quiet, studious, given to few gestures, driven by will power alone, he was the Generalissimo's most formidable adversary; and already his name was being whispered with dread and terror.

The Generalissimo followed the course of the long march closely, well aware that it boded grave danger. He took personal command of the Kuomintang forces, flew to Szechuan, organized an officers' training corps near Mount Omei, reconstructed the administration in Szechuan, and conducted an inspection tour which took him to nearly all the outlying provinces including Honan, Shansi, Kansu, Shantung, Hopei, Chahar, Suiyuan, and Shensi. The tour of inspection gave him a larger knowledge of the country than he had previously possessed, and helped to consolidate Kuomintang power over the provinces. Early in 1936 the Communists arrived in Shensi in the far northwest, to lick their wounds and prepare patiently for the time when their power would stretch out over all of China.

Meanwhile the Japanese had digested their previous conquests, and by the spring of 1935 they were preparing another assault on China. The plan was unchanged: they would destroy the Chinese will to resistance and then take the fortress at their leisure. By this time they were adept at creating incidents: at first these incidents would be given the names of obscure soldiers, later there would come incidents named after cities. Incidents and treaties were their chief weapons. With the restrictive treaties they were able to render the Chinese government nearly impotent. In May 1935 the Chinese were compelled to sign the humiliating Ho-Mei Agreement, named after the two generals who signed the document: General Ho Ying-chin, the Minister of War, and General Yoshijiro Umetsu, whose Chinese name was Mei Tsin. By this agreement China was forced to agree to the withdrawal of its troops from Hopei. In this province, too, all Kuomintang party activity was to cease, and the chairman of the provincial government was to be removed. There could be no military drilling by any students in the province, and throughout China there must be an end to all anti-Japanese agitation. Chiang Kai-shek might console himself that he was buying time with space; the Japanese could congratulate themselves that a country which was prepared to make so many sacrifices for peace was already on the way to extinction.

Most of the provisions of the unequal treaty were carried out. The Chinese armies were withdrawn to Chahar in good order, and there were no more incidents of importance until the autumn of the year when the Japanese began to grant autonomy to some regions of North China. In November the "East Hopei Anti-

Comintern Autonomous Government" was formed. Since the creation of local governments was not included in the treaty, the Chinese ordered the arrest of the new governor of the area with the formidable title. But the mischief had been done, the Japanese had never been more provocative, and they were now in a position of overwhelming power in the north. The skies of North China belonged to them. They flew wherever they liked, and built their own military airports on Chinese soil. They occupied the railroad junction at Fengtai, important for the defense of Peking. On December 16, 1935, they inaugurated the Hopei-Chahar Political Council. Two more provinces were added to the Japanese empire.

The momentum of the Japanese advance could not be stopped. On October 8, Koki Hirota, the foreign minister of Japan, had suggested three areas of negotiation leading to a lasting peace. They were: (1) suppression of all anti-Japanese movements; (2) establishment of a Sino-Japanese Manchukuo Cooperation Board; (3) institution of an anti-Comintern League between Manchukuo, China, and Japan. The first demand was already contained in the Ho-Mei Agreement, and was now revived because the Chinese government failed to suppress the growing anti-Japanese clamor among the students. The second demand involved China's recognition of the independence of Manchukuo. The third demand would have prevented any further Soviet aid to the embattled Chinese government. Soon after these demands were received, the Kuomintang held its Fifth National Conference, and Chinese independence was affirmed in tones deliberately intended to remind Japan that there were limits to China's humility. For the first time the Chinese seemed to be taking a propaganda offensive. Feng Yu-hsiang, who had been living in a hermitage on the sacred mountain Tai Shan, was one of the more vociferous attendants at the conference. Wang Ching-wei, recovering from long bouts of diabetes, attended long enough to be shot at by a student who believed quite rightly that he was in secret communication with the Japanese.

It had been a miserable year. The six-year-old depression was still darkening China, trade had fallen, the factories were closing their doors, Japanese tanks had attacked Chahar, the Yangtse and the Yellow river had flooded their banks, the fighting with the Communists was still going on. The Japanese, always excessively sensitive about references to their emperor, pretended to be outraged at what they thought was a derogatory adjective in the *New Life Magazine*, and there was a brief moment when China's fate seemed to depend on the interpretation to be given to a word.

On the credit side there was some satisfaction to be derived from the improvement in communications, the control of opium-planting, and the growing confidence of the government, which claimed to have abolished three thousand local and government taxes in a single year. Opium-smoking continued, but some 250 unlicensed opium peddlers were shot. While the general opinion was that the country was in grave peril, there were a few who believed that great successes had been accomplished. In an article entitled "An Optimist in a Sea of Pessimism," which he contributed to *The People's Tribune*, Dr. Hu Shih looked back at a period of enlightened progress. Vast numbers of schools had been opened, the civil law had been cleansed of its more magisterial horrors, fathers who drowned their infant daughters were no longer complimented but sentenced to long terms of imprisonment, and the worst forms of judicial torture were at least theoretically abolished, while footbinding was becoming a thing of the past, and a vast network of communications was opening up the country. It no longer took 104 days for a man to travel from Kansu to Peking. The journey could now be made in fourteen days, and soon, with the completion of the Lunghai railroad in sight, it would be made in three days. He ended the article with a quotation from the *Analects* of Confucius: "Scholars should be patient and courageous, for their future is great and their responsibility is heavy."

At the Fifth National Conference of the Kuomintang, the Generalissimo spoke in a mood of restrained optimism. He admitted that the country was in a state of turmoil, and that the international situation had never been more threatening, but he foresaw a time when China's most bitter enemies would become her friends. Then he continued:

> Our late leader warned us that there is more than one country that can destroy China. Mencius said: "A man must first despise himself, and then others will despise him; a kingdom must first smite itself, and then others will smite it." This was often quoted to us by Dr. Sun Yat-sen. So if we abuse ourselves and make no efforts to be strong and self-reliant, then those nations friendly to us today may become our enemies tomorrow; but if we become strong and self-reliant, it is not impossible that our foes of today may become our friends of tomorrow. There is an old adage—"People help those who help themselves." It is no more than the truth.
>
> We should seek harmonious international relations, provided there is no violation of our sovereignty. We should seek economic cooperation based upon the principle of equality and reciprocity. Otherwise we should abide by the decision of the party and the nation, and reach a resolute determination. As far as I am concerned I will not evade my responsibility. We shall not forsake peace until there is no hope for peace. We shall not talk lightly of sacrifice until we are driven to the last extremity which makes sacrifice inevitable.

At such a time and such a place the last words had the ring of truth. The most impassioned enemies of Japan must have realized that China was still unprepared for war, but possessed vast reserves of strength. Goaded to fight, she would give a good account of herself. But would she be more prepared when the Japanese had bitten off five more provinces? The students thought the patience of the government had gone beyond the limits of decency, and in Peking on December 16 there occurred a demonstration which the government could do nothing to prevent. It was a bitterly cold day with heavy snow on the ground, but the students marched out in disciplined order, for they were determined to be heard. Many were too poor to afford overcoats, and those cold, lonely figures marching in the snow were the easy prey of the police, who attacked with rifle butts and the flat of their swords. Some students mysteriously disappeared and were never seen again; others were beaten unconscious; a few died of pneumonia after the fire department drenched them in ice-cold water. They seized trains and demanded passage to Nanking, and displayed leaflets with the words:

"To the police, to our dear countrymen bearing arms, we are all Chinese together, let us help one another to save our country. Don't fight us, fight the Japanese!" All over North China, during the New Year celebrations, the students fanned out, bringing to remote villages the message that the time had come for the Chinese to oppose Japan. Some ten thousand students demonstrated in Hankow. Everywhere the students were arrested, and the jails were full.

Though the government attempted to obey the demands of the Japanese, suppressing all anti-Japanese demonstrations, no one had any illusions about the inevitability of a Japanese attack in force. By the end of the year there was only one subject of discussion: how would the war begin? The Japanese could produce incidents at will. On June 8, 1934, the Japanese vice-consul at Nanking disappeared without a trace. The Japanese government issued an ultimatum threatening military action. Japanese cruisers steamed up the Yangtse, while the police scoured the countryside and a large reward was offered by the Chinese government for information leading to the discovery of the vice-consul. Every schoolboy and schoolgirl in Nanking, every private detective and everyone who thought he had talents in the direction of detective work helped in the search. What the Chinese feared most of all was the discovery of a mangled body followed by the inevitable retribution. The mystery was solved by an old woman who kept a noodle shop at the foot of the Purple Mountains near Nanking. She reported that a stranger wearing foreign dress and speaking broken Chinese was living in one of the mountain caves behind the Ming tombs. He had come to the shop for noodles and, having no money, had offered her a gold button. She gave him the noodles, but declined the gold button. The old women had pity on him and kept feeding him until she was weary of it, and then she reported him to the police. They found the vice-consul in a cave, and shipped him off to Japan. He was quite mad. There were rumors that the vice-consul was thrown overboard during the journey to Japan, and there were other rumors that he had been ordered to commit suicide in the cave, thus presenting the Japanese with a pretext for entering the country. Many Chinese believed these rumors, and the fact that he was discovered alive was explained by his genuine liking for the Chinese and the knowledge that his death would bring calamities upon China. No one will ever know exactly what happened to the vice-consul. In the winter of 1935 there was no longer any hope that the threat of war could be held off by the kindness of an old noodle-seller at the foot of the Purple Mountains.

The Japanese were biding their time. They could well afford to wait, for Hitler's Germany was beginning to make overtures to Japan, and the expectation of a powerful ally bolstered their self-confidence. Already they could foresee the time when the world would be divided between the Germans and the Japanese.

For the Generalissimo it was a period of alarms and excursions, rebellions and mass arrests of students, with no certainties in sight. That summer there was a rebellion in Kwangtung. According to a popular legend one of the conspirators, a certain Chen, was given the task of consulting the auguries. He decided to travel to the Generalissimo's birthplace and determine the fortunes of the rebellion at a Buddhist monastery. A number of thin wooden sticks, each with a character carved on it, would be shaken in a vase until four fell out, and the future of the rebellion would depend on the four characters. Accordingly Chen lighted incense, prayed, and shook the vase. The four characters were *Chi Pu K'e Shih*. The last three characters meant "cannot be lost," but the first character could be interpreted in several ways. Finally he came to the conclusion that it meant "opportunity," and the message therefore read, "The opportunity cannot be lost." He returned to Canton with the good news, and the conspirators, believing in the auguries, came out in open rebellion. The rebellion was quickly crushed. Chen was arrested, and during his interrogation he mentioned the visit to the Generalissimo's birthplace. Asked to explain why the rebellion had failed, he suggested that he had probably misinterpreted the characters written on the little slender sticks. The old China of sorcery and spells, of prognostications and old wives' tales, still survived.

Since no Communists were involved in the rebellion, the perpetrators were given light punishments. "I firmly believe that the military leaders of Kwangtung are all patriots," the Generalissimo said. "If they will think deeply, they will come to the conclusion that the best thing is to obey the Central Government. With faithful and sincere heart I await a loyal response from them." There was no need for a punitive expedition; the loyal response came well within the stipulated time; and the Generalissimo could take some comfort from the fact that one more rebellion had ended in failure.

It was an age of rebellions. All over China and the occupied territories small armies were being formed, arsenals were being raided, guerrilla troops were marching, strange alliances were being fashioned. The Mongolian chieftain Wang Ying had long been dreaming of carving out of the three northwestern provinces—Kansu, Ninghsia and Chinghai—a vast Mongolian enclave to be known as the "Mongolian Great Yuan Empire." With the help of Japanese advisers, he was able to arm a large body of Mongolian irregulars who invaded the province of Suiyuan and attacked the town of Hunkertu. Nanking ordered an immediate counterattack, and in the battle of Pailingmiao the irregulars were routed. Some pilots who cooperated with Wang Ying were captured. No one was particularly surprised to discover that they were Japanese.

The "Mongolian Great Yuan Empire" went down to defeat and nothing more was ever heard of it. Chiang Kai-shek appears to have thought that these disorderly rebellions had come to an end, and that in the breathing space before the inevitable Japanese onslaught he might bring about the unification of China. He therefore gathered his forces for a final battle against the Communists. The battle plans were prepared; the armies were sent north; the bombers were readied; there remained only a few small details to discuss with the local commanders. All through the late autumn and early winter the Generalissimo was buoyed up with the prospect of a decisive encounter with the Communists. Nothing was more important than the extermination of the "Communist bandits." Only when they were destroyed would he be able to turn his full attention to the Japanese.

In this mood, putting last things first, absorbed in military affairs, quietly confident of his coming victory over the Communists, he began a tour of inspection of the northern provinces. It was to end in a small white-washed room, with armed guards standing outside the door prepared to shoot him down if he made any attempt to escape. He became the prisoner of men he had always regarded as his friends or subordinates. Scarcely knowing what he was doing, he fell into the trap.

AGAINST THE RISING SUN

IT WAS A TIME when many traps were being baited and many more were being sprung. All over Asia and Europe the makers of traps were either cynically observing the agonies of their victims or contemplating the greater agonies to come. A reign of terror stretched from Tokyo to Spain.

The Chinese, exhausted by interminable civil wars, were looking across the sea to learn what particular horrors the Japanese were preparing for them. The Chinese intelligence service, always strong in Japan, was beginning to observe a deliberate pattern in the secret decisions of the Imperial General Staff. Reports of Japanese troop movements gave the lie to Japanese pretensions of peaceful behavior. There came out of Tokyo a continual stream of warnings, but the government in Nanking seemed to be impervious to them.

For a long time the Generalissimo had known that a full-scale invasion was being planned. He had himself prepared plans for a Chinese withdrawal into the interior. Nevertheless he forced himself to behave as though the threat of Japanese invasion loomed far in the future, while he confronted dangers closer at hand. As long as there were warlords, as long as there were Communists, and as long as the Kuomintang was riddled with factions, he could not conceive of China mounting a counteroffensive against the Japanese. When people said, "We must fight Japan," he would answer, "We cannot fight—we must feed the animal a little more." Delaying tactics were an essential part of his strategy. Munich had not yet given a savage and sinister meaning to the word "appeasement." At whatever the cost in suffering, he must buy time on whatever terms were possible.

Through the centuries the classic strategies of Chinese generals followed the ideas of Sun Wu, a military commentator who is supposed to have lived about 400 B.C. In thirteen brief chapters he outlined a philosophy of war brilliantly designed to satisfy the needs of Chinese generals. It is in fact a potpourri of gnomic statements which can be interpreted variously, old saws, sudden illuminations, brutal truths, and psychological riddles. Usually the statements are very short, no more than a single sentence, but occasionally Sun Wu will pause long enough to deliver himself of a portrait of a general or describe a battle in progress. Chiang Kai-shek studied Sun Wu, and he may have seen himself mirrored in this description of a general facing a determined enemy:

> It is the duty of the general to remain calm and inscrutable, upright and strict. He must keep the army in ignorance of his plans by presenting false appearances. He must frequently alter his methods and schemes so that no one can be sure of his intentions. He must frequently change his arrangements and routes so that no one can anticipate his movements. The hour for battle should be decided suddenly, as when one climbs a ladder and unexpectedly kicks it away. After the army has penetrated deep into the enemy's territory, the general reveals his plans. When he wants to make a determined drive by burning boats and breaking up cooking pots, he should act like a shepherd who forces his flock of sheep to run hither and thither without knowing their final destination.

These ideas would not commend themselves to western strategists, but they were fundamental to a knowledge of Chinese warfare. When Sun Wu says, "A skillful attacker moves above the Ninth Heaven; a good defender hides beneath the Ninth Earth," he was saying something which is immediately intelligible to a Chinese soldier. When Chiang Kai-shek sought to buy time by imprisoning any Chinese who called for immediate war with Japan, he was acting according to a traditional logic. It was not particularly intelligent, but it was the best he could do.

Among the sayings of Sun Wu which every Chinese soldier knows by heart are the Five Ways:

> There are five ways in which a general may win victories.
>
> He will win who knows when to fight and when not to fight.
>
> He will win who knows how to match a large force with a small force.
>
> He will win whose army is animated by the same spirit throughout all ranks.
>
> He will win who, prepared himself, waits to take the enemy unprepared.
>
> He will win who possesses generalship and is not interfered with by the sovereign.

When he reflected on the Five Ways, Chiang Kai-shek could see that the advantages were nearly all on the side of the Japanese. A divided China was far from being "animated by the same spirit throughout all ranks," and there was no guarantee that he would be able to match his large forces with the smaller forces of the Japanese, who were highly trained. In his writings at this time we see him moved alternately by great hopes and fears, sudden exaltations and terrible depressions.

It was at this stage in the undeclared war between the two countries and shortly after the Japanese landing at Shanhaikwan in 1933 that he began to prepare his notes for three lectures given later to the Officers' Training Corps at Kuling. The lectures are important, because they emphasize the problems then uppermost in his mind and because they reveal the desperate stratagems which had become necessary. The three lectures were delivered in July 1934, at a time when the Japanese threats were mounting daily.

> The Japanese have already made preparations along the Chinese railways at strategic points where communications are easy, and at any moment they can occupy them. Consider the Kiaochow-Tsinan railway. Although they have not sent troops to occupy the railway, the Japanese merchants and workmen who are living beside the railway are all retired military men. The Japanese in important posts at Tientsin, Hankow, Chahar, and Kalgan are Japanese soldiers out of uniform. Accordingly, in the present situation, all the Japanese have to do is to issue an order, and in three days they can occupy all the strategic points in China and destroy China.

This was Chiang Kai-shek at his most pessimistic, employing hyperbole to reinforce an argument. There were spies everywhere, he went on. All the Japanese prostitutes, all the businessmen, all the coolies, all the small-town photographers, all the stevedores, all the clerks in the shipping companies—"all of them want to find out our condition, and all of them want to destroy our families." China was poor; Japan was wealthy. China could not even afford a twenty-four centimeter gun to protect the seacoast, at a cost of four million dollars, exclusive of shells. It was hideously true that the Chinese could not defend their coasts, because they were so vast and she could not train enough gunners. China was desperately poor in everything except men. So Chiang Kai-shek went on, comparing the strength of Japan with the weakness of China, but always at the back of his Japanese-trained Confucian mind there could be discerned the old Taoist faith that water by its very weakness could smash rocks and there were always advantages in being "drifting sand." A bomb disperses sand, but the sand settles again.

More than anything else he was afraid of the lack of unity in China. The wars against the warlords and the Communist insurgents return to haunt him, although he never explicitly mentions them:

> One of the conditions of our future resistance against the invader is unification. When unification has been accomplished, our strength can be concentrated, and once our strength has been concentrated, then one portion of it is capable of doing ten

> times the work. If there is no unification, and if the country is divided, then the effort to achieve anything will have to be increased twofold. If that happens, then the nation will eventually be destroyed. This is the significance of a modern state and the difference between civilization and barbarism. It concerns the preservation or destruction of the nation. I hope you will pay particular attention to this matter.

Though the mathematics of the argument are dubious, and though he proceeds less by logical progression than by a constant revolution around a fixed point, he was saying forcefully what needed to be said. Chinese arguments very often proceed without connecting links; it is enough that the main hypothesis should be restated in slightly different terms until the meaning has become abundantly clear. What was clear was that war was coming, and would have to be fought with the available weapons. It was not necessary to match the Japanese gun for gun, airplane for airplane. "We can resist the new inventions of the enemy with traditional Chinese weapons, many of them valuable and precious relics—they look useless, but if you examine them carefully they can be made into very effective weapons in wartime." He was thinking about blockhouses, which he had been using in an attempt to surround the Communists. The attempt failed, but he seems to have believed that he might be more successful against the Japanese. Once at least in the lectures, speaking about the paucity of Chinese weapons, he pointed to the possibility that even the Japanese with their vast resources might be outmaneuvered by armies possessing even more formidable resources. In the war of the future strange new weapons would appear:

> You must realize that Japan is still fighting our army with visible weapons, such as heavy artillery, airplanes, and tanks. But in the future world war the weapons will be electricity, chemicals, machines, and gases. There will not be anything visible, audible, or olfactory in the theater of war. At the present time Japanese armies and tactics seem to be very advanced, but I daresay that in the future world war the Japanese would be considered as backward. In this war fighting will take place in the air, under the sea, and below the earth. At that time not only

will blockhouses be futile, but also all the common types of arms and artillery used at the present time will lose their effectiveness. Yet the methods of military operation and strategy do not alter basically, and the military treatises of Sun Wu, composed two or three thousand years ago, are just as valuable as when they were first composed.

In this way, leaping from the remote past to the unforeseeable future, Chiang Kai-shek attempted to sketch out the new shapes of war. It must be admitted that the attempt was oddly unconvincing, and that there was little to be gained by drawing the attention of the cadets to a kind of war which they were not trained to fight.

These secret lectures were delivered in July. By autumn the Japanese were once again threatening to advance, and the situation of the government became desperate. For a while the Generalissimo seemed to be contenting himself with slogans, and a long series of newly invented slogans was broadcast through the country. "Loyalty to the party and love for the country," "Internal security and resistance against external aggression," "Let us do everything with singleness of purpose"—such were the slogans which originated in the Generalissimo's office. They reflected the Generalissimo's preoccupations, but were no help to the country. Toward the end of the year, as the Japanese danger became closer, there were widespread demands for the party to adopt dictatorial powers. These demands also originated in the Generalissimo's office, but there were many scholars who were inclined to believe that no other solution was possible.

Chien Tuan-sen, who later became a vigorous opponent of Chiang Kai-shek, wrote an article in the *Eastern Miscellany* in which he called for an ideal dictator. "I am of the opinion that what China needs today is a powerful and ideal dictator," he wrote. "It is imperative that China should come within the shortest possible time to be a powerful nation with great strength behind it. In the course of ten or twenty years the coastal provinces must be made to undergo a high degree of industrialization, so that agriculture in the interior provinces may form a complementary economy with the industrialized coast."

In later years Chien Tuan-sen, a trusted and much-loved professor at Tsinghua University, would wonder how he could ever have brought himself to believe that dictatorship would solve China's problems, and why he should have called for a dictator when one was already in residence. Already Chiang Kai-shek was assuming dictatorial powers, and his edicts had the force of law. He did not, however, employ that "totality of power" which is the mark of a dictator in the possession of a vast following and he did not yet see himself as the final authority on all matters concerning the state.

Chien Tuan-sen was only one of many calling for a strong central government with extraordinary powers. Dr. Tsiang Ting-fu called for a military dictator in an article in *The Independent Critic*. "We must have a strong centralized government," he wrote. "Under present conditions we have a dictatorship made out of scores of dictators. What I am suggesting is that a strong man should assume the powers now wielded by weak men." This thesis had sometimes commended itself to Dr. Sun Yat-sen, who saw himself as the strong revolutionary leader even when his party was in a state of disintegration. But Dr. Sun Yat-sen never had to face a threatened attack from Japan, and the "totality of power"—the dictator ruling in defiance of his subjects and with all the resources of the state at his command—was a conception which never penetrated his consciousness.

Into this battle of ideas there entered a third figure, Dr. Hu Shih, the man who had reformed the Chinese language. Noting that Chien Tuan-sen and Tsiang Ting-fu had thrown in their lot with dictatorship, he answered bluntly that there were three reasons why dictatorship was not only unnecessary but impossible in China:

> First, I do not believe that there is in China any outstanding personality capable of becoming a dictator, nor is there any political party or any class of people capable of shouldering the responsibility of dictatorship. Secondly, I do not believe there is in China today any vital problem of such a nature as to call for the emotional and reasoned support of the whole of the Chinese people, which would enable the whole nation to accept the

> leadership of any one single individual, or of a certain political party, or of a certain social class, in order to establish the authority of a new autocracy. Thirdly, I do not believe that either the intelligence or the experience of the Chinese people today is capable of carrying successfully into operation a modern dictatorship, which requires superior intelligence and highly specialized techniques for its operation.
>
> Looking over the political systems of the world during the past several decades, I feel that republican constitutionalism is a form of elementary politics best suited to training a people lacking in political experience. The essence of democracy lies in the fact that it does not call for exceptional intelligence; that political rights can expand gradually with a great degree of flexibility; that it promotes the welfare of all by seeking the advice of the many, so that the multitudes of *O Tou** can also put up a good showing by the display of its mediocrity; thus democracy affords to the masses of mediocre men the opportunity to participate in administrative affairs, so that they may be taught to protect and further their own interests and rights.

There were flaws in Dr. Hu Shih's argument, but they were the mistakes that a man makes honorably. Like Chien Tuan-sen, he looked forward to the time when a strong government would take command, but he insisted that it should have a mandate from the people. As for dictatorship, it seemed to him so complex and unmanageable in the circumstances of Chinese life that he despaired of finding any dictator who could assume the burden and carry it out successfully. "Few of those who are dreaming of an enlightened despotism," he wrote, "realize that a despotic political experiment is really the most complicated and difficult of human enterprises."

Chiang Kai-shek's attitude toward dictatorship was considerably more complex. He had no difficulty at all in finding adequate justifications for dictatorship in the writings of Confucius, who permitted the superior man absolute rule over his subjects. On the other hand he had sufficient knowledge of history to know that dictators fared badly on Chinese soil, and that the Chinese "who

* O Tou was the stupid son of Liu Pei, who made himself king of Szechuan. He is a character in *The Romance of the Three Kingdoms.*

suffer from too much liberty" were not likely to accept dictatorship with open arms. The party's influence scarcely extended outside the big cities, and as Chiang Kai-shek admitted later in *China's Destiny*, "there were very few in those years who were really for the National Government." To be effective a dictatorship needs a body of doctrine, a large and enthusiastic following, a devoted and obedient press. He had none of these things.

While the discussion on the need of a dictatorship was still going on, the government issued a short announcement intended to put an end to the controversy. The announcement read: "The present state of affairs and the trend of events in China today do not point to any necessity or possibility of instituting the kind of political system practiced in the Soviet Union and Italy."

In time Chiang Kai-shek would assume all the powers of a dictator, but this was forced on him by the nature of the war against the Japanese. The dictatorship came to him gradually, by small increments, not by a sudden seizure of power. In the coming years he would learn that dictatorship carries terrible penalties, and that there are no antidotes for the poison once it has penetrated the system.

BEFORE THE FIREWORKS

AS THE WINTER of 1936 drew nearer, it was observed that the Generalissimo became more abstracted and was less and less interested in the day-by-day activities around him, and his temper was shorter. He was forty-nine years old, and at the height of his powers. In the eyes of millions of Chinese he was the military genius who might yet save China from becoming a Japanese colony. The stern, lean figure who wore an immaculate uniform and seemed always strangely remote had become in their eyes the destined savior. No other high military officer possessed his charisma. He alone possessed the keys which would unlock the future.

The Generalissimo had no illusions about the nature of the Japanese threat. Sun Wu had written that a general must think only about victory, but everyone knew that in the coming war with Japan the Chinese would suffer innumerable defeats. In the eyes of the Generalissimo only a united China could survive. A small island was laying siege to a continent. A country of immense technical proficiency had fallen into the hands of militarists bent on world conquest. China was merely a stepping-stone. It would be a long war, with no end in sight. Speaking to cadets in 1934 he declared that the Japanese militarists believed that it was well within their power to conquer the Soviet Union, the United States, and the British Empire. He had not used these words. What he had said was even simpler and more cogent: "The objective of Japan's military preparation is the Soviet Union, whereas that of her naval expansion is America and England." Implicit in this statement was the realization that the conquest of China was merely incidental to the greater conquests of the future. The Japanese would reduce China to servitude and throw the weight of Chinese manpower into their own battles.

Although Chiang Kai-shek had spoken hopefully to the cadets in 1934, there was in fact little hope. Already there was an undeclared war fought with the weapons of subversion, espionage, and assassination. The Japanese had an overwhelming advantage in warships, airplanes, and heavy artillery. The Chinese had their Mausers and their courage of despair. On paper they possessed a formidable army, well equipped and well trained by German instructors, but few of the generals could be trusted, there were not enough dedicated officers, the soldiers were dispirited, and, worst of all, the supply trains and the commissariat were never in a state to bear the burdens of a long war. He knew all these things, and could do very little about them. For the first time the man who hated inactivity and worshiped energy found himself in a position where he was almost incapable of any kind of energetic action. He had hoped to dominate history, but now he was at the mercy of historic forces. History wore the familiar face of Japan.

In Europe World War II had already begun. The people of Madrid had flung themselves barefisted against the Montaña barracks, and in the University City and the bleak autumn hills of the Guadarramas the first shots were being fired which would define the destiny of Europe. Already the world was being divided into two camps. There was the totalitarian mystique, which offered simple, mindless solutions to the world's ills: the brute strength of domination in the name of the Führer, who cared nothing for his people but only for his self-aggrandizement. He offered the tempting creeds of obedience and sacrifice. Against the dictators were ranged the democracies, always slow to act, without any deepfelt need for obedience or sacrifice, yet ultimately as ruthless in their desire for their elementary freedoms as the enemy was ruthless in imposing its dictatorship. In Spain three fascist dictators were seeking to impose their will on a country which was close to anarchy. One end of the land mass which stretches from Spain to China was ablaze. In the long silences of meditation in the early morning Chiang Kai-shek could ponder on how soon Trotsky's prophecy that Spain and China would be the first to burn would come true. He had met Trotsky, and half-admired him, and he realized now that he would get no help from Russia, and that the great powers were fonder of Japanese order than Chinese anarchy.

With every day his difficulties only increased. Manchukuo was firmly established; the Communists were already entrenched in Shensi. There were a thousand adjustments to be made in the army, a thousand stratagems to be invented, a thousand high officials to be placated. He had always been most active in autumn, and now as autumn faded into winter, his restless and tormented spirit found solace in continually flying to remote battle posts where at least he could feel that his orders were being carried out—the shrill voice speaking across the parade ground, maps spread on the table, the gleam of leather, the glint of Mausers, the atmosphere of the camp. At such times he seemed to be at ease, in full command of the situation.

In October 1936 he flew to Sian to confer with Chang Hsueh-liang, who had been appointed acting commander-in-chief of the Northwest Bandit Suppression Corps, and with Yang Hu-cheng, the pacification commissioner of Shensi. The Bandit Suppression Corps could no longer be depended on to wage war against the Communists; dissaffection was rife; the Communists, with their slogan, "Chinese should not fight against Chinese," had scored at least a passive victory; Chang Hsueh-liang was no longer sure that he commanded the confidence of the Central Government, and far from certain whether he wanted to lead a crusade against the Communists. The Generalissimo patched up a long-standing quarrel between Chang Hsueh-liang and Yang Hu-cheng, or at least he thought he had patched it up. What he did not know was that the Young Marshal was already entering into secret negotiations with the Communists, and the trap was already being sprung.

The meeting with the Young Marshal and the pacification commissioner took place at the holiday resort of Lintung, near Sian, on October 21. Ten days later came the official celebrations of the Generalissimo's fiftieth birthday. By western calculation he would be forty-nine years old on October 31, but in China a baby is considered to be a year old at the time of its birth. Accordingly, festivities were organized all over China, with the most splendid celebrations taking place in Nanking, where a crowd estimated at a quarter of a million people attended a demonstration in his honor in the grounds facing the tomb of Dr. Sun Yat-sen. His birthday present consisted of seventy American airplanes bought by public subscription. The airplanes flew in formation over the crowd, writing his name and the number of his years on the skies. The Generalissimo was not present; he had slipped away to Loyang. There, in a brief interval between military conferences, he watched Madame Chiang celebrate his birthday in the American way, with two immense birthday cakes and fifty candles.

The purpose of his visit to Loyang was to discuss with his officers in the field the next stage of the war against the Communists. Chiang Kai-shek's speeches were still full of phrases indicating that it was virtually impossible to fight the Japanese while the Communists were still in open revolt. The Japanese were demanding the right to assist the Kuomintang armies in suppressing the Communists, and they were suggesting that there be a joint military occupation of the provinces of Hopei, Chahar, Suiyuan, and Shansi. The offer to take part in the occupation of the four northern provinces was a threat. It was generally agreed that the Japanese occupation of the northern provinces, with or without the help of the Kuomintang armies, was imminent.

A strange air of fantasy seemed to have settled on China. The Japanese were openly talking about the conquest of China, while the Kuomintang leaders talked about conquering the Communists. There were signs that the propaganda machinery of the Kuomintang was at cross purposes; and the Kuomintang party no longer possessed any clearly defined aims. All it could do was to insist that the party and the nation must close ranks around the Generalissimo in the face of the Japanese and Communist threats.

It was at this moment, shortly after the celebrations for his fiftieth birthday, that Chiang Kai-shek decided to issue a long message to the people, in which he hardly mentioned the Communists and never once referred to the Japanese.

This strange message could be read on many levels, for it involved many conflicting ideas and many subterfuges. It was at once a confession of failure and a cry of victory, a lament and a triumph. While offering himself to the Chinese people as their leader, he was also warning them against his own faults and imperfections. Like the Chinese emperors who in their speeches from the throne sometimes spoke of themselves as the least worthy of all the people of China, Chiang Kai-shek began his message in a mood of humility and even of self-abasement, but neither the humility nor the self-abasement correspond to these terms as they are generally understood in the west. Inevitably, since it was a birthday message, he evoked the figure of his mother. He described her at length, and his vision of her—this woman of great authority and singlemindedness—was inextricably involved in his vision of China as she ought to be, and might still be, if the Chinese would only learn to behave with decorum and simplicity and act with her singlemindedness. What is especially strange is that he should have chosen this moment of unparalleled peril to his country to demonstrate his enduring and terrible affection for the woman who more than anyone else was responsible for the driving ambition which brought him to a position of great power. He wrote:

> There remains for me the indelible impression of my mother, who endured so much in educating her fatherless son. Now, while the trees around her grave are tall and thick with leaves, I realize only too well how little I have accomplished and how singularly I have failed to live up to her high hopes. The dangers confronting the party and the state are so many, the misery of the people is so great and the road to recovery so long, that I am ashamed to think that I have allowed time to slip through my fingers without accomplishing my duty.

My mind full of such restless thoughts, I choose at this moment to make public the hardship and difficulties endured by my mother in bringing up her family, so that the world may better realize the sufferings of the helpless and the poor. I trust that these words may serve in some measure as an incentive for practicing self-restraint, and to remind us of the great tasks of national salvation.

I was born in a little village where my grandfather and father maintained a farm and pursued their studies. Through diligence and frugality, they acquired a little wealth. My father died when I was nine years old. After his death the family endured all kinds of tribulations and hardships. It will be remembered that the Manchu dynasty was then in its most corrupt state. Degenerate gentry and corrupt officials had made it a habit to abuse and maltreat people. From time to time usurious taxes and unjust public services were forced upon us, and once we were publicly assaulted before the court. To our sorrow and regret, not one of our relatives and kinsmen stirred from apathy.

Indeed, the miserable condition of our family at that time is beyond description. It was entirely due to my mother, to her kindness and perseverance, that the family was saved from utter ruin. With an iron determination she boldly undertook to save the family from its threatened fate, and with the same determination she resolutely undertook to rear the children in a proper manner. Her task was neither light nor enviable, for she had to look after everything herself. When I was a boy, she loved me very dearly, and her love was more than the love of an average mother. She was a very strict disciplinarian and never failed to hold me to account when I was unusually mischievous.

Whenever I returned home, she would ask me where I had been and what I had been doing, and when I came home from school she would question me on the lessons of the day. She taught me how to conduct and behave myself. She would make me do manual labor, trained me physically, and all her time and energy were devoted to my well-being.

When I reached manhood, I determined to go abroad for a military education. At first some of my kinsmen and relatives were surprised by my desire, and some of them were hostile to my decision. They would have prevented me from carrying out my wishes had it not been for my mother's resolute will and her efforts to provide me with money. Later, when the general principles of our national salvation had become more deeply rooted in my mind, I decided to dedicate myself to the party and the nation—a decision which involved great difficulties and dangers. At that time not one of my relatives would communicate with me. The only one who still believed in my purpose, and helped me spiritually and materially was my mother.

When the republic came, I was twenty-five. By then I was able to improve my mother's home and gratify her wishes a little. Unfortunately the establishment of the republic was not followed by the establishment of perpetual peace, and already internecine conflicts among warring militarists had occurred all over the land, the application of party principles was impossible, and for a time the cause of the revolution seemed hopelessly lost. At that time my mother again came to me with valuable advice, teaching me to make the principle of filial piety applicable to the whole nation. She taught me to recall how we overcame our difficulties at home, and wished me to apply the principle in a broader sense—in the national sense—so that injustice and oppression might forever disappear from human history. She impressed upon my mind that merely being a dutiful son hardly fulfills all the exacting requirements of filial piety. The principle demands also an unflinching devotion to the cause of the nation.

These good counsels were given by my mother for the purpose of guiding my life in the world. Although it was always my ardent desire to do everything in accordance with my mother's wishes, yet so far I have never been able to live up to her great expectations. Whenever I reflect on the conditions in which we two—a widowed mother and a fatherless son—lived in the shadow of cold realities, I cannot but pray for the day when I shall be able to fulfill my mother's wishes in a worthy manner.

Such is the great debt I owe to my country, and such is the great debt I owe to my mother. In some of my leisure moments I have reflected on my experiences during the last fifty years. I cannot but confess that the first twenty-five years were beset with difficulties, for I suffered the loss of my father, I was handicapped by lack of means, and again I was handicapped by my limited knowledge in the struggle for a larger life. The second twenty-five years were equally difficult, for upon my shoulders there had fallen the great task of national salvation. These long years of hard struggle appear to me as though they were but yesterday. Fellow countrymen and dear comrades, it depends upon our own endeavors whether we can bring back our past glories: the reflection of things past inevitably throws light on what is to come. So I take this opportunity to dwell a little more on the principles whereby a nation may establish itself.

There is a proverb which says, "From the family a nation is built." The causes by which families rise and fall are the same as those which cause the rise and fall of nations. Like a family a nation may be now powerful, now reduced to the weakest extremities; and whether a nation perishes or flourishes depends upon the endeavor or determination of the people. The past hundred years have witnessed a number of nations establishing themselves after years of bitter struggle: these nations have set us noble examples. No crops can be harvested without a due share of labor: no labor was ever denied its true reward. If we can continue the struggle with singleness of purpose, we are ultimately certain to triumph over our difficulties.

At this point I would draw an analogy from my own experience. During my childhood, as I have related, my family found itself in a most difficult situation; and yet, although we were oppressed by those in power, nevertheless my mother continued boldly to safeguard the sanctity of the home and she carried out the supreme duty of rearing her children. From this we may learn a profitable lesson. In our march toward national salvation there is no difficulty too great for us to overcome if we have the courage and resolution, but I must remark that our success depends entirely on our own efforts.

Ever since the death of Dr. Sun Yat-sen in 1925, China has encountered disaster after disaster both from within and from without. First the country was overrun by the Communists who almost succeeded in overthrowing the republic and the Kuomintang. There followed a series of foreign aggressions which almost succeeded in overwhelming us and which led to the loss of the three Northeastern provinces. In the midst of these disasters and sufferings, which covered a period of ten years and endangered the very life of the nation, the people began to lose confidence in their leaders and even to lose confidence in themselves. The situation was critical, the crisis confronting the nation unprecedented in our history, but nevertheless I still cherish a great hope. I neither despair over the defeat of international justice nor our own apparent impotence. Now my hope lies in the revival of the old national virtues of self-reliance, self-improvement, temperance, and self-consciousness.

If all of us devote ourselves to the cause of national salvation with the same persistence and endurance as my mother showed in raising her family, it will not be long before China takes her place among the great powers of the world. . . . The eight great virtues—loyalty, filial piety, kindness, love, faithfulness, righteousness, peace, justice—are in accordance with the true spirit and the time-honored characteristics of the Chinese race. No nation can ruin us unless we first ruin ourselves. If every one of us was to recognize his own weakness and endeavor to correct himself, then there will be no difficulty in removing all the obstacles we may encounter in life; if we do this collectively, we will remove all the obstacles confronting the life of the nation.

For my own part I have been painfully conscious of my inability to discharge my responsibility in a way which will fulfill the expectations of my countrymen and the fervent desire of my mother. Always I remember two things—as long as the people remain in distress, I shall have failed in fulfilling my mother's desire, and as long as the task of national salvation remains unaccomplished, I am responsible for the distress and suffering of the people. Therefore I call to my countrymen to help me to fulfill my mother's desire—to fulfill the great task of national salvation.

The birthday message has been quoted at considerable length because Chiang Kai-shek speaks more nakedly here than in his other writings. The man comes through in his pride, his strength, and his weakness. It is as though for a few minutes he permitted himself to abandon the inevitable masks of a dictator and showed himself as he was.

Yet that long meditation has ominous overtones and leaves many essential things unsaid. There is an air of uneasiness in the constant repetitions, in the *désinvolture* by which he now accepts the blame for the failures of the Chinese people, now exhorts them to obey the commandments, and now declaims against their impiety and lack of restraint. There is no sense of progress toward a definite goal. In the name of his mother he assumes responsibility for the distress and suffering of the people, and in his own name he places the burden of responsibility on the people for not having lived up to their ancient traditions.

There is something peculiarly disturbing in those continual references to the heroic mother, who mediates between the past and the future, acquiring almost supernatural powers as she presides over the destiny of China. It is difficult to avoid the conclusion that the son has finally identified himself with the mother. Such inversions are familiar to psychologists. The child loves the mother, assumes her characteristics, and becomes so identified with her that his whole existence disappears in her. Afterward there ensues a desperate struggle in which the child attempts to free himself from her dominating influence. He may succeed or fail, but the marks of the struggle remain, and always there will be moments when the mother returns and he sinks once again into her protective embrace. It would seem that in the silence of the long morning meditations he had heard her voice. She is there before him, and what is curious is that her dominating presence has not faded but has grown stronger with his passionate devotion through the years. In the face of the country's desperate peril he has performed a magical ceremony and raised her from the grave.

The meditation was published in the newspapers and in hundreds of thousands of handbills, and it was broadcast again and again on the radio, so that it came in time to be regarded as a document of historic importance, to be learned by rote by faithful party members and to be discussed endlessly at party meetings. But in fact it was a deeply personal and private document, addressed to his mother rather than to the nation, full of hesitations and ambiguities, and remarkable chiefly because it conveys a very real humiliation and anguish. He is conscious of failure. He has done everything that it was possible for him to do, he has trained himself rigorously for the task of governing China, he has raised great armies and fought grimly and earnestly for a vision, and nearly everything he attempted to do has crumbled into dust. At the end there are only the old Confucian appeals to virtue, the stern mother, a small whitewashed house among the pines, a lost grave amid the bamboos.

To the cynical—and China is a country where cynicism comes easily—there was something pathetic in his insistence on the ancient classical virtues. He was implying that he possessed these virtues, and if only the country would imitate him, then China would rise above all her present difficulties and final victory would be hers. Such self-indulgence was not calculated to disarm his critics. Many foresaw a war that might last a hundred years, with no hope of victory. One by one all the provinces of China would be overrun; every city would be fought over; every farmhouse would be put to the flames. It was not a prospect which gave satisfaction to anyone in China; the future loomed altogether too dark to permit a man to lose himself in dreams of redemptive virtue. The explanation of Chiang Kai-shek's long meditation would seem to lie in the realm of self-analysis; he was attempting to discover himself. There is a sense in which these reflections suggest a private *recueillement*, a soldier's half-hopeful, half-fearful collecting of his soul before the battle. "I am not afraid of death, and still less of fighting," said the great general Wallenstein, "but the waiting—the waiting—torments me!" Chiang Kai-shek was not afraid of death or fighting, but he was tormented by the waiting.

For the Chinese the autumn is the season of death and darkness. The crops are reaped, the leaves fall, the land lies empty, men prepare themselves for their long hibernation. Reading the *Tso Chuan*, the ancient history of Chinese dynasties, one is struck by how often the wars began in autumn, as though in fear of the winter death men took upon themselves the fierce excitement of war. Again and again modern revolutions have begun in autumn. That autumn the coming war could be felt in the air, while all of China seemed to lie under the shadow of Japanese guns.

Every day brought new threats, new demands. Rear Admiral Osamu Satu declared that because the situation was rapidly worsening, two flotillas of Japanese destroyers were being sent to Shanghai. Hachiro Arita, the minister of foreign affairs, announced that he was weary of Chinese "lack of sincerity," and demanded that there should be a joint Sino-Japanese air service, Nanking must employ Japanese advisers, the Chinese tariff walls must be reduced, and the Chinese army must put down the armies of Korean bandits on the borders of Korea. In the early days of November Japanese-trained irregulars crossed the borders of Suiyuan and occupied the town of Pailingmiao. They had tanks and aircraft, and some reporters noted that they were armed with gas bombs. A week later the city of Taolin was attacked. From obscure bases in Chahar the mysterious influence spread out, the armed irregulars drifting southward like a black cloud, so that it seemed as though still another province would soon be added to the three already acquired by the Japanese.

The situation in the north was so tense that on November 17 Chiang Kai-shek flew to Taiyuan and interviewed Prince Ah, the vice-chairman of the Suiyuan-Mongolian Autonomy Council. The situation was fluid. In this half-Mongol province, largely commanded by Mongol bannermen, the lamas still wielded great religious power and the Buddhist temples were centers of political strife. The completion of the Peking-Suiyuan railway had brought unparalleled prosperity to the province, where the flat grasslands offered no barrier to the invader. The Central Government was disturbed by the possibility that the bannermen would go over to the enemy. Prince Ah, however, had not the slightest intention of submitting to Japanese threats. The discussions advanced so well that on November 18 the Generalissimo could say, "We are fully prepared to cope with the situation in Suiyuan, and there is no need for undue alarm." Meanwhile there was the Japanese army in Manchuria, the flotillas of destroyers anchored off Shanghai, and the irregulars continually drifting across the borders. All signs pointed to the coming storm.

As so often in the long history of Sino-Japanese relations, threats of violence were followed by periods of dubious calm. On November 24 the irregulars were swept out of Pailingmiao, and in an old lama temple the victors uncovered documentary evidence of the complicity of the Japanese. The defeat of the irregulars was regarded as a good omen: it was said that the Japanese lines of communication were already too long, and that the Japanese high command had postponed the date for launching a full-scale attack on China on the advice of the foreign office in Tokyo. It was argued that they would need more time to digest Manchuria and to discipline their Manchurian puppet troops, but these arguments were not altogether convincing. More convincing was the argument that the Japanese were still wondering whether they could carry out their full-scale attack without the intervention of foreign powers, who had their own spheres of interest in China. Chiang Kai-shek urged his foreign office to inquire whether China could depend on aid from its allies; he was to learn that there were no allies, and China would have to fight alone. The Americans were still selling scrap iron to Japan, the Russians were obstinately neutral, the British were indifferent. Orders were suddenly issued to buy ammunition wherever it could be found, in as large quantities as possible. There remained one last slender hope, a hope which had often brought courage to the Chinese in the past: the hope that the enemy would make a move so false that the flow of history would turn aside and engulf the militarists who clamored for war. The Japanese high command was wary. The war drums were muffled, and men walking through the streets of Peking, where the snow was already falling, greeted one another and said, "Perhaps, after all, there will be no war."

There was no war. The delusory peace continued, though muffled drums were still heard on the northern frontier. The Chinese, playing their waiting game and hoping the enemy would make the first false move, were agreeably surprised to learn that the Japanese were capable of making errors of judgment. On November 26 Japan signed an Anti-Comintern Agreement with Nazi Germany, thus putting on record the common desire of the Japanese and German governments to attack Soviet influence wherever it could be met. Overnight Stalin became more friendly to Chiang Kai-shek. The agreement had been expected for a long time, but no one had suspected that the commitments would be so definite on both sides. Herr von Ribbentrop, a former champagne seller, was largely responsible for the first false throw in the game which would lead ultimately to the defeat of Japan.

The world was now warned that Japan and Nazi Germany were in close alliance. One did not need to be a visionary to know that there were secret codicils to the Anti-Comintern Agreement. Germany and Japan were preparing to carve out for themselves vast areas of Asia. They were already dividing the spoils.

The time had come for one last concerted effort to eliminate the Chinese Communists. Two days before the signing of the Anti-Comintern Agreement, Chiang Kai-shek received a telegram from the Young Marshal indicating that there was disaffection among his troops and that it would be impossible to mount an offensive against the Communists; he concluded the telegram with a request that they should meet in Loyang. Chiang Kai-shek made inquiries. He was not convinced that the Young Marshal's troops were disaffected, and he seems to have felt that the telegram was an expression of timidity and inexperience. He had no very high opinion of the Young Marshal, who lacked the rough human character of his father and was something of a playboy. Previous conferences with him had been unsatisfactory. He seemed to have a strange reluctance to attack the Communists when they could have been easily encircled with the forces under his command. The Generalissimo had always liked law and order—a clean desk, trains running on time, implicit obedience, long lines of people marching to some predestined and disciplined end—and the time had come to ensure that the Young Marshal would submit to discipline. Accordingly he accepted the invitation to fly to Loyang and discuss the question of the Chinese Communists and the disaffection in the Young Marshal's army.

In this way, almost casually, taking no precautions against treachery, Chiang Kai-shek flew to Loyang on December 3. There would be a few brief conferences, an inspection of the troops, a speech delivered from a parade ground, and an order for a general offensive. The field would be swept clear. The last, the most complete, the most carefully calculated plans against the Communists were in his pocket. He expected total victory, for his secret agents had produced incontrovertible evidence that the communist leadership was divided and that only a sudden blow was needed to destroy the entire communist army. He was on the eve of a great victory, and in his own good time he would turn his attention to the Japanese.

It was dark and cold in northern China. Snow and ice covered the ground, but the harvest had been good and the rice was plentiful. The peasants huddled on their *k'angs*, while the northern winds blew over the Gobi. In Peking men still took their singing birds to the park, walking through the snow under a sparkling blue sky, pretending it was a winter like any other winter. Even in distant Yunnanfu, where it is eternal spring, there were many who believed that blood would flow before the melting of the snows.

There are no iron laws of history, and no statesmen have ever been able to predict the erratic course of events. But there is a phenomenon which has been often observed before great movements of history. Before the great tragedy is played, the same actors perform a curtain raiser which takes the form of a farce, a comic interlude, or a divertissement performed for our amusement. The real blood will soon be spilled, but the actors are armed with wooden swords and buckets of red paint, and they amuse themselves by prancing across the stage wearing the costumes of clowns. Then, abruptly, the curtain rings down. When the curtain rises again, the tragedy begins.

FIREWORKS

ABOUT FIFTEEN MILES from Sian there is the small town of Huachingchih, famous for its hot springs. Huachingchih means "clear splendid pools," and during the T'ang dynasty the Emperor Ming Huang built a pleasure ground with ornamental palaces here for the imperial concubine Yang Kuei-fei when she became inconsolable for the loss of her snow-white parrot. There were sixteen bathing pools constructed of white marble with carved balustrades shaped like egrets and falcons, and broad marble floors where dances were held at midnight. Here the Emperor dallied with his favorite and wasted his kingdom away. Because he was obsessed with her beauty, he permitted affairs of state to be managed by unscrupulous adventurers, and ended his life a prisoner of his enemies.

When Chiang Kai-shek set up his headquarters at Huachingchih, the delicate T'ang palaces had long since passed away. He lived in a large house in the shelter of the overhanging mountains, with about twenty members of his bodyguard. He had met the Young Marshal briefly at Loyang, and was now busy putting the final touches to the master plan for the offensive against the Communists. In a few days he proposed to give the signal for a massive attack which would destroy them forever.

From the beginning there were ominous warnings. When he arrived at the airfield at Loyang, some hundreds of officers of the Northeastern Army demanded permission to present their ideas concerning the anticommunist campaign. He dismissed them summarily, saying that he would talk only with the Young Marshal. Nothing came of these talks. He went into seclusion. A strange dreamlike silence descended on his headquarters at Huachingchih. There were plots. There were threats. There were the strangest possible interviews. Snow fell; armed soldiers patrolled the streets; in the silence of a northern winter strange forces were being let loose. The past, the heavy remote past of China which is continually obtruding on the present, seemed to descend on the chief actors of the drama at odd intervals, unrecognizable by them but visible to the historian who remembers that the great T'ang dynasty almost perished among the hot springs of Huachingchih.

When he wrote about these days immediately after the coup, Chiang Kai-shek said he had absolutely no idea that treachery was contemplated. Writing twenty years later, he observed that he was perfectly well aware that treachery was in the air. On December 5 he had a long discussion with Chang Chi-lan, a journalist with wide contacts throughout northern China. The Generalissimo asked the journalist whether he had heard of the Young Marshal's secret negotiations with the Communists. The journalist said he had heard of them, but could not be certain whether they had in fact taken place; it was possible that the rumors had been spread by the Communists with the deliberate intention of compromising the Young Marshal. "When I heard this, I realized that the situation was serious," Chiang Kai-shek wrote in 1956. From his own secret agents in the communist capital Chiang Kai-shek had learned that the communist hierarchy was hopelessly divided and wanted only an excuse to make peace with the Central Government. Later the Generalissimo learned that the secret negotiations had been continuing for many months and that the communist hierarchy had never been less divided. In fact, at that very moment the Young Marshal's emissary was discussing with the communist high command what should be done with the Generalissimo.

Already, without knowing it, the Generalissimo was the Young Marshal's prisoner. The large house at the foot of the Lishan mountains was surrounded, his movements were being carefully watched, and there appear to have been agents of the Young Marshal inside the house, a hotel which had been hurriedly evacuated by its guests. The Generalissimo spent the days working over his plans for an offensive and interviewing people who might be able to throw light on the treacherous conspiracies of the Young Marshal. He announced that in the middle of the month he would summon a meeting of high military officers, at which he would reveal his plans. At the same time he was considering the arrest and punishment of some highly placed officers, but he had not yet decided who were the culprits. In this state of uncertainty, while mist and snow covered the Lishan mountains and mysterious automobiles went on mysterious errands, he wasted several days. In Nanking it was generally believed that the Generalissimo would make a momentous announcement as soon as he returned to the capital.

On the night of December 11 the Generalissimo invited three generals to dinner at the hotel. They were the Young Marshal, Yang Hu-cheng, and Yueh Hsueh-chung. Yang was the pacification commissioner for Shensi and Yueh was the commander of the Fifty-first Army. The dinner was a failure, because only the Young Marshal attended. He explained that the two generals were absent because they were entertaining high civil and military authorities in nearby Sian, an explanation which can hardly have commended itself to the Generalissimo, who combined in his own person the highest civil and military authority in the land. The generals had not attended because they were afraid they might be arrested. The Young Marshal attended in the belief that he was altogether too powerful to be arrested. In this he proved to be wrong, for he was to become the Generalissimo's private prisoner for the rest of his life.

The unsatisfactory dinner party broke up early, and the

Young Marshal returned to his headquarters to put the finishing touches to the coup which he had been planning since the Generalissimo's arrival in the north. The plan involved the arrest and imprisonment of the Generalissimo followed by a secret trial presided over by the northern generals, in the presence of communist emissaries. If the Generalissimo did not agree to his demands, the Young Marshal was prepared to order his execution.

The Generalissimo knew nothing whatsoever about the Young Marshal's plans, and it seems never to have occurred to him that he was in any danger. Earlier that day, while walking in the foothills of the Lishan mountains, he had observed two men in the distance watching him fixedly. They were not members of his bodyguard, and it occurred to him that they had been sent to spy on his movements, and then he dismissed them from his thoughts. At some time before nine o'clock, while the dinner party was still going on, the Young Marshal asked the Generalissimo's permission to introduce a young colonel called Sun Ming-chiu, saying that he was a young man whom he wished to send to the front on a special mission and who would benefit from a few words of advice. Seeing the young colonel, who was the commander of the Young Marshal's bodyguard, the Generalissimo remembered that earlier in the day he had had an unexpected visitor, the Young Marshal's chief of intelligence. This man had entered his room unannounced, and immediately harangued him on the subject of the Communists, saying that it was foolhardy to attack them at a time when the whole nation should be preparing to fight the Japanese. The Generalissimo had reprimanded the chief of intelligence severely, but there was no reason to reprimand the young colonel. Instead, he spoke kindly, inquired about the "special mission," and then dismissed him. At nine o'clock the dinner party broke up, the Young Marshal ill-at-ease and the Generalissimo faintly perturbed by the events of the day. He worked for a while on military plans, and then went to bed. He could hardly have foreseen that in the morning he would be arrested by the young colonel, or that this was the last meal he would enjoy for forty-eight hours.

He slept well, and when he awoke in the early morning a light snow was falling, and it was still dark. He got up, did his exercises, splashed his face with ice-cold water, and he was about to get dressed when he heard shots being fired outside. He sent one of his aides to report, and when the aide failed to return, he sent two more. It occurred to him that there might be a mutiny, but whether it was a mutiny of his own soldiers or of a local garrison he did not know. The mutineers, whoever they were, had not cut the telegraph wires and he was able to communicate with the small force of guards in a barracks on the other side of the mountain. He asked about Lieutenant Mao, the chief of his bodyguard, and learned that he was at the front of the hotel, guarding the approaches. The mutineers were already invading the grounds of the hotel, and firing was going on continually. A runner from Lieutenant Mao informed him that his best chance of safety lay in the mountains behind the hotel. Asked about the uniform of the mutineers, the runner said they wore fur caps and belonged to the Northeastern Army. None of the mutineers had yet entered the hotel and the situation was not desperate, but might become so at any moment. The Generalissimo decided to take to the mountains. He was in his nightshirt, barefoot, and without his false teeth.

He imagined that the whole of the Northeastern Army was in revolt, "possibly," as he wrote later, "under the instigation of the communist bandits." He felt certain that the Young Marshal was innocent, because it was inconceivable that he would dare to assume the responsibility for such a coup. On both these counts the Generalissimo was wrong: the Young Marshal was perfectly capable of attacking his headquarters and the Communists were not responsible for the revolt. The soldiers attacking the hotel belonged to the Young Marshal's forces and were under the direct command of the colonel who had been introduced to him the previous evening. Accompanied by an aide-de-camp and one of the officers of his guard, the Generalissimo made his way out of the back of the hotel, crossed a stone bridge, and reached a gate, which was locked. Precious moments were lost in trying to open the gate, but there was no key and they were forced to scramble up a ten foot wall.

If there had been no moat on the other side of the wall, if the attackers had surrounded the hotel on all sides, and if the morning had been brighter, the history of Chiang Kai-shek might have been entirely different. He fell into a moat thirty feet below, sprained his ankle, wrenched his back, suffered contusions and bruises, and for three minutes he was incapable of moving. He moaned and called to his aides, afraid of raising his voice above a whisper, and with their help made his way to a small temple, where some of his bodyguards were waiting. Together they began to climb the mountain.

In the darkness there were only the rocks and the gray crags of the Lishan mountains in front of them. It was bitterly cold, there were no paths, and it was so dark that they had to keep together for fear of losing one another. At any moment they knew the mutineers might fall upon them. They dared not go west, in the direction of Sian. They turned east, where there were the most precipitous slopes and the greatest possibilities of refuge. In about half an hour they reached the top of the mountain, took a short rest, and sent one of the bodyguards to reconnoiter. This was probably the worst mistake the fugitives made, for the bodyguard was seen standing on the edge of the cliff in the early morning light. Soon the hills, which were honeycombed with soldiers, were echoing with rifle shots from all directions. Chiang Kai-shek was now certain that he would be found and murdered, and it was merely a question of time until his bullet-riddled body would be carried in triumph to Sian. There were dead and dying guards all around him, and there was still shooting in the hotel, which could be seen below. He now realized that it was wrong to have left the hotel and the main body of his guards, and that every move he had made had been foreseen by the invisible and relentless enemy. But who was the enemy?

In despair he began to crawl down the mountain. He was in agonizing pain from his wrenched back and could make his way only very slowly. Then, as he told the American correspondent Hallett Abend some weeks later, at the moment of deepest despair he surrendered himself to God, prayed earnestly, and asked that if God had chosen him to lead China, He should send a sign showing the way to safety. When he opened his eyes he saw two white hares and knew instinctively that this was the sign which God had sent him. He followed them haltingly over the barren rock, and when they slipped under a shelving rock he crawled after them. With the two whites hares as his companions, he hid in the cave.

He thought he would eventually be found and probably shot out of hand, and he was now almost beyond caring. He was appalled by the indignity of his flight and heartened by the signs of God's mercy, and between despair and hope he moved helplessly. During the following days he wrote an account of the incident in the form of a diary, which was later published with a few significant and perhaps necessary omissions. The diary reads as though it were written with transparent honesty, but there is more than a suspicion that the omissions have shifted the focus away from the battle of ideas to the portrait of the leader contemptuous of danger, determined to dominate the situation by moral force alone. Here is his account of his discovery and arrest:

> As the day gradually dawned I could see from the cave that the Lishan mountain was surrounded by a large number of troops. Then I heard the detonation of machine guns and hand grenades near my headquarters. I knew that my faithful bodyguards at the headquarters continued their resistance and that the rebels were using artillery to attack them. It was about nine o'clock, after which time no more firing could be heard. The rebels sought for me. Twice they passed the cave in which I took cover but failed to discover me.
>
> About twenty or thirty feet from my refuge I heard someone hotly arguing with the rebels. It was Chiang Hsiao-chung's voice.* The rebels made a more thorough search. I heard one of the mutinous soldiers above the cave saying: "Here is a man in civilian dress; probably he is the Generalissimo."
>
> Another soldier said: "Let us first fire a shot."
>
> Still another said: "Don't do that."
>
> I then raised my voice and said: "I am the Generalissimo. Don't be disrespectful. If you regard me as your prisoner, kill me, but don't subject me to indignities."

* Chiang Hsiao-chung was the Generalissimo's aide-de-camp.

> The mutineers said: "We don't dare." They fired three shots into the air and shouted: "The Generalissimo is here."
>
> Sun Ming-chiu, a battalion commander, then approached me. He knelt before me with tears in his eyes and requested me to go down the mountain. Then I knew that the soldiers attacking the headquarters belonged to the second battalion of Chang's bodyguards. Sun accompanied me down the mountain. When we reached my headquarters I intended to go in for a rest. I saw through the doorway that things were in great disorder and the ground was strewn with dead bodies. Sun asked me to go by motor car to Sian. He said that my room was already in a state of confusion and that he had received orders from his superiors to invite me to Sian. I ordered Sun to find the deputy commander [Chang Hsueh-liang], who, he said, was in Sian waiting for me. He added: "We don't dare to mutiny against our superior officers; we wish to make a personal representation to Your Excellency in the hope that he will kindly grant our request."
>
> To this I shouted in anger: "Hold your tongue, you rebels! If you want to kill me, kill me right now! "

The rages of the Generalissimo were famous, and he was now in a rage which was to endure for nearly two weeks. From time to time he would give the order, "Kill me!" and he seems to have been genuinely surprised that the order was not carried out. He expected to be killed, and his reactions can only be understood in the light of his knowledge of what happened to men captured by mutineers.

When Sun Ming-chiu, the chief of the Young Marshal's intelligence, politely invited him to go to Sian, the Generalissimo had no alternative. He observed that the car was driven by the Young Marshal's favorite chauffeur, and it suddenly occurred to him that the entire conspiracy was the Young Marshal's work. When they reached the East Gate of Sian, the Young Marshal's car came in sight: more proof that the Young Marshal was responsible. But the only person in the car was an officer who ordered the Generalissimo to be taken to the house of General Yang Hu-chen, the pacification commissioner who had so singularly failed to arrive at the dinner party the previous night. Worse still, the armed guards in the street wore the armbands of the Seventeenth

Army, which was directly under General Yang's command. Armbands, however, are easily changed, and more than one warlord had ordered his men to wear the armbands of the enemy to create confusion. Yet General Yang had for long been a trusted member of the Kuomintang, and he was the trusted appointee of the Generalissimo. It could *not* be General Yang who was responsible for the uprising. But the Generalissimo remained uncertain, still confused by the events of the morning, still dazed by his fall and by the slaughter at the hotel. What was the explanation? He was as perplexed as the members of the Central Government in Nanking who received at about this time a telegram from the Young Marshal reporting the mutiny and the fact that the Generalissimo had completely disappeared.

What was the explanation? Even today there is no simple solution to the problem. The Young Marshal gave the order for the arrest of the Generalissimo: so much is certain. But what he intended beyond putting him on trial and using him as a hostage is unknown, and it is possible that even the Young Marshal did not know. There is evidence that many different plans with different aims were prepared, and they were never coordinated, because the rebels were divided among themselves. Faced with their own *fait accompli,* they did not know how to proceed, for there exists no protocol which orders the behavior of men who have just captured the chief of state.

The Generalissimo was kept waiting in the house of the pacification commissioner for half an hour, while the plotters deliberated among themselves. At last the Young Marshal arrived, looking pale and frightened. He said he knew nothing about the mutiny, a statement which was certainly untrue. "In that case," said the Generalissimo, "your proper course is to see that I return immediately to Nanking or Loyang, and the whole affair can be quickly settled." The Young Marshal then corrected himself, saying that he knew nothing about the actual developments of the mutiny, a statement which may very well have been true. "Meanwhile I wish to lay my views before Your Excellency the Generalissimo."

The flourish of titles offered many clues to his behavior, and the Generalissimo said sharply: "Do you still call me the Generalissimo? If you still recognize me as your superior, you should send me to Loyang; otherwise you are a rebel. Since I am in the hands of a rebel, you had better shoot me dead. There is nothing else to say."

There was a good deal more to say, and during the following days the implications of the words "rebel" and "superior" would be examined at length by people who found a strange pleasure in perverting their obvious meanings. The Young Marshal was no match for the Generalissimo at the game of playing with words. He found the utmost difficulty in explaining his intentions, while the Generalissimo, secure in the knowledge of God's protection and his own invincibility, had no difficulty in explaining his intention to override all his enemies. The Young Marshal had the courage of despair, and he seems to have known that he would have to assume the responsibility for the coup and suffer the consequences.

So they took up their positions and debated at length, without coming to conclusions. In his diary the Generalissimo recorded a portion of the debate, which gives every appearance of having been remembered accurately:

> CHANG: If Your Excellency will accept my suggestions, I will obey your orders.
>
> GENERALISSIMO: Which are you, my subordinate or my enemy? If you are my subordinate, you should obey my orders. If you are my enemy, you should kill me without delay. You should choose either of these two steps, but say nothing more, for I shall not listen to you.
>
> CHANG: My motive is revolutionary, not mutinous.
>
> GENERALISSIMO: Why do you still disclaim any previous knowledge of the mutiny?
>
> CHANG: Even if we are enemies, there is still the possibility for us to enter into negotiations.
>
> GENERALISSIMO: Can there be any talk between enemies? What kind of man do you take me for? Can the rebels and my enemies compel me to surrender to force?

There followed a short discussion with Shao Li-tzu, the portly chairman of the provincial government, and then Chiang Kai-shek was left alone with the mysterious Sun Ming-chiu. He was offered blankets, a fur coat, food, and he refused them all. With his face turned to the wall, overwhelmed by a sense of savage indignation, contemptuous of his captors, he waited for an unknown end. It was obvious that his captors had the power to kill him; it was also obvious that they had not yet decided on a plan of action.

So the day passed in the small unheated room, the door unlocked, Sun Ming-chiu keeping constant guard in the corridor outside and entering the room at intervals to ask whether the Generalissimo would like tea or food, and receiving no answer, though from time to time the prisoner would drink tea. He refused to eat, refused medical attention, and refused to speak except in the most peremptory manner to the Young Marshal, who came twice a day with tears in his eyes, begging for forgiveness, expatiating on his own unworthiness, making demands, reducing them, beseeching the Generalissimo to have a change of heart, at a loss to explain the sense of urgency which sustained him even in those terrifying moments when he was greeted with the dull, withering glance of the Generalissimo, who despised him. The Generalissimo was the son of a Chekiang salt merchant and had raised himself to prominence by his own efforts. The Young Marshal was the son of a warlord, and he had risen to power only because it had come to him effortlessly after his father's murder. The warlord's son and the former private faced each other, and neither could convey to the other the peculiar urgencies which occupied his mind.

There were worse moments than those terrifying silences, moments when the Generalissimo would simply refuse to recognize the other man's existence, when he would turn his face sharply to the wall, when instead of silence there was a vast indifference which was not scorn or contempt so much as a soldier's weary recognition of his own error in permitting himself to be captured. He continually asked his captor to kill him, and his captor continually asked for forgiveness. It was a spectacle which would have delighted Corneille, who loved above all to describe the weariness which comes from pride and the meeting of implacable forces. For at least thirty centuries north and south China had been engaged in a confused debate which could never be resolved, because neither could communicate with the other. So now, in a small room in Sian, the debate was being continued over barriers of incomprehensibility. The Generalissimo would continue to face the wall, while the Young Marshal pleaded, cajoled, spoke of the need for a united China, and demanded that at the very least there should be some attempt at communication between them.

In Nanking nothing was yet known about the silent duel which was being fought in Sian. The newspapers had flaming headlines, there were the wildest of inaccurate surmises, there were premature announcements of the Generalissimo's death. Ho Ying-chin, the minister of war, was seriously contemplating a massive bomber attack on Sian; in this way he hoped to dispose of both the Generalissimo and the Young Marshal. Madame Chiang, fearful for the life of her husband, was attempting by all the means in her power to open communication with the Generalissimo and to prevent the bomber attack. The war ministry was adamant, and the strange debate in Sian was accompanied by a still stranger debate in Nanking between the wife of the Generalissimo and the minister of war.

Within forty-eight hours the Young Marshal began to show signs of wavering. As Shao Li-tzu remarked to the Generalissimo, he had not been able to summon up the courage to kill his prisoner. He lacked the Generalissimo's singlemindedness and contempt for death. The Generalissimo's mind was limited, but rigidly disciplined. He could think hard, he had a sense of his own authority and a logic of his own. Because he thought he might be put to death at any moment, he could afford to be more authoritarian than he had ever been in his life; and his silent war was fought implacably. But it is necessary to insist that he was not the unchallenged victor in the contest: the challenger possessed powers of his own. Dissatisfaction with the Generalissimo was rife in China, and it was necessary that he should be warned. He had long since established a form of dictatorship, and it was necessary that he should think out his relationship with the Chinese people afresh.

The eight demands which the Young Marshal later presented to him represented a consensus which could not be ignored. It was said later that these demands were drawn up by the Communists, but they were not essentially communist in nature. They were:

(1) Reorganize the Nanking Government to include members of other parties.
(2) All civil wars to be stopped at once.
(3) The political prisoners in Shanghai to be released at once.
(4) A free pardon for all political offenders.
(5) Guarantee the people's liberty of assembly.
(6) Allow the people to maintain their own patriotic movements.
(7) Sun Yat-sen's will to be faithfully carried out.
(8) A National Salvation Conference to be held at once.

If he analyzed these demands, the Generalissimo could see that they were designed to restrict his own dictatorial power and that they would inevitably favor the Communists. They were aimed at the Kuomintang party as much as at himself, and they were curiously lacking in respect for himself, since each demand implied a diminution of his authority, and the authority of the party. Since he saw himself as the chosen leader of the Chinese people, and the party as the chosen instrument of his will, he rejected the demands out of hand. He could not do otherwise, for he was incapable of agreeing with any arguments but his own. On the evening of his capture the Young Marshal asked him why he was so obstinate. He answered:

> What do you mean by obstinate? I am your superior, and you are a rebel. According to military discipline and the law of the land, you as a rebel deserve not only reprimand but also punishment. My head may be cut off, my body mutilated, but I must preserve the honor of the Chinese race, and must uphold law and order. I am now in the hands of you rebels. If I allow the honor of the four hundred million people whom I represent to be degraded by accepting any demands in order to save my own life, we should lose our national existence. Do you think that by using force you can compel me to surrender to you rebels? Today you have lethal weapons: I have none, but instead

> I am armed with the principles of righteousness. They are my weapons of defense. With these I must defend the honor of the people I represent, and with these I must be a faithful follower of our late leader. I shall do nothing to betray the trust imposed on me by the martyrs of the revolution. I shall not bring shame or dishonor to this world, to the memory of my parents or to the nation. You, young man, do you think you can make me submissive by force? You mistake my firm stand on the principles of law and order for obstinacy. If you are a brave man, kill me; if not, confess your sins and let me go. If you do neither, you will be in a dangerous position. Why don't you kill me now?

Another man might have been driven to murder by these taunts, but the Young Marshal was restrained by a sense of his own inadequacy and by the knowledge that the Generalissimo, whatever his faults, was preferable to Ho Ying-chin, the minister of war, who would inevitably seize power if the Generalissimo was killed. The Generalissimo's argument defining the difference between obstinacy and righteousness was less impressive than the unspoken argument which said in its simplest form: What is to be gained by killing me?

For the Generalissimo, the question was ultimately a very simple one, for he had nothing to lose except his life. He had identified himself with the Chinese people and could say without any feeling of betrayal: "If I allow the honor of the four hundred million people whom I represent to be degraded by accepting any demands in order to save my own life, we should lose our national existence." But what if the demands were reasonable, or even necessary? He spoke of the honor of the people, but was not the honor of the people involved in those periodic wars of extermination between rival Chinese factions? His mind was never logical. He saw himself as one of those princely rulers who are to be found in all ages of the history of China. A certain Prince T'ung, according to the *Tso Chuan*, said before battle, "A man who fights in three campaigns perishes, and this is my third campaign," and thereupon he sent his lute to a neighboring lord with the message, "Farewell, my lord, I shall not see you again." Another prince wrote on the eve of battle, "I shall hear the drumbeats which summon us to the battlefield, but I shall never hear the sound of the cymbals which bring the battle to an end." The Generalissimo had heard the sound of drums and was waiting patiently for the cymbals.

The whole atmosphere of the capture remains mysterious to the western observer, but we shall understand it better if we remember that the feudal past weighs heavily on China. The ancient princes were at the mercy of conventional treacheries; the savage encounters between the feudal states usually ended in the murder of one of the rulers. We should remember, too, that the Chinese emperor was in theory subject to the mandate of the people, and that Confucius regarded the killing of a bad emperor as a proper act. The Young Marshal evidently toyed with the idea of killing the Generalissimo or at least of removing him from office on the grounds that he no longer possessed the mandate of the people. He said:

> I am not alone in this affair. There are many other people who are in the movement, which should be referred to the people for their verdict. Should the people be in sympathy with this movement, then it would prove that I am representing the common will of the people, and Your Excellency will realize that my actions are not wrong. Then you may retire from office, and let me do the work. If the people are not in sympathy with this movement, then I shall admit my own fault and Your Excellency may resume your work. I believe I have not in any way disobeyed your teachings. Please don't be angry, but consider the matter carefully.

The Generalissimo was no more inclined to accept this argument than any of the other arguments which had been put forward. He was outraged by the appeal to a popular verdict, and equally outraged by the Young Marshal's offer to do the work of governing China. He shouted:

> You are crazy! Do you think that the people are in sympathy with your mutiny? Even the so-called Popular Front will not give you their support. You claim that your motives are revolutionary. Can a mutiny be called a revolution? Chen Chiung-

> ming* also claimed to be a revolutionist, but who in the world could believe him? Since you are a rebel, how can you expect to command the obedience of your men who surround this house? How can you be a man yourself? How can you be sure that your men will not follow your example and do as you are doing to me? Remember that four years ago the people wanted to get hold of you and punish you, but I took the blame for you I do not know how many times. Because I took a generous protective attitude toward you, you were able to go abroad. From now on, in spite of the size of the world, where will you find a place for yourself? Living, there will be no place to put your feet; dead, there will be no place to bury your bones. You still do not realize your predicament, but I do. I am really afraid for you.

The Generalissimo had sized up his enemy and was playing an astute game of psychological warfare against a man who had never staked his life on a psychological game. His task was to find the weakest point in the Young Marshal's armor and drive the attack home. So might a feudal emperor of the Spring and Autumn dynasties have spoken to some chieftain who thought he might take the crown by force. But although the argument was maintained on a personal level, and the Generalissimo was determined to inflict a moral defeat on his opponent, there were impersonal forces which could not be won over so easily. Once, lying in bed, he heard people whispering outside and thought he could make out the words: "To refer the case to the people for judgment." These words were ominous, and he was perfectly aware of their implications. "I must maintain the same spirit which led Jesus Christ to the Cross," he wrote a little later, "and I must be ready to meet any death which the mutineers may bring upon me by the so-called people's verdict." In long passages of the diary he returns to the subject of his own death as though it had already occurred, as though he could see clearly all the events that led up to it and everything that happened afterward. His death would be remembered in all future ages, and the future Chinese leaders would all be imbued with his spirit of sacrifice. Because he had maintained

* Chen Chiung-ming was civil governor of Canton and commander-in-chief of the revolutionary army when he revolted against Dr. Sun Yat-sen in 1922.

his integrity until death, his spirit would live forever, guiding the destiny of China. "Then, though I die, the nation will live."

It was a simple and rewarding answer to insoluble problems, for it permitted him to believe that whatever happened to him, whether he lived or died, all the advantages were on his side. These arguments were set before the Young Marshal, who appears to have found them conclusive. "My sacrifice will be my achievement," the Generalissimo told the Young Marshal two days after his arrest. "On the day that I sacrifice my life for the sake of principle the revolution will be a success." In a letter to his wife which was smuggled out of Sian on December 15, he wrote, "Since I was born for the revolution I will gladly die for the same cause. I will return my body unspoiled to my parents." If much of this was posturing, the deliberate assumption of a heroic role, it was also an attempt to come to grips with his own legend. He was living vicariously, permitting the legend to live for him.

As the days passed, the Young Marshal became increasingly careless, fearful, and awkward. While the Generalissimo increasingly adopted the posture of the heroic martyr, the Young Marshal found himself in a quandary, because it was inconceivable to him that heroic martyrdom had any place in modern civilization. It was not only that he could not understand the Generalissimo, but the more the Generalissimo explained the attitude he was taking, the more incomprehensible he became. Once the Young Marshal said, "You always have in your head such men as Yueh Fei, Wen Tien-hsiang, and Sze Ko-fa,* and are therefore behind time in your mentality. Why do you insist upon sacrificing yourself for the sake of principles and not think of the possibility of achievements? I think you are the only great man of this age, but why won't you yield a little, comply with our requests and lead us in this revolution so that we may achieve something instead of your merely sacrificing your life?" To this argument the Generalissimo had a ready answer. "Sacrifice and achievement are the same thing," he said, and went on to elaborate how his own sacrifice would effec-

* These three generals had sacrificed their lives for the country, and were repeatedly mentioned in the Generalissimo's speeches. The Generalissimo had made a special cult of Yueh Fei, who was accused of rebellion against the emperor and died in prison.

tively bring about the triumph of the revolution. "If I become afraid in the face of danger, my character as a military man will be destroyed, and the nation will be in a precarious position," he said, and the equation between the man and the nation was never so nakedly expressed.

As he spoke these words, Chiang Kai-shek knew perfectly well that vigorous and sometimes ill-considered preparations were being made to rescue him, and he may have known there was a continual shifting of forces in Nanking and Sian, and this was dangerous, for inevitably there would come a time when a final decision would have to be made, and it would come about through an alliance of those strangely mobile and ghostly forces. Meanwhile a winter dance was being performed around the prisoner, who was in no position to know who was conducting the orchestra or whether there was any orchestra at all, for the dance seemed to be performed in silence. He could only clutch at straws, guessing what was happening by an intonation, a gesture, the way the Young Marshal formed his sentences, the fear in his eyes.

In Nanking Ho Ying-chin was determined to put an end to the rebellion by force, even if it meant that the Generalissimo would be placed in even greater danger. He sent airplanes to bomb Hwahsien, near Sian, where there was a concentration of Chang Hsueh-liang's troops. Many soldiers were killed. The Young Marshal was properly incensed, and urged the Generalissimo to forbid any further bombing, which would only exasperate the armies loyal to him and make a solution of the problem more difficult. This, within the context of the elaborate fantasy, seemed reasonable enough, and the Generalissimo thereupon wrote a letter to Ho Ying-chin, demanding that there should be no further bombardments by Nationalist planes. The letter was sent by courier on December 17, arriving in Nanking the following day. Ho Ying-chin decided that the letter had been written under compulsion, and no particular attention need be given to it. He ordered a brief cessation of the bombing, which would be resumed at 6 P.M. on December 19.

By this time it was becoming clear to the Generalissimo and even to Nanking that the Chinese Communists were in close contact with the Young Marshal and that no final decisions would be made without their concurrence. The final judgment was perhaps being made by Mao Tse-tung in Yenan. Certainly many Chinese Communists had arrived in Sian, and there was a brisk communication between Sian and Yenan, as the Young Marshal's conversations with the Generalissimo were being reported to the communist headquarters. And when Madame Chiang, accompanied by the Australian adviser W. H. Donald and her brother T. V. Soong, arrived in Sian on December 22 in a daring attempt to free the prisoner by a display of brute courage, the Generalissimo said, "Why have you come? You know it is a death trap." So it might have been, for the Chinese Communists were still weighing the possibility of condemning him to death or perhaps carrying him off to Yenan.

Two more days passed before the Chinese Communists and the Young Marshal finally reached an agreement. It was decided to spare the life of the Generalissimo because he was essential to the conduct of the war against the Japanese, which could not be long delayed. As the Chinese Communists explained later in Yenan, they were confronted with a bitter alternative. They detested the Generalissimo, but they detested Ho Ying-chin more. They were afraid that Ho Ying-chin would come to terms with the Japanese, and they were now satisfied that the Generalissimo would behave toward the Japanese exactly as he had behaved toward his captors—with courage.

They had taken the measure of his dedication; they knew now that he would fight to the bitter end. Although, for obvious reasons, the Generalissimo did not mention in his account of the Sian incident that he had had several conversations with Chou En-lai, these conversations did in fact take place, and there is little doubt that the Generalissimo spoke to this Chinese Communist ambassador in exactly the same way that he spoke to the Young Marshal. Just before leaving for Nanking, the Generalissimo summoned the Young Marshal and once more delivered himself of a homily on the subject of a man's proper duty. It was a long homily, which has survived because Madame Chiang took careful notes:

> We must remember that the life of a nation is more important than anything else. We should not care for ourselves although our personal integrity must be preserved in order that the

nation may exist on a firm foundation. Our lives may be sacrificed, but the law and discipline of the nation must be upheld. Our bodies may be confined, but our spirit must be free. My own responsibility to the country and the Central Government will always be willingly borne as long as I live. That is why I have repeatedly refused to give any orders or sign anything you wanted me to sign while under duress. It is because I consider life or death a small matter compared with the upholding of moral principles.

He spoke these words, and many more, while lying down, for his back was still aching from the fall. At first the Young Marshal had stood rigidly at attention, but he was prevailed upon to sit down by Madame Chiang, who observed that the Generalissimo had some difficulty in talking up to a man who stood as stiff as a ramrod. Already the Young Marshal had decided to accompany the Generalissimo to Nanking. It was his privilege, he declared, to submit to whatever punishment lay in store for him; and the Generalissimo answered that he would serve the nation better by remaining with his troops. He was ordered to remain in Sian, but he was so determined to be punished that the Generalissimo finally relented. When the airplane flew off to Nanking, the tables were turned, for the Young Marshal was now the prisoner of the Generalissimo.

Some days later, in the manner of a tribal chieftain supplicating a Chinese emperor, the Young Marshal addressed a petition to the Generalissimo:

> I am by nature rustic, surly, and unpolished, due to which I have created an incident which was at once imprudent and illegal. I have committed a great crime.
>
> I have shamefacedly followed you to Nanking in order sincerely to await my punishment by you, punishment befitting in severity the degree of my crime, so that it may not only uphold law and discipline, but also serve as a warning to others in future against repetitions of such a crime.
>
> Whatever is beneficial to our country, I shall never decline, even if it means death. I beg you to leave aside sentiments of personal friendship, and let nothing hold you back from giving me the kind of punishment I deserve.

The punishment was perhaps greater than the Young Marshal had expected, for he was to become the perpetual prisoner of the Generalissimo, traveling about like a parcel in the retinue of his captor, never permitted to speak for publication or to explain himself. He became a nonperson, deprived of all rights. His report to the Generalissimo, which was never published, showed that he had been in secret correspondence with the Chinese Communists for six months before the Sian incident; the arrest of the Generalissimo had been carefully planned, and the decision to sentence him to death unless he obeyed their demands had already been made. For these reasons the Generalissimo thought he deserved the highest punishment short of death. When he stepped off the airplane at Nanking, the Young Marshal vanished from the pages of history.

THE WAR COMES

IN 1937 THERE WERE MILLIONS of Chinese who knew that the year of decision had come, but no one could have guessed that the war would come so casually or so quietly. The Chinese expected the Japanese to attack along an immense front with huge armies; battle plans of vast intricacy would be devised; all the resources of both nations would suddenly be thrown into the war. Instead, the Japanese blundered into war like sleepwalkers, without realizing what they were doing. They attacked with a handful of troops and seemed surprised to discover that they were confronted by a nation in arms.

The year began quietly, with the Generalissimo leaving Nanking to recuperate from his experiences in his native village of Chikow and to give thanks at his mother's grave. He was ill and tired, in need of medical treatment, and he wanted time to digest his experiences away from the intrigues of Nanking. While he was still at Chikow, Wang Ching-wei returned from France, but his arrival caused little comment; his power had vanished, and while he remained an important member of the Kuomintang party, he was in no position to wrest supreme power from the Generalissimo, who alone made the important decisions. The Sian incident had increased his popularity. Few people knew what had happened in Sian: it was enough that he had been a prisoner and emerged unscathed. In the eyes of the people he was the one man on whom they could rely for the prosecution of the inevitable war with Japan.

When spring came, hope revived, for had not President Roosevelt announced that further Japanese aggression would not be tolerated by the great powers? China was at last in a state of military preparedness. Airplane squadrons were being formed, prodigious efforts were being made to train the troops, plans were being formed for a vast retreat to the hinterland, and every day ships came up the Pearl river loaded with ammunition from Belgium and Czechoslovakia. Dr. Sun Yat-sen had once spoken of a war with Japan lasting ten days, but now people were speaking of a hundred years' war, a war of slow attrition and endless brush fires, which would ultimately exhaust both nations. Meanwhile the Generalissimo was still doing everything possible to postpone the final confrontation. "We shall not forsake peace until there is no hope for peace," he had said at the fifth plenary session of the party in November 1935. "We shall not talk lightly of sacrifice until we are driven to the last extremity which makes sacrifice inevitable. Individual sacrifice is trifling, but the sacrifice of the country is great. Individual life is of short duration, but the life of the country is endless." These words reflected the mood of the country in the spring of 1937.

In their own way, without insisting too loudly, the rebels in Sian had won many victories. The eight demands were widely discussed, and if they were not immediately adopted, they were regarded as basic instruments of policy to be studied at the People's Political Assembly to be set up later in the year. The attitude of the Kuomintang toward the Communists was no longer so militant. At the February session of the party, the Generalissimo denounced the Communists as "bandits," but the denunciation was combined with the offer of "a chance to repent." The words could be interpreted variously, but there was a general assumption that in exchange for a tacit agreement to put an end to further propaganda outside their own territories, the Communists would be left alone. The Soviet areas were "reorganized" as a "Special Border District" under the supreme authority of the Central Government, elections were held, and landlords were allowed to return. The landlords did not get back their lands, the elections were controlled by the Communists, and the authority of the Central Government reached only as far as the borders of the Special Border District. Nevertheless a precarious truce was maintained.

Meanwhile in Japan the situation was improving. In the elections of February 1936 the liberal Minseito party had gained seventy-eight seats, the Trade Union party fifteen, and the Independents twenty-one. The growing democratic temper of the Japanese people might have produced reforms within the army if the militarists had not suddenly realized that they were in danger. They seized Tokyo and assassinated four of the most notoriously liberal cabinet ministers. The effect of these murders was felt in widespread strikes, but the liberals and the left were hopelessly at the mercy of the army. The Emperor was also at the mercy of the army, which he favored because it was fanatically devoted to the institution of the monarchy and thus served his own purposes. The Emperor was therefore in no position to protect the rights of the people, and though outwardly he gave evidence of a desire for peace, he was not averse to war in China if victory could be bought cheaply. Moreover, victory in China might lull the dissident elements within the empire who were clamoring for social reforms. Japan and China faced each other across the narrow seas, and the chiefs of state of both countries were alarmed at the presence of those powerful ghosts—the Communists. Perhaps they could be exorcised by war.

It is one of the fallacies to which all dictators conform: a national war will prevent people from thinking of their hunger. But hunger, which is sharpened by the terrors of war, becomes implacable in times of reverses, and Japan could hardly look forward to unmitigated victories. There are good grounds for believing that the Emperor did not desire war at this time; he was prepared to wait, for he possessed inexhaustible patience; and when at last he permitted the war to take place, it was only because, like so many autocrats, he was misled by his advisers into the belief that all the obstacles raised by the enemy could easily be overcome. Nor could he always control the army, which possessed a logic of its own.

Like the Kuomintang in the early years of its power, the Japanese army owed its strength to the secret societies. The cloak-and-dagger game had been played for centuries by the *ronin* and the samurai, who dedicated their daggers to the highest bidder and thought of death as no more than a cloak of darkness which would carry them into a posthumous paradise. Trained to instant obedience, the Japanese soldiers were prepared to die for something more worthy than themselves. They had an instinct for death; the Chinese soldiers preferred to live, though they could be ferociously heroic when they were well led. The Chinese also had their secret societies. They knew that a whisper could murder, and that a man might walk out of his house to buy a package of cigarettes and leave no trace behind him. But they could hardly have known that a single whisper and a single disappearance would lead to one of the bloodiest wars in history.

The war began at ten o'clock on the night of July 7 when the Japanese troops who had been illegally maneuvering in the neighborhood of Lukouchiao re-formed, having discovered that one of their soldiers was missing. Lukouchiao (Marco Polo Bridge) commands the main highway between Peking and Hankow. It was a massive and beautifully designed bridge, decorated with one hundred and eight stone lions. Nearby, about fifteen miles southeast of Peking, was the small walled town of Wanping.

On the excuse that the land would be needed by the Peking-Mukden railway administration, the Japanese had been surveying the neighboring land and making offers to purchase it from the farmers, who refused to part with it. The Japanese were not particularly disturbed. They were using the land for maneuvers, which took place once or twice a month in the spring of 1937, but as the summer approached they began to have maneuvers every three or four days. They used live ammunition, and the farmers were terrified. At night the fields were lit with tracer bullets, and by day there was the continual rattle of machine-gun fire.

The maneuvers which took place on July 7 were also with real weapons, and even noisier than before. The farmers complained bitterly. They complained even more bitterly when Japanese on motorcycles began to scour the villages during the late evening, saying they were searching for a missing soldier. It was not unusual for Japanese soldiers to disappear toward evening: what was unusual was that the Japanese were making threats and demanding compensation. At the same time they were firing with their rifles beneath the walls of Wanping. They were hysterical, brusque, and meddling, and could not be argued with. They went through Wanping house by house. There was a great deal of confusion and a lot of shouting. At 2:30 A.M. the soldier was found in a brothel. He gave himself up to the Japanese, and the villagers went back to their beds.

At the time it was thought to be just one more of the many incidents that would inevitably continue as long as the Japanese troops were in north China. When the villagers were asked later what they remembered about the incident, they said they were puzzled that the Japanese should have spread the rumor that they had killed the soldier. They were much too frightened of the Japanese to kill them, and they had gone out of their way to be accommodating to the enemy in their midst.

But the Japanese had not yet finished with Wanping and the surrounding villages. At three in the morning a company of Japanese troops, in eight trucks, made for Lukouchiao under the command of a certain Colonel Terahira, whose name in Chinese characters means "peaceful temple." At a sandhill to the northeast of Wanping and about half a mile from the town, they took up their positions, preparing to assault the walls. By this time Chinese commissioners had arrived from Peking, and when they learned that a small force of Japanese troops was about to launch an attack on Wanping, they asked Colonel Terahira for an explanation. He replied that the Chinese had kidnaped the soldier, and that the town of Wanping must make restitution. Since restitution had not been made, they intended to break through the walls and take what properly belonged to them. Only if all the Chinese troops in Wanping left by the western gate would they act peacefully. It was then clear to the Chinese commissioners that the Japanese were determined to occupy Wanping whatever the cost.

Colonel Terahira, an officer of the Japanese Special Service Corps, had come to China only three months previously, but he spoke Chinese well. He announced to the Chinese commissioners that he was acting on orders from above, and was prepared to offer a time limit of ten minutes; otherwise the town would be bombarded with heavy artillery and then taken by assault. The negotiations failed. At 4:50 A.M., when it was still dark, bullets began to sweep over the walls, and although firing stopped shortly afterward to permit the Japanese colonel and one of the Chinese commissioners to be lowered into the city, by the afternoon of the next day fighting was resumed. The direct telegraph with Peking was cut. General Ho Chi-feng brought up his troops to engage the Japanese, and by nine o'clock in the evening the Japanese were being pressed back. Once again there was a lull. Negotiations were resumed. The Japanese soldiers remained in the sandpits, and from time to time they would shoot at random at the walls of the town.

At first the Chinese commissioners felt that they were dealing with a man who was acting without authority. Nothing quite like this had happened before. The soldier who had vanished into a brothel had long since been forgotten, and he was not mentioned in the negotiations. What was clear was that the Japanese were determined to take possession of Wanping. The seat of the negotiations was removed to Peking. It was hoped that in the calmer atmosphere of the capital city good sense and reason would prevail.

At first the Japanese seem to have been moved by a strange sense of uncertainty and insecurity. They parried, thrust, retreated, offered to negotiate, and broke off negotiations in a manner which suggested that they were waiting for some final decision, which never came. It was like a strange, unwieldy dance. Finally, at 2:30 A.M. on July 10 they made the long awaited frontal attack on the town. While the Chinese pondered the solution of an affair which still seemed to be of minor importance, reports came in that Japanese troops were marching from Tientsin and Shanhaikwan, while artillery, tanks, and armored cars were moving toward Fengtai.

Wanping held out, and was bombarded again on July 20. The Japanese had cut the Peking-Hankow railway, and the train which set out from Peking on the twenty-second was turned back. On the twenty-sixth there was a savage clash between Japanese and Chinese troops at Nanyuan. The local war was assuming larger proportions. Suddenly the Japanese demanded that the entire garrison at Peking be removed. The demand was instantly rejected by the Chinese authorities, but it showed that the Japanese were no longer thinking in terms of brief skirmishes.

Fengtai, which the Japanese had captured, was recaptured by the Chinese a few days later. Nanyuan became the scene of a fierce battle, in which General Tung Lin-keh was killed. The war reached the suburbs of Peking. Lieutenant General Kiyoshi Katsuki, the commander of the Japanese forces in north China, announced that the Japanese could no longer tolerate the presence of Chinese troops and he intended "to chastise the Chinese for their outrageous behavior."

The battle, which had begun on a sandpit near Wanping, now raged from Tientsin to Peking. Astonished observers watched the troopships entering Tientsin without any resistance from the Chinese. Nankai University in Tientsin was bombed into a heap of smoking rubble. It was the first time the Japanese had bombed a Chinese university, and it was justified on the plea that Chinese soldiers had taken refuge in the buildings. Not a single Chinese soldier had been permitted to enter the university, but the Japanese were not concerned with facts: their aim was to break the spirits of the Chinese students, who had always opposed them. Peking fell on August 9, with little opposition, the Japanese announcing that they had come to protect the inhabitants.

Even then it was thought that the blaze might be put out. The Japanese were behaving with wanton disregard for international opinion, and it was unthinkable that they would dare to carve up the whole of north China. Soon there would be a day of awakening: the battles which had begun so casually would end just as casually, there would be a few carefully selected diplomatic concessions, a few more privileges. But it was too late. After the fall of Peking and Tientsin the war moved along the Peking-Hankow and Peking-Pukow railways, but it was observed that the main force of the Japanese was still moving along the Peking-Suiyuan railway, slowly drifting down from supply bases in Manchukuo. They may have thought that China was still "a tray of shifting sand," but it was not so. For the first time since the fall of the Manchu dynasty China was united. Telegrams of support came from all sides, and once more the Communists pledged themselves to fight to the last man against the Japanese invaders. In the first week of August, Yen Hsi-shan, Pai Hsiung-hsi, Lung Yun, and a host of other generals who had fought against the Kuomintang leadership pledged their services to the government. The Generalissimo became the symbol of revolt against the Japanese, no longer the leader of the party but the leader of the whole nation.

During that hot interminable summer China was confronted with defeat after defeat. Sometimes, before engaging in battle, the Japanese would go through the motions of accusing the Chinese of committing some crime which must be expiated. So it happened on August 9 that two Japanese sailors were dispatched by imperial headquarters in Shanghai to spy out the Chinese airfield at Hanchiao; the sailors killed a Chinese guard, and were shot down while attempting to escape from the airfield. The two sailors took the place of the soldier in the brothel: they were the ceremonial figures who announce the opening of the play. The Japanese demanded the withdrawal of the Chinese troops in Shanghai and the dismantling of the defense works. If this was not done, they would storm the city.

On August 13 Japanese cruisers entered the Whangpoo, and the battle for Shanghai began. From Nanking the Generalissimo announced a five-point program for the defensive war against the invaders. It was written in his characteristic style, which was simple, direct, and urgent. The five points were: (1) there must be determination for sacrifice; (2) there must be belief in final victory; (3) the resistance must be carried out with all the strength and native ability of which the Chinese people are capable; (4) the people must be united in a spirit of affection; (5) they must maintain their positions, only advance and never retreat. The last of the five points was by far the most important, and the others merely served as introduction. He had said in July, "If we allow one inch of our territory to be lost, then we would be guilty of committing an unpardonable offense against our race." More inches had been lost than anyone could count, and the "unpardonable offense against the race" was the most painful endured within living memory.

The Japanese militarists were determined, pitiless, and completely uncontrollable either by the government or by the Emperor, who appears to have had little desire to control them and little interest in their activities. Shanghai was being battered into insensibility. It was a strange war, because the International Settlement was left unmolested, the Japanese not yet feeling that they possessed the power to destroy the foreign enclaves on Chinese soil. They were perfectly prepared, however, to destroy the Chinese section of Shanghai, and the working-class district of Chapei was attacked by soldiers, bombers, and naval guns. Two divisions of Chinese troops were rushed up to form the Chapei-Kiangwan line, which was battered continually for seventy-two days. A "lone battalion" of Chinese troops held out in a barricaded warehouse in sight of the International Settlement long after Chapei had fallen, but the heroism of the Chinese soldiers, who were badly led and ill-equipped, was no match for the suicidal bravery of the Japanese, who destroyed everything in their path and seemed not to care how many of their own soldiers perished.

From his headquarters in Soochow the Generalissimo took command of an army which amounted to a quarter of a million men, of whom about a quarter died in the fighting. It was the biggest bloodletting China had yet experienced in modern warfare. The Japanese losses amounted to about sixty thousand men. At the end the whole of Chapei was in flames. Astonished observers saw a wall of fire six miles wide, blotting out an area of the city where more than a million people had once lived.

Although the Japanese carefully refrained from attacking the International Settlement, which was under the jurisdiction of Japanese, French, British, and American nationals, they were determined that there should be no misunderstanding about their right to inspire fear among the democracies. Any ship traveling in the Yangtse was in danger; they bombed British cargo boats and fired on British gunboats. These provocations were deliberately contrived by Colonel Kingoro Hashimoto, one of the mutineers who had assassinated Premier Keisuke Okada the previous year. Colonel Hashimoto gave orders that "everything that moved" above Nanking on the Yangtse river should be bombed out of the water. The climax of these provocations came on December 12 when the American gunboat "Panay" was sunk by Japanese airmen, who swooped low and machine-gunned the survivors as they attempted to escape in a rowboat. On that same day several Standard Oil vessels were bombed and destroyed, and H.M.S. "Ladybird," a British gunboat, was fired upon by Japanese batteries at Wuhu. Colonel Hashimoto's aim was to embroil Japan immediately in hostilities with the United States and Great Britain. His superior officer, General Iwane Matsui, the supreme commander of the Japanese armies in the Yangtse valley, was more cautious in his dealings with foreign powers, but he showed very little caution in his dealings with the Chinese. An old man, called back from retirement, he seemed to take an exquisite pleasure in killing as many Chinese as possible.

Just as everything that moved along the Yangtse river was regarded as legitimate prey by Colonel Hashimoto, so too was everything that moved along the Nanking-Shanghai road. The British ambassador, Sir Hugh Knatchbull-Hugessen, was fair game, and as he drove to Shanghai along the main highway from Nanking a Japanese aviator flew low enough to see the Union Jack flying from the staff and machine-gunned the car at his leisure. The Ambassador was permanently disabled by a bullet in the spine.

An even more distinguished visitor to Shanghai was attacked in October. Madame Chiang was driving along the same road and had already reached the outskirts of Shanghai when the Japanese recognized her car and ordered artillery fire to open up along the road and airplanes to machine-gun it. The driver pressed hard on the accelerator. The car was traveling at more than sixty miles an hour over a badly damaged highway when a tire exploded while he was taking a fast turn. The car careened off the road and turned upside down. Madame Chiang was thrown clear, falling into a puddle of mud. W.H. Donald, the Australian who acted as confidential adviser to Chiang Kai-shek, was also thrown clear. He found Madame Chiang lying unconscious in the puddle, mud all over her blue woolen slacks and shirt. When she recovered consciousness, she was dazed and incoherent; she was in pain; some ribs were cracked or broken; she could scarcely walk. He carried her into another car, and they continued the journey to Shanghai, where Madame Chiang remained in seclusion. According to the official biography, "when the news of her injuries was brought to the Generalissimo, tears filled his eyes for the first time since the beginning of the war."

The war was no longer a war: it was reaching into that indeterminate stage when it becomes scarcely distinguishable from a massacre. The Japanese had crushed Shanghai and were now about to advance up the Yangtse river, crushing everything in their path. Kiating, Soochow, and Wusih fell, and then it was the turn of Nanking. Emboldened by success, General Iwane Matsui ordered the surrender of Nanking intact, threatening frightful consequences if his order was disobeyed. He was as good as his word. The field commander of the Japanese army attacking Nanking was Lieutenant General Prince Yasuhiko Asaka. Since the Chinese troops had put up a pitiful defense, and the city had therefore not been surrendered intact, the field commander gave the order for a general massacre. The Imperial Japanese Army was given license to butcher, mutilate, and rape any Chinese who fell into their hands. For two weeks there was a reign of terror, and some 150,000 Chinese perished. Nanking became a ghost town.

The spectacle of a modern army assuming the role of murderous hooligans was not one which the Japanese desired to advertise. They therefore did everything possible to conceal the crime. The Prince, who was closely related to the imperial family, was recalled. Mass graves were dug. The gutted buildings were rebuilt. Nanking was given preferential treatment; and after being obsessively murderous, the Japanese soldiers went to great pains to show a kindly regard for the survivors. Apparently this was done at the order of the Emperor Hirohito, who had approved the massacre and realized too late that it would reflect on the honor of the royal house. Prince Yasuhiko was married to Princess Nabuko, the Emperor's aunt. The Prince belonged to the small circle of princely advisers to the Emperor, and he carried great weight at the court. In later years the Emperor would claim that he knew nothing about the massacre until many months later, but this was merely to compound the crime. He was not only well aware of the unprecedented reign of terror, when the streets of Nanking ran with blood and were littered with mutilated bodies, but as Emperor he bore the full responsibility. It was a responsibility which weighed lightly on his shoulders.

For the Chinese the losses in Nanking were almost too unendurable to contemplate. The shock waves traveled across the country. At long last they realized they were confronted by a pitiless enemy who would not be satisfied until the Chinese people were annihilated or reduced to slavery.

In the eyes of Chiang Kai-shek, who had slipped out of Nanking only a few days before its fall, there was not the least doubt that the Japanese proposed to colonize China. Ten years before the rape of Nanking the Tanaka Memorial had stated: "Once we have acquired the entire resources of China, we shall proceed to conquer India, the Archipelago, Asia Minor, Central Asia, and even Europe." Japan was now helplessly embroiled in insane plans for world conquest. The bloodbath in Nanking was merely a very small and unimportant incident in the great design.

For the Chinese now there was only one overwhelming principle: they must resist at all costs, even if it meant being thrown back to the borders of Tibet. The government, with hundreds of thousands of refugees, retired to Hankow, and then to Chungking, where plans were made for an eventual withdrawal to Sikang. Somewhere in the remote interior, perhaps in the upper reaches of the Yangtse river, the Chinese and Japanese armies would confront each other in a battle to decide the future of Asia.

This battle was never fought, and in fact the Chinese and Japanese armies never met again in any great battles. Secure behind the Ichang gorge, the Chinese government remained on the defensive, knowing that the time would come when the Japanese would embark on even more dangerous adventures. They would wait until the Japanese had exhausted themselves, and then like the Yangtse river in flood they would carry everything before them.

THE EAGLE'S NEST

CHUNGKING IS A CITY made for breaking people's hearts. For half the year it is covered with humid clouds, rain drips interminably, and darkness comes early. The city is built on a rock at the confluence of the Yangtse river and the Chialing river, and the river damp seeps into the rock. In summer the winding streets carved out of the rock are deep in scorching dust, and the sun strikes like a hammer. Only the very tough, and the very determined, survived on that rock, which had been the capital of Szechuan since the time of the Han dynasty. The city dominated the two rivers, and something about it suggested a stone dragon crouching, quivering, and ready to spring.

Any ordinary Chinese town gives an impression of continual violent activity, the people darting about at a pace which, one might think, would reduce them in a few days to a state of exhaustion. But Chungking was no ordinary city. It was bursting at the seams with refugees from all the provinces of China. The poor, the desperately poor, were everywhere. They crowded into matshed huts built into the side of the cliffs, and they made their living by scavenging, by carrying their leaking buckets of water up the cliffside, and by bending their shoulders beneath the sagging, swaying bamboo chairs which carried the rich up the endless stone steps. You would see men walking stark naked in broad daylight. They were not mad or exhibitionist; they were too poor to afford the luxury of clothes. A permanent chorus was provided by the screaming of women, the grunting of men carrying burdens too heavy for them, the barking of dogs, and the dull explosions of dynamite, as the engineers honeycombed the rock for air-raid shelters. Especially when the river was in flood, the city seemed to live in a state of frenzy.

In Chungking everything that was modern—steamboats, telegraph, automobiles, radios, even matches—seemed in some strange way to be anachronistic. That there should be government offices and foreign embassies and newspapers and militiamen with guns slung over their shoulders sometimes seemed to be wildly and ludicrously improbable: the city resembled a stone fortress built at a remote period in some lost province of Central Asia. The invaders in their dark blue Sun Yat-sen uniforms, with fountain pens in the upper left pocket, could be recognized at a great distance; they were taller, stronger, lighter than the dark Szechuanese. These newcomers were the government officers, the clerks, the businessmen, the hustlers, and the students who had fled from the east to find refuge behind the Ichang gorges, which protected them from Japanese soldiers, and below the damp winter clouds, which protected them from Japanese airmen.

In some ways the Generalissimo gave the impression of being the greatest anachronism of all. He was austere and passionless in a city given over to violent passions. He walked slowly and gracefully, with the calm of a man who knows his own mind, where nearly everyone else was in a state of frenzied excitement and despair. He was precise and doctrinaire, cautious and reserved, where others were awkward and only too aware of their inadequacy. He had come, it seemed, from another planet where everything was simple and displayed in a proper order. Chungking was a rock converted into a junk pile, and there was no order in sight.

Chiang Kai-skek lived very simply and quietly, taking little part in the life of the city, remote from it. He lived in an unpretentious mansion called "Ying Wo"—the Eagle's Nest—with a small staff of servants and a handful of armed guards. When someone reminded him that the same name had been appropriated by Hitler for his house at Berchtesgaden, he was angry and quickly pointed out that Hitler had spent a fortune on building his mountain eyrie while his house in Chungking might have been occupied before the war by a superior bank clerk. He had no taste for expensive food or sumptuous entertainments. Except when he was ill—he was ill quite often in Chungking and went to considerable lengths to prevent his illnesses from becoming known—he spent his days in monotonous regularity, working by the clock.

His habits had scarcely changed since he was a young officer. He rose before dawn, spent half an hour doing his exercises, usually "boxing exercises," which consist of assuming swift and graceful postures against an invisible enemy. He took deep draughts of air beside an open window. He then wrote in his diary—that voluminous diary which by this time amounted to several hundreds of volumes so carefully preserved that only a very few had been lost by the wayside. He had a habit of permitting close friends to read from it, and on rare occasions he would permit some fragments to be published. At half past eight he took a light breakfast—a small dish of vegetables, a bowl of noodles or half a bowl of porridge. At Nanking he had developed a taste for bamboo shoots. Since they were not easily procurable in Chungking, he turned to the famous "great head vegetables," for which Szechuan is famous, but found them tiresome; they lacked the exquisite delicacy of the bamboo shoots. After breakfast he attended a cabinet meeting, read and dictated dispatches, answered petitions. At some period in the day there was always a discussion with the minister of war or one of the high officers on his staff. At intervals he would pick up a book, as often as not a translation of a foreign work. His secretaries were kept busy translating articles and even whole books into Chinese. Of modern books he was inclined to complain that they lacked the serenity of those written by the great sages.

At one o'clock he took lunch, usually with guests. He preferred not to talk at length during meals, but he was annoyed when others were silent. At lunch, too, the food was simple—pickled bean curd, salted turnips, rice congee, a little meat, nothing more. He bolted his food, and would sometimes sit back with an amused expression, watching the others who were only halfway through their meal. In China a man's character can be revealed in many ways. You can learn a great deal from watching a man play mahjong, and in the old days you could learn a good deal more by watching him making the preparations for lighting his opium pipe. The Generalissimo liked to watch people eating, having formed the conviction that people reveal themselves in the private ceremony of meals. He liked people to eat fast, with scarcely any outward movement of their features and with disdain for the food.

In the afternoon he would sometimes practice calligraphy, humming to himself. Humming was another of his vices. He would hum when he was out walking or when he was in a fit of concentration, but he could not abide others humming in his presence. Sometimes there were presentation scrolls to be prepared for close friends, for generals who had distinguished themselves, or for foreign dignitaries. He had a horror of making them, but he knew that they would be highly valued and discussed. Like Dr. Sun Yat-sen he showed very little proficiency in calligraphy. His Chinese characters are square, upright, rigid, like the man.

Between four and five in the afternoon there were regular meetings with cabinet ministers and party representatives. Occasionally he would find himself entertaining visitors from outlying provinces. He was usually well prepared for them by his secretariat, and he would give the impression of knowing a good deal about their problems. When they asked questions, or requested assistance, he had a ready answer. It was his habit to answer quickly—sometimes too quickly. When Dr. C. H. Wu, a well-known Catholic scholar and editor, came to discuss a new translation of the Bible into Chinese, he was prepared to find a sympathetic listener in the Generalissimo. The problems involved in translating the Bible into Chinese are of such immensity that scholars have been known to go mad under the strain. To Dr. Wu's surprise the Generalissimo seemed totally unaware that any problems existed. He presented the scholar with a rare and expensive copy of the Jesuit translation made in the eighteenth century. "Just follow the old Jesuit translation, and make it more up to date," the Generalissimo said. He had a passion for words like "up to date," "modern," "new," "exact," and he was not always aware that things are rarely exact and cannot always be solved by rules of thumb. Impatient with verbosity, he could sometimes—especially during the long Monday morning memorial meetings—be extremely verbose himself.

These speeches, delivered in a high-pitched voice of quite extraordinary monotony, so that the words had a hallucinatory effect, were always variations on the themes of Dr. Sun Yat-sen's three principles. He spoke without notes, and most of his audience knew what he would say during the speech after hearing the first words. He never entertained any new concepts, never permitted himself the least deviation from the accepted doctrine. His mind possessed an enviable serenity, but no elasticity. He was the ancient sage endlessly repeating the unchanging tablets of the law, following a ritual which had been handed down through the centuries. In fact these doctrines were scarcely twenty years old, but they appeared to have acquired the patina of a remote antiquity.

Just as his ideas did not change, so the man himself seems to have remained unchanged. He showed no signs of advancing age. His skin was clear and rosy; no one could detect on his features the traces of suffering. There were no wrinkles, no sagging muscles. The strains of an interminable war had left no mark on him.

As he grew older, his habits changed a little. In wartime Chungking he usually did no work at all in the evening. In the past he had enjoyed working through the night, beginning a day's work the next morning, showing no sign of tiredness, but those days were over. He would take a rest between five and six in the afternoon. Supper was at seven, and there might be a short nap before supper. There would be a few guests: usually very close friends or relatives, and on very rare occasions there might be the showing of a film after supper. It was a calm, sedentary, unexciting existence, for the fighting had come virtually to a standstill and little was demanded of him except that he assume the role of symbolic ruler, while the officials went through the motions of government.

While the Generalissimo was content to assume a symbolic role, the Japanese were concerned to push the war to a successful conclusion. Chungking lay invisible under the winter mists, but when the spring came they were free to continue the war from the air. Two frightful air-raids took place on May 3 and 4, 1939. Large areas of Chungking were destroyed. Cameramen on the south bank of the Yangtse recorded the fires which swept across the city and the cloud of black smoke which appeared to tower half a mile into the sky. Business and government offices crumbled into black powder, but the Japanese aim was not simply to paralyze trade and reduce the government to ineffectiveness: the raids were designed to break the spirit of the Chinese people. The government had made no preparations. There were almost no shelters, and there were no anti-aircraft guns. During the long summer the Japanese raided Chungking with impunity.

As he walked through the burning city on those tragic May nights, the Generalissimo was seen to be visibly shaken, and it was reported that he shouted, "It is all my fault! It is all my fault!" But it would be wrong to see in these words the expression of a profound acceptance of guilt, for they were no more than the conventional expression of grief. Thousands died in the inferno. The mat-shed huts burned like paper, and much of the working-class quarter was destroyed. The Japanese hoped to reduce the city to a pile of cinders.

The Generalissimo was perfectly aware of the danger presented by the air-raids. He summoned the generals of his air force and demanded to know why no fighter planes had been sent up to intercept the Japanese bombers. In a towering rage he ordered the punishment of high air force officers and placed them under arrest. The army was ordered to prepare an immediate plan for the evacuation of Chungking. There were urgent conferences to discuss the defense of the city or its abandonment in the face of continuous attacks, and at the end of a week of conferences the Generalissimo retired to a nearby mountain to meditate on the cataclysm confronting China. It was apparently during these meditations that he came to the conclusion which was stated in his official biography: "The raids were Japan's direct reply to China's Spiritual Movement which the Generalissimo had put afoot as a morale booster."

Although the Chinese officials were compelled to pay lip service to the Generalissimo's interpretation of events, there were very few who unreservedly accepted it. The Japanese were indifferent to the New Life Movement, which caused barely a ripple on the surface of Chinese life. What concerned them was the need to deliver a series of explosive shocks to the body of the Chinese people. The sack of Nanking was a deliberate attempt to deliver a shock of overwhelming proportions; the aim was to terrify the Chinese into surrender. The same aim was pursued in the savage bombing of Chungking, which continued sporadically during the summer, sometimes with devastating force, more often with the knowledge that it was enough to drop a few incendiary bombs in order to bring the city to a standstill, for the whole population would flock to the shelters. The plans for evacuating the city, like so many other plans, were abandoned. Whether the government wanted it or not, the Chinese were determined to remain. Chungking had become their bastion, their rock of salvation, their act of defiance.

In those heroic times, before cynicism and indifference set in, the Chinese showed a magnificent endurance. Chungking burned and bled. The mat-shed huts went up in flames, were rebuilt, and went up in flames again. The roads were impassable to wheeled traffic, the electric cables were down, the telephones were usually out of order, and the city itself resembled nothing so much as a charred, overturned anthill. Soon the rock was being honeycombed with caves, and the Chinese living under Kuomintang rule were as much cavedwellers as those who lived under communist rule in Yenan.

With Chungking crowded with refugees and exiles, the quiet provincial life of Szechuan began to change. Szechuan is a wealthy province with a teeming population and rich resources in food and minerals. It is well watered, and the valleys and plains are perhaps the most fertile in all of China. But at some period in the Middle

Ages the province seems to have come to a dead stop. In the villages scarcely anything had changed since the Han dynasty. Now, violently, Szechuan was opening up to modern ideas. Roads were being built, telegraph wires followed the line of the mountains, there were airfields, buses, technical schools, universities. Szechuan was being shaken out of its ancient lethargy.

The Chinese showed themselves at their best during those early years when they clung to the rock and refused to abandon it. Their gift for improvisation was put to good use; buses ran on alcohol produced from potatoes and urine; paper lanterns strung on high gallows announced the coming air-raids; out of a few boards a burned-out shop would be resurrected the next day. The energy and determination of the Chinese people was never so powerfully expressed. Hollow-eyed, ill-clothed, reduced to a kind of half-madness by the continual summer bombings, the people of Chungking went about their affairs with unconscious heroism.

The Japanese played with Chungking like a child playing with a toy. They knew the city was virtually defenseless; there was no radar; the anti-aircraft guns were obsolete; there was no efficient fire brigade and no pumping equipment; the fires simply burned themselves out. They were therefore in a position to introduce refinements into their bombing raids, carefully calculating the interval between one raid and the next, dropping their bombs just at the moment when the city was recovering from the last attack. There were night attacks, and the people of Chungking feared the nights of the full moon. Sometimes the bombing raids continued uninterruptedly for two or three hours.

All through the summer of 1940 the raids continued, but the worst raids were reserved for the summer of 1941. It was as though the Japanese were determined at last to tear the city to pieces. For seven successive days and nights waves of Japanese planes came over Chungking, dropping their bombs at random, until the city seemed to vanish in its own fires. There were no more saturation raids, but for months afterward Chungking reeled from the attack.

About this time Hitler invaded Russia, and the Japanese were putting the finishing touches to their plan to conquer the American, British, and Dutch possessions in the Far East.

"Make your plans as dark and impenetrable as the night, and when you move strike like a thunderbolt." Such had been Sun Wu's advice to his generals, and the Japanese, who were familiar with Sun Wu's writings, acted accordingly. Pearl Harbor and Singapore were attacked on December 7, and the Pacific war began in earnest. The Chinese had been waiting for this moment in fear and trepidation, never quite believing that it could happen, accustomed to fighting alone. Now they had powerful allies, who would surely rush to the assistance of China. A restrained Chiang Kai-shek sent a brief telegram to President Roosevelt on December 8: "To our new common battle we offer all we are and all we have, to stand with you until the Pacific and the world are freed from the curse of brute force and endless perfidy." Similar messages were sent to Churchill and Stalin, who replied that the time had not yet come for the Soviet Union to enter the Pacific war. Meanwhile President Roosevelt instituted a series of high-level conferences in which the problem of bringing aid to China would be discussed in detail. China, so long an outcast, deprived of any aid except the comfort of words, was now promised all the military equipment she needed. At long last help was coming from the western world.

These discussions were scarcely under way when Chiang Kai-shek announced that a great and decisive battle had taken place at Changsha from January 14 to January 17, 1942. An entire Japanese army, advancing out of Yochow, had been cut to pieces. The government claimed that fifty-seven thousand Japanese had perished during the campaign, but the foreign correspondents who rushed to the scene were puzzled by the claim. Here and there on the frozen fields they saw the bodies of the Japanese lying where they had fallen, stripped of their clothes, their faces turned to the sky. The Japanese had penetrated into the outskirts of Changsha, for clumps of bodies lay on the deserted roads, and some Japanese soldiers had penetrated into the heart of the city. But nowhere was there any evidence of a great holocaust. The correspondents came to the conclusion that a comparatively small column of Japanese had blundered into a trap, leaving at most some six or seven thousand dead. On the evidence available the battle of Changsha was no more than a series of hard-fought skirmishes.

The Generalissimo viewed the battle of Changsha as a signal victory, and perhaps the turning point of the war. In *China's Destiny*, a book which he began writing later in the year, he described how the Japanese were suddenly confronted by the massed might of the Chinese army:

> At this time American and British preparations in the Pacific were inadequate, and Japanese aggression was able to spread in all directions, so that the situation was almost entirely in her favor whatever direction she decided to follow. But unexpectedly, while she was sailing before the wind, the Chinese with their "warfarc of annihilation" dealt a crushing defeat to the Japanese at the battle of Changsha, a blow so fatal that it is now impossible for her to recover her strength in China.
>
> Thus, in the first stages of the Pacific war, Japanese morale suffered a severe blow, and Japan was compelled to recognize the power of the Chinese army. So it happened that on her western front, having occupied Malaya and Burma, she dared not advance into India, while on her southern front, having occupied the Philippines and the Dutch East Indies, she abandoned her plan to invade the Australian mainland; and after attacking the Aleutians, she could not carry out her long-cherished plan to invade the Soviet Union.
>
> While the Japanese were hesitating and giving way to indecision, Britain and the United States were given the opportunity to prepare their battle lines in western Asia and the South Pacific, and the Soviet Union was able to devote herself to the war against Germany.

In this way Chiang Kai-shek enumerated the benefits resulting from the victory at Changsha, demonstrating how this battle had influenced the entire Japanese strategy. As a result of the battle of Changsha the Japanese were compelled to abandon the invasion of India and the Soviet Union and Australia, and the Allies were given a much-needed breathing space in which to prepare their massive counterattacks. It was a breathtaking claim, but it had very little relation to reality. Nor were the Japanese reduced to impotence by the battle of Changsha. For the remaining years of the war they continued to harass the Chinese armies, recapturing Changsha in the spring of 1944 and threatening Chungking and Kweichow later in the year.

With the opening of the Pacific war, the lifelines connecting Chungking with the western world were broken. Hongkong had fallen, and there was no longer any possibility of bringing supplies through Burma and Indochina. Overnight India had become the inevitable staging-ground for the vast quantity of supplies which would have to be flown into China. But India was in turmoil, with Gandhi and the Indian Congress demanding freedom from British rule as the price of supporting the war effort. Chiang Kai-shek decided to fly to India to sound out the Indian leaders. At all costs he must know whether his supplies would flow freely through India.

There was little comfort to be had from the Indian leaders, who were inclined to regard the war against Japan as secondary to their own nonviolent war against the British. In an extraordinary interview in Calcutta on February 18, 1942, Gandhi and Chiang Kai-shek debated the merits of their own wars. Gandhi delivered a long lecture on the advantages of nonviolent opposition to the Japanese, while Chiang Kai-shek politely insisted on the need for a powerful and militant India, which would help China to throw off the Japanese yoke. He reminded Gandhi that half the world's population was contained in India and China, and if they exerted themselves to the utmost they would ensure freedom for themselves and for all mankind. It was an argument which Gandhi was not disposed to accept, for he was concerned only with Indian freedom. A few days later Gandhi wrote to Sardar Patel a brief account of the interview with Chiang Kai-shek:

> He came and went without creating any impression, but fun was had by all. I would not say that I learned anything, and there was nothing that we could teach him. All that he had to say was this: Be as it may, help the British. They are better than others and will now become still better.

Since helping the British was not one of Gandhi's intentions, he appears to have felt that Chiang Kai-shek had fallen into a British sphere of influence. He had no desire to pluck Chiang Kai-shek's chestnuts from the fire, and for the remaining years of the war he displayed no interest in the fate of China.

In spite of Gandhi and the Indian Congress, American and British supplies began to flow into China at an increasing tempo. At first there was a thin trickle. Later the skies over the Himalayas were to grow dark with American planes laden with guns and fuel. Kunming, a small walled city lost in the provincial backwaters, was to become a vast airbase supplying the machines of war to the whole of free China.

Chiang Kai-shek's meeting with Gandhi had been inconclusive. So, too, was his meeting with President Roosevelt, which took place in Cairo in November. The President had long wanted to meet the Generalissimo, but not for reasons which would have given the Generalissimo any pleasure. He had no great faith in China's ability to conduct a war against the Japanese, and he was inclined to ascribe China's failures to the fact that the Generalissimo commanded a political party which was more fascist than democratic. He felt strongly that the Chinese Communists were agrarian reformers, and therefore closer to the heart of the Chinese people. Nevertheless, he was prepared to give the Generalissimo the benefit of many doubts. Churchill, who also attended the Cairo conference, showed only a minimal interest in Chiang Kai-shek and was impatient to attend the Teheran conference with Stalin, which would take place as soon as the meeting in Cairo was over. In his book, *Closing the Ring,* he describes his magisterial impatience: "The President, who took an exaggerated view of the Indian-Chinese sphere, was soon closeted in long conferences with the Generalissimo. All hope of persuading Chiang and his wife to go and see the pyramids and enjoy themselves until we returned from Teheran fell to the ground."

But while Churchill maintained a studied silence, Roosevelt was beginning to see unsuspected virtues in the Generalissimo, who spoke gravely and sensibly about the huge problems confronting China and showed not the slightest disposition to pontificate on China's role in the war. It was agreed that Manchuria, Formosa, and the Pescadores should be returned to China. When President Roosevelt suggested that there might be a need for an American base on Chinese soil after the war, the Generalissimo offered him Port Arthur. They discussed the future of the Japanese imperial house, and while the President hinted that he would like to see it abolished, the Generalissimo replied intelligently that this was a matter which should be left for the Japanese people to decide after the war, and when they went on to discuss the occupation of Japan, the Generalissimo showed no particular enthusiasm for sending a Chinese occupation force. He asked that the Japanese should eventually make reparations in the form of warships, merchant ships, rolling stock, and machinery. They were feeling their way, and though there was never a meeting of minds, there was a growing tolerance for each other's ideas and opinions.

The most pressing questions involved Burma and China's lifelines to the west. "Burma is the key to the whole campaign in Asia," the Generalissimo said. "After the enemy has been cleared out of Burma, his next stand will be in North China, and finally in Manchuria. The loss of Burma will be a very serious matter for the Japanese and they will fight stubbornly and tenaciously to retain their hold on the country." The Generalissimo's prophetic utterances were rarely rewarding, and in fact there were no great battles in North China and Manchuria. But the problem of Burma could not be ignored. The Generalissimo wanted the British and Americans to mount a combined air, sea, and land assault on Japanese positions in Burma. Churchill had no intention of sending his ships to Burma, and no amphibious operation was undertaken. He considered Burma to be an appendage of the British Empire, and he objected strongly to the idea that the Chinese and Americans should have any share in its liberation.

The Generalissimo had taken Churchill's measure. He realized that Churchill had little knowledge of China and was indifferent to her fate. For Churchill, China was Hongkong, Shanghai, the treaty ports, and British gunboats on the Yangtse river.

Nevertheless there were some gains at the Cairo conference. For the first time China was welcomed into the fraternity of great powers. The Cairo Declaration, composed in haste by Harry Hopkins, included a momentous paragraph on "the Three Great Allies" who were "fighting this war to restrain and punish the aggression of Japan." And though the Cairo Declaration was little read and had no binding effect on the signatories—history was moving too fast for such declarations to be heeded, and the Soviet Union had not yet been consulted—the Generalissimo could take comfort from the fact that President Roosevelt was determined to help China to the utmost.

A few weeks later, on January 12, 1943, the Generalissimo was able to announce over Chungking radio that the United States and Great Britain had finally signed a treaty abrogating all their rights to extraterritoriality on Chinese soil. The treaties granting these rights, which the Chinese always called "the unequal treaties," had been a continual and heartbreaking reminder of Chinese weakness. They were the theme of innumerable speeches by Dr. Sun Yat-sen; the Kuomintang was dedicated to the task of abolishing the treaties, but had never dared to abrogate them; and now at last by the fortunes of war they had become meaningless and absurd. With unusual tact, the British and American governments had already made the announcement that they were voluntarily abrogating the treaties on October 10, the anniversary of the revolution. For three months the international lawyers worked on the draft of the new treaty now formally presented to the nation. With justifiable pride the Generalissimo declared that the humiliations of a century had been swept away and that China was all the stronger for not having to bear the weight of humiliation any longer.

As he spoke over the radio, he became once more the Confucian moralist. He claimed that the unequal treaties were the cause of all the ills that had affected China; the treaty ports had been centers of corruption and degeneration; the evil had entered the bloodstream of China, and the poison had spread into the remotest villages. It was necessary that the people should purge themselves by continual self-examination and self-criticism. Selfishness and greed must be abandoned; instead, there must be thrift, obedience to price controls, absolute devotion to the state.

But if he was scarcely convincing when he spoke of a nation devoted to impossibly high ideals, he was more credible when he expressed his joy over the passing of the treaties:

> It is a century since these unequal treaties were concluded. Now, as a result of her fifty years of revolutionary struggle and five and a half years of resistance, the tragic history of the unequal treaties resolves itself into the glorious history of their abrogation. A new lighthouse has been built by our allies, Great Britain and the United States, to guide man's progress toward freedom and equality for all the peoples of the world. We now have before us the evidence that the allies are truly fighting for humanity and justice.

Those who were in Chungking during those sunless January days felt that for once the words "humanity," "freedom," "justice," and "equality" were being used in their proper sense. An intolerable wrong had at last been righted. The abrogation of the treaties, the dream of so many Chinese, was long overdue, and there was some significance in the fact that it should have come about when the armies were deadlocked in a dreary winter, at a time when no one could say with certainty that the enemy would be defeated.

CHINA'S DESTINY

IN THE SUMMER, fall, and winter of 1942 Chiang Kai-shek worked on a book he had been planning for nearly twenty years. In this book he hoped to present a blueprint for the China of the future. All his most intimate and secret thoughts, his dreams and expectations, everything he had written in the personal diary which he kept with meticulous care nearly every day of his life, all his ponderings about the future of the nation he had ruled for so long, all these would be quarried and shaped and built into a permanent edifice of thought. If he should die, this book would be his testament to the Chinese people, and if he should live, the book would be a stepping-stone to further achievement.

He was perfectly aware of the importance to be attached to the book and went to great pains to see that it accurately reflected his thought. He had read widely in the memoirs of the scholar-soldiers of the nineteenth century and was determined to follow in their path. He would write the book gravely, even ponderously, with a full awareness of his responsibility as the leader of a great country in time of war. It was a book he hoped to be remembered by; and a grateful posterity would be expected to include it among his major achievements.

Unfortunately, a good many things went wrong in the writing of the book. The secretaries who helped in the writing of the book did their work too well. So many people saw the manuscript and commented on it, suggesting a deletion here and an emendation there, that the final work resembles a patchwork made out of many patchworks. Here and there it is possible to recognize the authentic voice of the Generalissimo: a passage from one of his speeches or his diary would remain unaltered, but all around it there would be the supporting arguments of his secretaries and advisers. Dr. Sun Fo and the members of the Legislative Yuan were employed to do the final polishing, but by this time there were so many confusions and complications that their contributions resembled nothing so much as the crown of icing on a many-layered Christmas cake.

Nevertheless the book reflects the Generalissimo's mind, for he was the motive force behind it, the generator of the ideas and the chief artificer. His secretaries and editors knew his mind well, and they were sufficiently awed by the personality of the Generalissimo to attempt to reproduce his thought faithfully.

If *China's Destiny* had been written at any other time, it might have been a better book. The Generalissimo was writing when the first wide cracks were appearing in the monolithic structure of the Kuomintang. The party was riddled with corruption, prices were soaring, the war in China was at a stalemate, and the Chinese themselves were losing confidence in his leadership. All his life the Generalissimo had clung to the Confucian ethic: discipline, obedience, respect for the ancestors, the cultivation of simple virtues. His mind was tempered by a wide reading of the classics. Rituals, benevolence, the golden mean, recognition of the absolute power of the Emperor as the mediator between earth and heaven—all these fundamental ideas had become as much a part of him as his own skin. Now, obscurely aware that the walls were cracking open and the foundations were shaking, he sought refuge in those Confucian concepts which he had learned at his mother's knees. There was no longer any trace of that thin veneer of Christianity which had colored his mind at the time when he inaugurated the New Life Movement.

"The human mind does not change," the Generalissimo wrote. "We are dealing with the same problems which were dealt with by the philosophers of old." But if the human mind had hardly changed, the landscape in which it had its being had changed beyond recovery, and Confucian philosophy offered no measuring stick for evaluating this changing landscape. New urgencies, new problems, new social patterns, even new forms of consciousness had arisen; and Confucius, if he had been brought back to earth, would not have recognized in the young Chinese walking through the streets of Chungking the same people who once inhabited the state of Lu, where he had been the prime minister. What the Generalissimo wanted was a China modeled on the ancient Confucian state, without foreign entanglements, secure within its own boundaries, benevolent and feudal, shorn of all foreign philosophies. He wanted the past, while the future was threatening to engulf him.

In *China's Destiny* the Generalissimo's xenophobia was permitted to have full rein. He had always detested foreigners, and when he employed them, it was always on sufferance. He found them useful, but never trusted them. It never seems to have occurred to him that China was profoundly and unalterably influenced by the west, and that western technology had come to stay. In the China of his dreams all western ideas were banished, and the Chinese remained proud, undefiled, unassailably pure and devoted to Confucius. He found both democracy and communism distasteful, and he was inclined to regard them with equal loathing:

> The various political parties each revere one particular foreign country and worship one particular theory, forming groups of their own, proud before their countrymen but submissive toward foreigners. Since the theories of the various countries are forever changing, therefore the theory of each of these groups has to change unceasingly in accordance with the changes abroad. As to the struggle between liberalism and communism, it is merely a reflection of the opposition between Anglo-American

> thought and the thought of the Russians. Such theories are not only unsuitable for the national life and the people's livelihood of China and opposed to our original culture, but they reveal that their promoters have forgotten that they are Chinese and have lost their learned respect for China and fail to apply their learning to the Chinese situation.

In this way he would ascribe all the diseases afflicting China to the intervention of foreigners: prostitution, opium-smoking, gun-running, banditry, warlordism, socialism, communism, and liberalism are all ascribed to foreign influence. Wherever he looks, he discovers the malignant evidence of foreign intervention. At the same time he celebrates the advances of Chinese technology and the growth of the Chinese railroad system under the Kuomintang government. Such contradictions were perhaps inevitable, and he took them in his stride.

The most disturbing part of the book is found in the opening chapters, where he presents a simplified history of China from its remote origins to contemporary times. China is represented as a nation superlatively graced with virtue and benevolence, wherc all men are brothers and no trace of vainglory has ever been seen, where everyone lived in contentment and therefore there was no urge for conquest. She fought battles only "to help the weak and support the fallen." Not only had China never taken any part in wars of aggrandizement, but she had resolutely maintained in the face of countless provocations a pacific attitude toward the world, calm in her majestic power. There had been, he admitted, a certain amount of "nation-blending," by which he meant that foreign nations had in some way become assimilated to China, but all this had happened peacefully and inevitably. China was vast and self-supporting, and therefore had no need for alien territory. "She benefits other people by extending her blessings and asking nothing in return."

As he traced the development of China through the ages, Chiang Kai-shek found himself depicting an ideal kingdom, which possessed no existence except in his imagination. This portrait had no relevance to the time, for China, as he well knew, was disintegrating all around him. He spoke of a triumphant China at a moment when it was close to defeat, its armies immobilized and at the mercy of the Japanese. This portrait of China derived a kind of hallucinatory strength from the continual repetition of the theme of inherent virtue. Here, for example, he rationalizes in a characteristically Confucian manner:

> Through five thousand years of alternate order and confusion and the rise and fall of dynasties, our nation has acquired the virtue of modesty, a sense of honor, and the ability to endure insult and shoulder hardships. Because of its modesty, it is capable of contentment with its lot. Because of its sense of honor, it is capable of developing its own power. Because it is contented with its lot, it does not trespass upon other nations. Because it is capable of developing its own power, it does not tolerate the aggression of other nations. Because it can endure insults, the strength of the nation is accumulated inwardly and not exposed outwardly. Because it can shoulder hardships, the aspirations of the nation are enduring instead of spasmodic. Because of the development of these virtues, the various clans and branches of the Chinese nation are capable of sacrificing their personal interests for the benefit of the whole community.

The last sentence is perhaps a clue to the real meaning of those introductory chapters. Chiang Kai-shek is not so much attempting to describe the ideal China as to describe the ideal leader. He is continuing that self-examination which he had cultivated from the time of his adolescence and perhaps even earlier. Self-examination has given place to visions, dreams, and hallucinations; and sometimes in his weakness he has permitted himself the luxury of imagining himself stronger than all his enemies.

Like so many apologists, he prefers not to name the enemy. Throughout the whole course of *China's Destiny* there is no mention of the Chinese Communists, perhaps because he felt that they had no part in China's destiny. Though Mao Tse-tung never appears by name, his presence can be felt at intervals throughout the book like a haunting presence. To lay the ghost, Chiang Kai-shek has recourse to Confucius, and so he relates at length the punishment which befell a certain Shao-cheng Mao who was put to death by Confucius. Confucius gave his reasons for killing the man:

> There are five kinds of evil people in the world and thieves and robbers are not among them. The first are those whose hearts are rebellious and dangerous. The second are those whose conduct is consistently depraved. The third are those whose words are false but unconvincing. The fourth are those whose learning is extensive in undesirable fields. And the fifth are those who are acquiescent and helpful toward misbehavior. A person with any one of these five faults should not escape execution by the superior man, and Shao-cheng Mao possesses them all: his dwelling serves as a gathering place for his disciples, forming a party; his theories serve to beautify unorthodoxy and please the multitude; his stubborn arguments are sufficient to upset the right and constitute a new and independent theory—he is thus a villain among men and must be eliminated.

According to the Confucian ethics, a superior man not only had the right to kill such men, but he was under the obligation to do so, and their killing would be accounted an act of righteousness.

In this way, concretely and without malice, putting his trust in the ancients, Chiang Kai-shek was saying that it was necessary to outlaw and crush the Chinese Communists. It is significant that the five crimes committed by Shao-cheng Mao correspond to the negative aspects of the five Confucian virtues: *jen*, benevolence; *yi*, righteousness; *li*, correct behavior; *chih*, correct knowledge; *hsin*, loyalty. Shao-cheng Mao was doomed because he opposed not some small segment of Confucian doctrine, but all of it. The Chinese Communists were doomed because they opposed Confucian doctrine, as Chiang Kai-shek understood it.

China's Destiny is a complex work which accurately mirrors the Generalissimo's complex character. It represents a deliberate and sustained attempt to provide both a philosophy and a plan of action suitable to the time. An exactly comparable event would be a book written in wartime by Winston Churchill, with suitable quotations from Plato and Spinoza, describing the nature of the state and the responsibilities of the state officers, planning boards, and government agencies, together with a recital of recent history. The trouble with the book was that it was fundamentally irrelevant, and had absolutely no relation to the confused and tortured country over which the author ruled. He was speaking from some remote eyrie about an idealized China which had no existence outside his dreams. Through the pages of *China's Destiny* the Chinese learned that the Generalissimo was out of touch with reality. The first printing was massive, with about half a million copies being printed, and then the book was suddenly withdrawn from circulation. It was never again printed in China until Mao Tse-tung, after conquering the mainland, ordered a new printing in Peking.

The foreign embassies protested against the book because it was inclined to place the British, French, and Americans in the same imperialistic light as the Japanese; and Chinese scholars protested even more loudly because it did not meet the standards of Chinese scholarship and because it represented an attitude of mind which was essentially reactionary and inconclusive. There were no firm outlines. China, as seen by Chiang Kai-shek, melted into dreams. The book told more about the limitations of China's wartime leader than anyone had expected to learn, and in the universities there was a sense of profound shock and disenchantment. The kinder critics ascribed the failure of the book to his secretaries, but no one doubted that the Generalissimo assumed responsibility for the work and that it accurately reflected his opinions.

It was about this time that loyalty to the Generalissimo's leadership began to erode. The man who had been regarded so long as the savior of China, the charismatic figure who alone possessed the keys to the future, was seen to be weak and mortal, like any other man. In the controlled press nothing could be said against him, but there were lively discussions in the universities about his character, his use of power, his military ability, and his complicated alliances with the provincial warlords, who retained their private armies and sometimes engaged in profitable deals with the Japanese. Criticism became epidemic, and it was the custom to speak about him in guarded language, referring to him as "Mr. Wang." When these criticisms reached him, he would fly into a temper, angrily rebuke his critics, and accuse them of being agents of the Chinese Communists. Students who criticized him in the universities were in special danger, for the Kuomintang

Youth Corps had received orders to report on all students who were not totally loyal to him. Some were thrown into prison, others were tortured, and still others vanished. The secret police under General Tai Li went into action against the universities, arresting professors and creating incidents calculated to expose the dissidents. But by this time there was only a small handful of people in the universities who were prepared to follow him blindly.

Although Chiang Kai-shek could not be expected to realize it, these criticisms were a sign of returning health. For too long the Chinese had given him unquestioning obedience. It was as though the shock of the sack of Nanking had paralyzed their springs of action, and during the long retreat to the southwest, while hard-pressed by the Japanese, they had voluntarily relinquished the right to examine him closely. They knew his faults—his violent temper, his arrogance, his nepotism, and his lack of any real contact with the people—but they were prepared to forgive these faults in the light of his determination to resist the Japanese at all costs. Like the conspirators at Sian, they recognized that he would never compromise with Japan, and there was scarcely any other Chinese political figure who could be trusted to hold out to the bitter end. But now it was no longer a question of holding out to the bitter end, for the war in China was at a stalemate and the ultimate military defeat of the Japanese was no longer in doubt, since the huge American war machine was already in full operation. Chiang Kai-shek's usefulness to the Chinese diminished as American power in the Pacific increased. If he had died in the spring of 1943, he would have been remembered as the man who had single-handedly led the Chinese during the years of their greatest danger and a grateful posterity would have showered him with honors such as no emperors or presidents had ever received. It was his tragedy that he outlived his usefulness.

The more the critics examined him, the more they found to alarm them. What was most alarming was that he was completely incapable of accepting criticism rationally. He had been so long accustomed to absolute power that he regarded anyone who questioned his motives as an enemy of the state. It was impossible to argue with him, for he permitted no new idea to enter his brain. To suggestions that he should broaden the base of the power structure, he answered that the existing power structure had served the country well enough and there could be no changes in wartime. When the war was won, there would of course be a popular assembly with advisory powers. He still spoke about a more or less lengthy period of tutelage, during which the Chinese people would be led along the paths of the Three Principles of the People. It never seems to have occurred to him that a cultivated and brilliant people with four thousand years of recorded history did not deserve to be treated like children.

In a somewhat distant fashion he recognized that not everything was going well. Once, traveling in an automobile in the outskirts of Chungking, he saw twenty farm boys all roped together, prodded by soldiers with fixed bayonets. He jumped out of the car and asked what was happening, only to learn that the farm boys were draftees. "Why are they roped up?" he asked. He was told they had resisted the draft. "Why were some of them bleeding from bayonet wounds?" Because they had not marched fast enough. He made a speech to the farm boys, telling them that it was a great honor for them to fight for their country, and they were the flower of the country. He ordered them to be unroped, and they cheered him and promised faithfully to conduct themselves like good soldiers. Later the order went out that draftees should never be roped together, but the custom persisted. Every village and small town saw those wretched processions of roped draftees lurching along the country roads.

Prices were soaring, inflation had set in, the poor were reduced to living on a subsistence level, while the rich merchants of Chungking and Kunming grew richer. To survive, minor government officials practiced corruption, sometimes on a breathtaking scale. Rice, the staple food of the land, was being hoarded, but although there were laws against hoarding on the statute books, they were rarely enforced, for many of the hoarders were government officials or were protected by them. When reminded that hoarding was having a calamitous effect on the economy, the Generalissimo replied that this was a matter for the Legislative Yuan, and it was not in his province to act as an economic dictator. Economics, indeed, was a subject which he had never studied and never understood, although a long concluding section of *China's Destiny* was devoted to an analysis of China's economic future.

One of the most disturbing charges made against him was that of nepotism. Nearly everyone in the higher echelons of the government was related to him. Madame Chiang Kai-shek was commander-in-chief of the Nationalist air force. The minister of finance, Dr. H. H. Kung, was his brother-in-law. So, too, was T. V. Soong, who was given many high positions in the government, although the Generalissimo regarded him warily and never completely trusted him because he had sided with the left wing of the Kuomintang in the past. The minister of education was Chen Li-fu, a nephew of Chen Chi-mei. He had been adopted by the Generalissimo after Chen Chi-mei's death, and was treated like a son. His older brother Chen Kuo-fu had an equal place in the Generalissimo's affections, and held the position of director of his secretariat. No document would pass across the Generalissimo's desk until it was first examined by Chen Kuo-fu, approved by him, and given authority by the mere fact that he approved it. The Chen brothers formed a government within the government, for they controlled propaganda, education, and a vast number of government appointments. They supervised the Generalissimo's daily program and set up his appointments. Only on the very rarest occasions would the Generalissimo override their decisions, for he was bound to them by ties which were even closer than ties of blood. As nephews of the martyred Chen Chi-mei, they were regarded as above the law and incapable of wrongdoing.

The Chen brothers had their own following, which was known as the "CC clique." Their influence extended to the provinces, for they had appointees in all the towns of free China, and they were closely affiliated with General Tai Li's secret police. They were organization men, greatly feared and clever at manipulating opinion, for they possessed vast reserves of power through their control of the press and their alliance with the secret police. Chen Li-fu controlled the universities, and after 1943 he was continually at loggerheads with the great complex of Chinese universities which had traveled across the whole length of China and established themselves in Kunming. The professors of Peking,

Tsinghua, and Nankai universities were generally liberal in their opinions and found little comfort in the authoritarian statements issued by the minister of education. Chen Li-fu regarded himself as a profound scholar of education, but his scholarship was suspect. He was responsible for the passage excoriating Chinese scholars, which was inserted in *China's Destiny:*

> From 1911 to the Nationalist revolution, academic traditions underwent changes in unison with the changes in academic teaching, and all the ideologies of the nations of the world, such as liberalism, nationalism, communism, and anarchism, were subject to examination. If we look at them closely, we may observe that although a large degree of progressiveness was diffused in the social structure, a tradition of genuineness, sincerity, stability, and honesty failed to materialize. *Scholars did not seek truth through practical effort.* Some concentrated on thinking about learning, closing their eyes to facts, and engaging in hollow discourse and setting up rival schools of thought. Others learned without thinking, uncritically selecting a theory here and there. Those who admired westernization abandoned China's own culture in favor of allegiance to foreign theories. Those that upheld the national culture reverted to an isolated chauvinism.
>
> Scholars became careless and irresponsible in their lectures, uncritically echoing the popular trend in order to court favor with the people. Their concept of "liberty" was based on their own selfish desires, while their theory of "democracy" was based on their desire to advance their own material interests. Observance of the law was regarded as humiliating, and resistance to orders as clever. They took advantage of the ignorance of youth and called themselves "teachers of youth." They wantonly spread superficial propaganda and called themselves "academic torchbearers." The ultimate consequences were turmoil in the state and the decline of the nation to the point of extinction. While such trends existed, it was difficult to find many persons who accepted the principle that the rise and fall of the state was the responsibility of every individual. Such being the condition of education and academic teaching, the attempt to reform social and political customs was as futile as climbing a tree to look for fish.

The bewildering attack on education—all education at all levels over a period of more than thirty years—was not calculated to make the Generalissimo or the minister of education more popular in the schools and universities. What was still more bewildering was that all students and professors were officially urged to buy copies of *China's Destiny*, to discuss it at length in their personal diaries, and to send copies of these discussions to the proper authorities.

In the summer of 1943 Chen Li-fu announced that a public subscription would be opened for funds to erect three large ceremonial tripods of bronze in honor of the Generalissimo. They were to be set up in three cities, with appropriate inscriptions. Such tripods had been erected to commemorate the victories of the emperors of the Chou dynasty, and it was felt that the Generalissimo's wars against the Japanese deserved a similar commemoration. Chen Li-fu had consulted Ho Ying-chin, the minister of war, and various generals and staff officers, and they had demonstrated so much enthusiasm for the plan that it was generally thought to have originated with them. In fact, it originated with Chen Kuo-fu, who had passed on the idea to his brother. The officials favored the plan, and a considerable sum of money was collected. Then letters began to arrive at the Generalissimo's headquarters, pointing out that he was not a Chou dynasty emperor and that it might be better to spend the money on relieving the poverty in China. The groundswell of criticism increased in intensity, especially in the universities, and the Generalissimo gracefully abandoned the project. In a letter addressed to his general staff, he wrote that "such a memorial is not only inappropriate to the spirit of the time, but suggests that my generals are wanting in respect for the great emperors of the past."

At the time when the highest honors were being paid to him, he was experiencing his greatest defeats. They were not the visible defeats of the battlefield, but the invisible defeats which take place in the hearts and minds of people. Outwardly, nothing had changed. He still performed the duties of a Generalissimo, still attended cabinet meetings and gave orders and studied maps, but the threads which attached him to the people were being snapped one by one. Time was running out, and soon the people in despair would turn to another leader.

ALARMS AND EXCURSIONS

SHORTLY AFTER the Pacific war broke out, when China found herself in alliance with the Americans, British, and Dutch, Ho Ying-chin, the minister of war, gave a banquet to honor the ambassadors of the new allies. The minister of war was a short, solidly built, choleric man who was not accustomed to banqueting with ambassadors and their staffs. He was very voluble, drank too much, and became more and more ill-tempered as the evening advanced. Finally, after many toasts, he offered the toast which was to make the evening memorable. He raised his small cup of rice wine and said, "Let us drink to the day when every damned foreigner has been run out of China." In the stunned silence that followed, a secretary said, "The minister is drinking to the defeat of the Japanese."

But the minister was not drinking to the defeat of the Japanese. He was drunk, but he meant exactly what he said, for he detested all foreigners. The remark would have had no significance if he had been merely a low-ranking government official, but he was in fact one of the triumvirate—Chen Li-fu and H. H. Kung were the other members—who were the effective rulers of China under Chiang Kai-shek. The minister was affirming his right to be xenophobic, and though he apologized later and sometimes went out of his way to be kind to foreigners, he would often give the impression that he regarded the allies with less favor than he regarded the Japanese. Like the Generalissimo, who tended more and more to disappear into the remote regions of disembodied power, he was impatient with allied defeats and could rarely bring himself to understand why the allies, fighting a war on twenty different fronts, were impatient with Chinese defeats.

The allies were in an angry mood, for the war was going badly. Moreover, their representatives in Chungking had very little knowledge of the traditional delicacies of Chinese diplomacy. Winston Churchill announced bluntly that the war in the Far East must be regarded as a holding war, while the more important war against Hitler must be pursued with fury. The statement was issued by the British embassy in Chungking in the form of an official memorandum and did nothing to soothe Chinese sensibilities. It was a meaningless statement, for in fact the war in the Far East was pursued with the same fury as all the other wars which were being fought in the air over Europe, on the high seas, in the jungles of Asia and the deserts of Africa. With the transfer of Sir Archibald Clerk Kerr, the British ambassador to Chungking, to his new position as ambassador to Moscow, British influence in China went into a catastrophic decline. For more than a century the British had played the leading role in opening up China to the west. They had the largest banks, the biggest investments, the greatest influence. From the moment the Pacific war broke out they counted for little in the affairs of China and their place was taken by the Americans.

The Americans had even less understanding of the problems confronting a nation which had been fighting a losing battle for five years. Chinese nerves were at the breaking point. The Chinese were relying desperately on the Pacific war to save them from the Japanese, but when the war broke out they learned to their horror and surprise that the Japanese were perfectly capable of fighting simultaneously in China and all over southeast Asia. Early in January a mood of profound apathy settled on Chungking. People were beginning to realize that the war in China would never be more than a holding operation, that there would be no honor in it, and that the civil war between the Nationalists and the Communists would continue unabated, even though it would be a silent war, kept out of sight, with no official bulletins to report its progress.

Meanwhile the Americans were making their presence felt in Chungking. Lieutenant General Joseph W. Stilwell reached China early in March and briskly set to work to reorganize the Chinese army, insofar as that was possible, and to integrate Chinese fighting power into the global struggle. He had no illusions about the difficulties ahead, for he had been the military attaché at the American embassy in 1938, spoke Chinese, had many Chinese friends, and was well aware of the frictions in the Chinese government. He cordially detested Ho Ying-chin and was not overly impressed by the Generalissimo's capabilities as a military leader. A sharp, intense, wiry man, he was not one of those who spend their lives pouring oil on stormy waters. He liked to quarrel, and he quarreled bitterly and vehemently with the Generalissimo, who was accustomed to immense deference from all his inferiors. But in fact General Stilwell was not an inferior. He possessed vast powers, which had been carefully spelled out in Washington by General George Marshall. He was in command of all the American forces in the China-Burma-India theater, he acted as chief American representative at all Chinese war councils, he supervised all military aid to China, and he was the liaison officer between the Generalissimo and General Wavell, the commander of the British forces in Burma and India. He was also chief of staff to the Generalissimo, and was thus equal in rank to Ho Ying-chin, the minister of war. All these powers had been granted him for a specific purpose, in order to bring the Chinese armies effectively into the war. The Generalissimo complained that it was embarrassing for him to discuss matters of command with a subordinate who took orders only from General Marshall or the President of the United States. What the Generalissimo failed to realize was that General Stilwell was not a subordinate, and that all questions about who ranked higher or lower were irrelevant. The American general had been charged with the task of bringing life to a dying army. In the eyes of the American government the Generalissimo was expendable; the Chinese army was not.

No doubt many of the disagreements between the Americans and the Chinese would have been avoided if men with greater tact had occupied positions of authority. General Stilwell's private papers, published after his death, give the impression that the Generalissimo and his American chief of staff quarreled interminably and were united only in dislike of each other; in fact their relations were outwardly friendly and over large areas of policy they were in general agreement. In the General's diary the Generalissimo was "the Peanut" or "the little rattlesnake." These were, of course, terms of abuse, but when he was writing up his notes late in the day after exhausting conferences he was inclined to abuse everyone in sight, including the President of the United States. Sometimes he would speak half-affectionately of "the Peanut" as a man who seemed to exist in a remote world where nothing happened according to logic and all decisions were taken as a result of Chinese "intuition." "The G-mo has a cockeyed conception of warfare," wrote General Stilwell.

The exasperations of the Americans were compounded by the Generalissimo's insistence on large unsecured loans for the purpose of bolstering up China's failing economy. Immediately after the opening of the Pacific war he asked for and received a loan of half a billion dollars; later he asked for a billion. Since he had very little knowledge of economics, and depended largely on the information supplied to him by Dr. H. H. Kung, the high-level discussions of Chinese economy sometimes achieved an extraordinary level of unreality. The American ambassador in Chungking wanted strict accounting of the loans, since it was necessary to have some assurance that the money would be well spent. Dr. Kung indicated that a strict accounting would be an invasion of Chinese sovereignty and must be opposed by his government; he also made it clear that the loans would be regarded by his government as outright gifts, an indemnity for all the sufferings and sacrifices imposed on the Chinese people. The argument was puzzling to the Americans, who knew that much of the corruption in China could be traced to the Ministry of Finance, and they had no desire to compound the felony.

Through all the remaining years of the war a bitter financial tug-of-war was fought between the Treasury of the United States government and the Chinese Ministry of Finance. The Generalissimo demanded in 1944 that the dollar be converted into a Chinese *yuan* at the rate of 1-to-20 at a time of galloping inflation when a proper exchange rate would have been 1-to-150. He insisted that unless this rate of convertibility was maintained he would refuse to permit the Chinese to build airfields for the American forces. Madame Chiang Kai-shek maintained that every American soldier on Chinese soil cost the Chinese government three hundred *yuan* a day, a sum which would feed a Chinese soldier at the current value of military rice for a month. She threatened to cut off all food supplies to the Americans unless the Americans supported the Chinese government with a billion-dollar loan. While the Chinese government demanded vast amounts of gold to shore up the Chinese gold reserves in the hope of halting the inflation, the inflation continued unabated, the profiteers went unpunished, and the private fortunes of the ministers increased. The Americans had to deal with these matters cautiously, for there was always the remote possibility that the Generalissimo would make a separate peace with Japan if his demands were not met.

There were other matters which had to be treated with the utmost caution. Just as it was well known that the Generalissimo would grow heated if anyone suggested that the exchange rates established by the Ministry of Finance had no relation to existing circumstances, so he would grow wildly excited whenever anyone suggested that the Chinese Communist army was successfully fighting the Japanese. The Kuomintang had established a blockade; no military observer or journalist was permitted to enter communist territory. In their broadcasts from Yenan the Chinese Communists claimed to have fought a succession of bitter engagements against the Japanese, but the official Kuomintang line was that all these claims were unfounded, and that the Chinese Communists were only interested in securing their own positions in preparation for a struggle for power at the end of the war. There was some truth in the second accusation, but none in the first. The Chinese Communist armies had fought vigorously and well. They had abandoned positional warfare for guerrilla raids against the enemy, but there had been so many raids, and they were in effective control of so much territory, that they constituted a fighting force of quite extraordinary strength. They fought better than the Kuomintang armies, and they made no demands on the American government. If success in war consisted in destroying Japanese, the Chinese Communists were doing more than their fair share.

The Americans were caught in a dilemma: if they sent arms and ammunition to the Chinese Communists, they risked the anger of the Generalissimo. If arms and ammunition were not sent to the Communists, then there was the possibility that Japan would be able to launch larger and larger offensives against the Kuomintang forces and perhaps destroy them. The Chinese Communist army had numbered about fifty thousand in 1937; it had multiplied four or five times in the intervening years, and more than half of Japan's mainland army was occupied in defending the fortified areas of northern and eastern China from their attacks. It was a force to be reckoned with; it was growing daily; and the Americans wanted to know more about it, and if possible to help it.

The Generalissimo put every obstacle in their path. A few journalists were permitted to enter communist territory in 1943, and eventually the Americans sent a small observation group to Yenan, but they were never in a position to give the Chinese Communists any effective assistance. The Americans who came in contact with them found qualities notably lacking in the Kuomintang. They were in close contact with the peasants, they had a vast knowledge of China and a great ignorance of the outside world, and they knew how to fight. They could not be corrupted by money, because they were supremely indifferent to money. They were ruthless and unscrupulous, but they acted like men, not like office-seekers.

Throughout the war President Roosevelt made it known that he hoped for a coalition government, but Chiang Kai-shek had no intention of permitting such a government to come into existence. In his own way and in his own time he was determined to destroy the Communists completely, until no trace of them remained. If there had been a coalition government, China might have been spared a civil war which cost the lives of uncounted millions.

In this way the stage was set for the greatest bloodbath that China had ever known.

DESPERATE STRATAGEMS

IN CHINA the news of the end of the war came with jolting suddenness. It was evening when the news began to spread through the cities, and by eight o'clock there was pandemonium. In Chungking and Kunming the crowds came out on the streets, shouting themselves hoarse, waving flags, milling about in a kind of spontaneous delirium, scarcely believing what they heard. Firecrackers spluttered, while the long victory processions wandered aimlessly through the darkening streets. The Americans, who had dropped the atomic bombs and thus brought the war in the Far East to an end, had never been more popular, for they had given the Chinese the gift they had been dreaming of for nine long terrible years of humiliation and defeat. For most of those years peace had been beyond their utmost hopes, and they were a little frightened of it, as one is frightened by something totally strange and unfamiliar.

While the victory processions filled the streets of Chungking, the man who had led the people through their darkest days smiled quietly and said, "*Hao, hao,*" as he watched the searchlights crisscrossing the skies and made his way through thronged black masses of people to the white broadcasting station in the center of the city. It was observed that though he smiled, he looked drawn and somber. He had worked through the previous night, reading reports and dispatching orders over the length and breadth of China. His voice was weak as he spoke into the microphone:

> Recalling the nation's bitter struggle and thinking of the ruin and destitution all over our land, I am moved beyond words. . . . So that our past sacrifices should be made truly worth while, we must now introduce democracy and constitutionalism and consolidate national unity. Our people have united in their war effort. Let them now unite to bring in democracy and carry out the Principles of the People's Livelihood in an environment of social security and peace.
>
> Three major tasks confront the present government. The first is the implementation of the Three Principles. Now that the war has been won, the heavy load on the shoulders of the farmers and workers must be relieved at once. The National Government on this day decrees that conscription shall be suspended for one year throughout the country. The National Government has also completed plans to allot land to the soldiers in accordance with the program adopted by the Sixth National Congress of the Kuomintang. Land tax will not be collected for one year in the provinces occupied by the enemy. Responsible officers and local governments will be charged with the task of formulating plans to reduce land rent in accordance with the general principle of "reduction by twenty-five per cent," taking into consideration the local conditions. These reduction plans will be completed and submitted to the National Government before November 12 of this year for examination and enforcement.
>
> The second task is the adoption of constitutionalism. When the war first broke out, we thought we could achieve victory and attain constitutionalism at the same time. We believe there is an imperative need for the early realization of constitutionalism, and we must not admit any further delay in the convocation of the National Assembly.
>
> Thirdly, national unity is the absolute requirement of a modern state. After the war our national unity will have the strong guarantee of the whole people. We know we achieved vic-

> tory by national unity. We must realize also that national unity is the prerequisite of democracy and constitutionalism. Only a united nation can fully reap the fruits of victory. There should be no private army within the country's boundaries, nor should armed forces be kept by any political party. Only when the armed forces are no longer directed by private interests of individuals and are no longer guided by the private wishes of any political party can national unity be secure.
>
> On behalf of the government I solemnly state that all armed forces, if they submit to reorganization by the government and obey all military orders, shall receive the same treatment without discrimination. The Kuomintang branch headquarters that existed in the armed units during the past twenty years have been entirely abolished as the first step toward nationalizing the armed forces. We hope that the whole nation will realize that the unity of military command and the integrity of political authority are the factors that determine the survival or extinction of a country. With the greatest sincerity I make this appeal for the future of our country and our people.

On that stifling hot summer evening the Generalissimo's speech, with its ominous undertones, came like a dash of cold water. Instead of rejoicing in the victory, he was describing the somber prospects ahead. Indeed, this was his duty, and he could no more avoid it than he could avoid the prospects of defeat which had haunted him throughout the long years of war. Victory, he knew, was insubstantial as long as China was divided; and the Chinese Communists, who had been merely a nuisance before the war, had emerged at the end of the war more powerful than ever, and in a strategic position to dominate Manchuria and vast areas of northern and northeastern China. Most of the Generalissimo's speech was therefore directed toward the problem presented by the existence of a gigantic communist enclave, which threatened to bring about a civil war more terrible than any that had been fought in the past.

By remitting, or promising to remit, land rents by twenty-five per cent, and by putting a moratorium on conscription, the Generalissimo was stealing some of the communist thunder; for the first time he was appealing to the peasants for their support. To the middle classes and the intellectuals he appealed with his promise of "constitutionalism," by which he meant an elective parliament and a more democratic government, with the Kuomintang no longer in the saddle or at least no longer in a position of arbitrary power. To the Chinese Communists he appealed by urging them to incorporate their army into a national army free of control by any political party, pointing out that he had decreed the abolition of the Kuomintang party headquarters which had become the political arm of all the army units under his control. He realized that the new, emerging China could not afford the luxury of political armies.

Nevertheless, while he was speaking, the political armies had already resumed the civil war. At that very moment the radios in Chungking and Yenan were transmitting orders to their troops to occupy the territory formerly held by the Japanese. Chinese Communist troops were racing northward to meet the Soviet army in Manchuria. Russia had declared war on Japan on August 8, and the Chinese Communists hoped to acquire Manchuria and vast quantities of Japanese arms. Chu Teh, the commander-in-chief of the Chinese Communist army, ordered all troops under his command to accept the surrender of the Japanese, and if the Japanese refused, they were to be attacked. North China immediately became disputed territory, for Kuomintang troops were being airlifted into territory which the Chinese Communists regarded as their own.

On August 14, the very eve of the Japanese surrender, the diplomacy of the National Government scored one of its greatest triumphs. A Sino-Soviet treaty was signed in Moscow. Stalin, who had no high opinion of the Chinese Communists, was prepared to sacrifice them in return for the advantages that could be wrung out of the National Government. By this treaty Outer Mongolia was to have full independence, Port Arthur was to become a Soviet naval base, and Dairen a free port with special rights reserved for the Soviet Union. Privately, Stalin indicated that he had no faith in the Chinese Communists and was prepared to tolerate and give assistance to the Nationalist Government. He seems to have believed that the Nationalist army, with its American equipment, would make short work of the Chinese Communists and that within a few weeks Mao Tse-tung would no longer exert any effective power over the territories he had once ruled.

While the Sino-Soviet treaty hurt the Chinese Communists, the massive supplies falling into their hands encouraged them, for these weapons could be turned against the Nationalists. Chiang Kai-shek had no desire to confront the Soviet presence in Manchuria, and soon the Chinese Communist armies were moving at will along the Manchurian railroads, with the obvious connivance of Soviet army officials. Stalin's disapproval of the Chinese Communists, who had usually slighted him and always refused to obey his orders, did not prevent him from permitting them a lion's share of the feast. Later, when he thought they were becoming too strong, he gave orders that the Manchurian heavy industries should be transported bodily into Russia, so depriving them of a powerful industrial base. He regarded Manchuria as enemy territory to be looted at his pleasure. The Chinese Communists were outraged; so were the Nationalists and the Americans. Manchurian heavy industry was the cornerstone of China's industrial wealth, and without it China was reduced to industrial beggary.

The safest and surest method of dealing with the problem was to arrange a confrontation between the two leaders. Mao Tse-tung was invited to come to Chungking. The invitation, addressed to Elder Brother Mao Tse-tung, was twice rejected in accordance with Chinese usage. Finally, professing a cordiality shared by neither of the two leaders, he agreed to fly from Yenan on an airplane provided by the American army. Chiang Kai-shek guaranteed "on the honor of my life" to protect the safety of his guest, and he must have known that he did not possess the ultimate physical means to protect the safety of any man. If a lunatic had attacked Mao Tse-tung in Chungking, the civil war which had already begun in an oddly tentative manner would have flared up in a storm of explosive violence. Extraordinary measures were taken for his safety. He arrived on August 28, and remained in Chungking for six weeks.

In later years Mao Tse-tung would say that "Chiang Kai-shek treated me like a peasant." He disliked the Generalissimo's unbending manner, his assumption of superiority, his implied recognition of Mao Tse-tung as the leader of a small and recalcitrant minority. In public they spoke politely to one another and drank toasts to one another's health; in private they spoke with corrosive bitterness. For more than two thousand years it has been the custom of opposing Chinese generals to meet in order to penetrate the secrets of each other's character. So now, in an atmosphere shot through with danger, they parried and thrust and fought quietly with words, as later they would fight with weapons. They had last seen each other in Canton in 1924, but the intervening years had only made them more intolerant. Mao Tse-tung believed as an article of faith that Chiang Kai-shek had ordered the execution of his wife and that he was guilty of innumerable treacheries. Chiang Kai-shek believed with equal assurance that Mao Tse-tung threatened the entire fabric of Chinese civilization.

Between these two adversaries there could at best be only a partial meeting of minds. The classic encounter produced few surprises, for they behaved in character. When Mao Tse-tung arrived in Chungking, he wore a gray solar topee, which made him look like a visitor from the South Seas. Later the topee was abandoned, and he presented a more conventional appearance to the world. Chiang Kai-shek, observing that his visitor chain-smoked throughout the forty-one days of bargaining, seems to have concluded that Mao Tse-tung was weak and self-indulgent, while remaining a hard bargainer. Shrewdly, Mao Tse-tung accepted all the demands, which he regarded as meaningless. He agreed that peace, democracy, solidarity, and unity should form the basis of the nation, that Dr. Sun Yat-sen's Three Principles of the People should be implemented, that the political parties should have equal status, that the army should be nationalized, that every effort should be made to avoid internal strife, and that Chiang Kai-shek should be the president of China. But with regard to the Chinese Communist army he was adamant: he wanted forty-eight divisions, and Chiang Kai-shek was prepared to let him have only twenty divisions. He also demanded that the Chinese Communists should have the power to appoint the governors of Manchuria and the northeastern provinces and the vice-governors in Hupeh, Anhwei, Honan, Suiyuan, Kiangsu, and Kwangtung, far in the south. The conference intended to bring peace to China was being used to exacerbate the cumulative tensions arising from an interminable civil war. Inevitably the two leaders dominated the conference, and inevitably they were at loggerheads.

When Mao Tse-tung returned to Yenan, the stage was set for the resumption of the war between the Kuomintang and the Communists—a war which Chiang Kai-shek feared, and Mao Tse-tung regarded with increasing elation. In Chungking he had detected the smell of fear. He had observed, too, that the Kuomintang seemed totally incapable of stopping the inflation, that it had almost no following among the intellectuals, the peasants, or the lower middle classes, and that having depended so long on American aid, it had lost the initiative.

Both Chiang Kai-shek and Mao Tse-tung were ruthless men, continually seeing themselves as great historical figures dominating the stage. Neither of them had ever felt the least scruple about sending men to their deaths; the deaths of cities meant little to them; each was determined on conquest. But in the aftermath of the war, Chiang Kai-shek no longer possessed the charismatic power which had carried him safely through the Sian days; his legend was fading. The legend of Mao Tse-tung was growing clearer, though it had very little relationship to the real man. According to the legend he alone possessed the power to rejuvenate China by means of his intellectual brilliance and his widespread support among the peasantry; he was the herald of a new spring or a new sunrise. He presented himself as a man dedicated to the cause of China's poverty-stricken peasants, with no thought of personal ambition. The man was already vanishing in the legend.

In the last months of 1945 Chiang Kai-shek felt the need to assert his power over the armies of the provincial warlords. This was necessary if he was to turn the full strength of the Kuomintang army against the Chinese Communists. On October 4, while Mao Tse-tung was still in Chungking, he ordered an attack by loyal Kuomintang troops on the headquarters of General Lung Yun, the Governor of Yunnan. Lung Yun had powerful forces and was well supplied with military equipment stolen from the American air base in Kunming. Although he was a ruthless man and a peculator on a breathtaking scale, he was popular among the Yunnanese who had never felt any close ties with the Nationalist government. There was a short savage battle, Lung Yun's peasant soldiers fought well but were no match for the more disciplined Kuomintang troops, and soon the defeated Yunnanese soldiers were being led out to execution and Lung Yun was being flown to Chungking. The Generalissimo's intention was to secure his rear and to ensure the loyalty of Yunnan, but there was the further intention that Mao Tse-tung should be made aware of Kuomintang strength. Mao Tse-teng had no more sympathy for Lung Yun than he had for Chiang Kai-shek, and he seems to have observed this minor civil war with amused detachment.

There were others who observed the civil war in Yunnan with considerably less detachment. The three most important Chinese universities, known as Peita, Tsinghua, and Nankai, had traveled across the whole length of China and found refuge just outside the North Gate of Kunming. The professors taught in cattle sheds built over an ancient cemetery. They lived in great poverty, dedicated to the ancient traditions of Chinese scholarship and to their students, who lived in even greater poverty. The Kuomintang military government, which took power in Yunnan after Lung Yun was deposed, decided that the university was encouraging sedition because the professors and students were protesting vigorously against the civil war in Yunnan and the far greater civil war which was about to break out. They wanted a government of the talents, an end to dictatorship. The military governor received orders from Chiang Kai-shek that the university must submit wholly to the demands of the Kuomintang; no more criticism of government policies would be tolerated. During a demonstration on the university campus, shots were fired over the heads of the students and some days later hand grenades were lobbed over the walls. Four students were killed, and thereafter there was no peace between the Kuomintang and the university.

With the deaths of the four students the Kuomintang lost its remaining support from among the intellectuals. No breath of fresh life flowed through the party; it was very tired, and much weaker than anyone could have guessed. Its chief support now came from its beneficiaries: army officers, bureaucrats, bankers, and rich merchants. In order to remain in existence it was compelled to rely increasingly on the weapons of the secret police, and since the secret police attacked blindly and erratically, without recognizing the real enemy, the effect was to strengthen the opposition. The silent war between the people and the government had begun in earnest.

Outwardly little had changed. There were the same familiar faces in the government offices in Chungking, with the friends and relatives of the Generalissimo occupying all the important positions. The Generalissimo was in command, prices were rising, the boundaries between the Kuomintang and Communist armies were continually shifting, but the Communists were not yet threatening the authority of the Central Government. There were ugly rumors about the fortunes made by the Kung family, but they were the same rumors heard during the war. It was said that the capital would shortly be removed to Nanking, and already an advance guard of bureaucrats was making its way down the Yangtse river. The godowns of Shanghai were piled high with relief goods sent by UNRAA, but they would soon fall into the hands of generals and merchants. Nowhere was there any sign that the government intended to introduce social reforms or took any serious interest in the plight of the landless peasants or the lower middle classes. Every Monday morning the Generalissimo addressed his soldiers, or the members of government, and sometimes he would quote the words of Dr. Sun Yat-sen's will: "The revolution has not yet been accomplished." He would say, as he had said so often, that everyone must bend his energies to the task, dedicate himself anew, subordinate all his private desires to the public interest; and there would be polite applause. Everything was the same, but everything had changed.

Sometimes when a sheet of glass is struck there will appear faint, almost invisible cracks. The glass seems unmarked, as strong as before. Then quite suddenly a single shout or even a whisper can shatter the glass into a thousand fragments.

A new enemy had appeared in China. It was not the enemy which continually occupied the thoughts of the government and the Generalissimo. The name of the enemy was despair.

DEATHS AND ENTRANCES

THE AMERICAN GOVERNMENT was well aware that the Kuomintang government was losing the confidence of the people. Something had gone wrong, and it was necessary that the wrong should be righted if China was to play a useful role in international affairs. Accordingly President Truman sent General Marshall to China to examine the situation and to see what remedies could be applied.

General Marshall arrived in Chungking on December 22, 1945. He came as the President's special representative with the rank of ambassador. In a very real sense he came as a plenipotentiary, "with full powers," for there was no doubt that whatever decisions he made would be approved by the President and by Congress. He was already a legend. When he spoke, nations listened, and when he was silent, his silence was oppressive. He possessed in abundance all those qualities which the Chinese recognized in the "superior man." To the Chinese he seemed larger than life, and for a few weeks a vast hope surged through China. In some miraculous way, it was believed, he would put an end to the quarrels of twenty years and bring about a real peace.

At first everything went well. Nineteen days after his arrival, the Government and the Communists signed a truce. Six weeks later they signed a formal agreement to merge their armies and to reduce the standing army from three hundred divisions to sixty within eighteen months. Marshall received from Chiang Kai-shek full powers to arbitrate the dispute, and it was agreed that the Kuomintang dictatorship should be dissolved and replaced by a government of all the parties, including many small splinter groups and the growing Democratic League, which largely represented the universities. To the Kuomintang and the Communists alike Marshall presented the case for compromise, and he pointed to the small parties as being more representative of the real feeling of the country than the two powerful colossi who continued despite his advocacy to regard all the agreements as a means to an end, building up their armies and preparing secretly for civil war. The small parties had no armies, no newspapers, no radio stations, and no well-known leaders. Even in those early days it was clear that only a miracle would save them from extinction; and when in the summer of 1946 Wen Yi-tuo and Lo Lung-chi, the two most prominent leaders of the Democratic League, were assassinated by the Kuomintang secret police, even this slender hope could be abandoned. The war which would decide the future of China for generations to come was merely being postponed. Marshall's influence, which at first seemed to encompass the whole of China, was gradually whittled away until at the end of his mission he realized that both sides had used him as a cloak for their own conspiracies, that in fact he had no influence at all. His immense prestige had not saved him from being the tool now of the Communists, now of the Kuomintang. "I am not willing to allow myself to be used by either party, nor do I intend to serve as an umpire on the battlefield," he wrote, but he had been used by both parties, and for many months he had served as an umpire, as the two armies maneuvered for position. In a statement made at the time of his departure in January 1947, he pointed to the small parties as being the hope of China, since they represented the desperate desire for peace among the common people. His departure was a signal for the resumption of the civil war.

In later years the Nationalists would argue bitterly that Marshall by insisting on compromise had favored the Communists, and that the embargo on American military assistance, which came into force in July 1946, was designed to weaken the Kuomintang position. In fact it was designed to dampen the Generalissimo's hopes of annihilating the Communists by an overwhelming use of armor, hopes which were doomed to failure because the Kuomintang army would have been incapable of using armor effectively; and while the Generalissimo dreamed of thousands of tanks crushing the Communist foot-soldiers, the Communists wondered what they would do with the tanks when they captured them. Asked by a journalist in Yenan how the Communists proposed to fight against tanks, Mao Tse-tung answered, "We will tear them to pieces with our bare hands."

Compromise might have been possible if Mao Tse-tung and Chiang Kai-shek had elected to step down from their high places. There was no lack of good will among the lower ranks, but there was only ill will at the top. Mao Tse-tung and Chiang Kai-shek confronted one another like medieval emperors, with the pride and insolence of royalty. From the beginning they had determined to destroy one another.

As the months passed, the civil war increased in violence. The Chinese Communists were masters of the sudden raid and the quick withdrawal; they were able to cut the Kuomintang lines of communication at will; they fought on many scattered fronts and would melt into the countryside when the fighting was over; there were no pitched battles, for their aim was to drain the energies of the Kuomintang troops and to conquer by propaganda. The Kuomintang possessed an inefficient and lethargic bureau of propaganda, and its troops had no practice in guerrilla warfare. When General Wedemeyer was sent to China in the summer of 1947 to report on the situation, he returned to America with the feeling that the Kuomintang was in the last stages of decay. He had been friendly with the Generalissimo in the past. Now he could only report that "recovery awaits inspirational leadership," thus disposing of the Generalissimo. He added that "the existing Central Government can win and retain the undivided, enthusiastic support of the bulk of the Chinese people by removing the incompetent and/or corrupt people who now occupy many positions of responsibility in the government." In this way he disposed of the government. Chiang Kai-shek was inclined to regard the Wedemeyer report as an inexcusable personal affront, the most damaging he had received in his long career, but this was not Wedemeyer's intention; he was discussing larger issues than the Generalissimo. In public the Americans had taken great care to avoid summary judgments on the Nationalist government; in private they would complain that they were being driven almost out of their minds by the barefaced corruption, nepotism, and lethargy of government officials, even the most highly placed government officials. When Wedemeyer spoke of "the reactionary leadership, repression, and corruption" of the Kuomintang, he was indicating that the Kuomintang was doomed and no further hope could be placed in it. Two years after victory the party that claimed to have led the Chinese to their ultimate triumph against Japan was dying at the roots, no longer trusted or respected by the people, hated and despised. The time had come for a revolutionary upheaval within the party, the ousting of its leaders and their replacement by younger, more efficient, and more dedicated men, but the party bureaucracy was in no mood to surrender its power and the party leader still regarded himself as essential.

The students protested, demanded last minute changes in the Kuomintang, and were accordingly suspected of being infiltrated by Communists. The Wedemeyer report discusses the plight of the professors and the students sympathetically; as a result of the inflation "the money that once would have supported a student for one year might buy him a notebook." Professors disappeared, or were killed, or were ordered to remain silent under penalty of immediate arrest. Student demonstrations were outlawed. There was no free press, for all the newspapers were under government control, and the students therefore had recourse to handbills and wall newspapers. Government officials dismissed their pleas as though they were the lucubrations of hotheads. The government no longer governed; it merely applied certain archaic principles to the rapidly changing times, enlarged its bureaucracy, increased the power of the Generalissimo, arrested everyone who called for the end of the dictatorship, and continued to sign documents and to issue statements about inevitable victory which no one any longer believed.

While the Chinese Communists were advancing on a hundred separate fronts, all of them quite small and none of them decisive, the Generalissimo was still thinking in terms of massive frontal attacks on wide fronts. He resisted all efforts by American military advisers to plan a campaign of withdrawal on fronts which could no longer be held successfully. The Chinese Communists controlled all the villages and most of the highways of Manchuria; the Nationalists held the cities. With the Nationalists penned up in Chilin, Changchun, and Mukden, with no way of receiving reinforcements except by air, their supplies running out and their morale at a low ebb, the youngest and most inexperienced military instructor might have known that the proper solution was to abandon Manchuria to the enemy and order the garrisons to fight their way to the south. When General Barr, the American adviser, suggested such a plan, the Generalissimo was "stupefied." "On no account," reported the American general, "would he give serious consideration to such a project." Changchun was the ancient capital of Manchuria; it must be held at all costs; political considerations demanded that it would remain in Nationalist hands. So throughout the spring and summer of 1948 the garrisons remained in the cities and the Communists harassed them. In the autumn the garrisons attempted to fight their way out, but it was already too late. The Nationalists lost three hundred thousand troops, the flower of their army, and the way to Peking was open.

In Peking, there hung over the Tien An Men Gate—the Gate of Heavenly Peace—a banner bearing the likeness of the Generalissimo. The banner was about seventy feet long and forty feet wide. As winter came down, the people of Peking observed that the banner was beginning to fray at the edges and to lose its color. In the middle of December the banner was removed. The Chinese Communists were very close, and there was no longer any need to flaunt the Generalissimo's power over Peking.

From Peking and Nanking the Generalissimo continued to

direct his far-flung armies. It was rumored that he slept badly and sometimes gave way to sudden bouts of ferocious ill temper, and at such times he would order the immediate execution of officers who failed to live up to his expectations. He was drinking heavily, and every night he would drink himself to sleep. These rumors were denied, but some echo of them reached his official biographer, who wrote, "A drain on his endurance during these exhausting days was a continuing insomnia which deprived the Generalissimo of his needed rest. Sleeping aids gave him no relief. Finally he found slumber by the habit of drinking a cup and a half of whisky each night to induce drowsiness." An official biographer need not be accurate when relating the drinking habits of his hero.

Drawn and thin, distrusting all his advisers, at a loss to understand why his army fought so badly and why his generals went over to the enemy, the Generalissimo continued to command the army, while leaving to others the government of the country. Wherever he looked, his forces were reeling back in disorder. Tientsin fell on January 14, 1949, and a week later, after a five-week siege, Peking surrendered, the entire garrison and the commanding general going over to the Chinese Communists.

A far more important event, little reported in the foreign press, had already taken place in northern Kiangsu. There, around the town of Hsuchow, traditionally the gateway to the Yangtse valley, two massive armies, each numbering about half a million men, fought for more than a month in blinding snow and rain. The Generalissimo's troops were equipped with tanks and heavy armor, which were of little advantage to him because the roads were deep in mud or slush. Once again the Generalissimo took direct command by telephone from Nanking. Supporting troops were rushed up, only to fall into carefully laid communist traps. It was the biggest battle which had ever taken place on Chinese soil, and in forty days of fighting a quarter of a million men perished. When Hsuchow fell on December 3, Nanking and Shanghai were as good as lost, and the way was open for the conquest of all southern China.

On January 21, 1949, the day of the fall of Peking, the Generalissimo abruptly laid down all his powers and retired from the scene. For three months he went into retirement in his native village of Chikow, refusing to read messages or telegrams, giving no orders and cutting himself off completely from the war. He visited the temples where his mother had prayed and solemnly inspected the school children at the village school, which had been built at his orders and according to his specifications; and it was observed that he enjoyed the company of the village elders. Sometimes he walked in the fields, accompanied by his son, Chiang Ching-kuo, to all appearances a country gentleman strolling across the family property without any thought of returning to the city. Occasionally couriers would come, bringing news of impending disasters, more battles lost, more generals surrendering to the enemy. The government was scattered; some ministers were in Nanking, others in Canton, and still others had vanished from the scene. The China which he had ruled for so long was disintegrating like a sandcastle crumbling before the onrush of the sea.

He had already laid his plans, and a few loyal agents were attempting to carry them out. Salvation, he believed, lay in the islands off the coast of China. There were many islands and all of them could be used against the Chinese Communists, who fought well on land but had no knowledge of naval warfare. Formosa especially attracted him. In February he sent secret orders to the Governor of the Central Bank of China to transfer the entire gold reserve to Taipei to prevent it from falling into the hands of the Communists. Li Tsung-jen, the President of China, who was then attempting to negotiate with the Communists, was not informed. The Generalissimo acted on his own responsibility. Since he retained the position of director-general of the Kuomintang party, he could claim that the transaction was perfectly legal. This is the only decision he is known to have made during his exile in Chikow.

There had always been an air of mystery around him; he enjoyed the secrecy which attended so many of his journeys; and now at last, the three-month exile over, he decided to survey the islands which would be his last line of defense. In April 1949 he left Chikow and sailed up the coast in a small gunboat, which anchored off Point Island near Shanghai; there, except for some brief excursions on shore, he remained for about eleven days, superintending the defense of the city which would fall in the following month. It occurred to him that the Chusan islands, which guard the approaches to the Yangtse estuary, would, if heavily fortified, prevent any ships from entering the Shanghai anchorage. He therefore paid particular attention to these islands, made a prolonged tour of inspection, and planned their fortification. But Formosa, as he well knew, offered more inviting prospects. The island was very nearly impregnable, being separated from the mainland by a hundred-mile-wide strait; there were excellent ports, an industrious people, a temperate climate, an easy approach to the Philippines and Malaya; and all these advantages weighed heavily with him. It was a matter of entire indifference to him whether the Nationalist government would follow him, for in his own eyes he was still the government. He had only to announce from the capital of Formosa that he had returned to power, and all the Kuomintang officials would flock to his side.

On May 6 he began a leisurely progress along the coast of China, examining the islands and their inlets. There are hundreds of small islands scattered off the coast of China, but very few are large enough to provide any of the facilities needed for defense. He examined one by one the small groups of islands known as the Pooto, Tungshachueh, Meishan, and Likang islands. It is not clear what he expected to discover, and he seems to have made this tour of inspection simply in order to have something to do. On May 20, two weeks after leaving Shanghai, he sailed into the harbor of Taipei on board the coastal steamer "Kiang Tsing," and immediately vanished from sight. When Shanghai fell to the Chinese Communists five days later, he was living in a small secluded mountain village called Tsaoshan, eight miles north of Taipei.

Since he no longer commanded the armies in the field, and was no longer in the government, it was assumed that he had abandoned the struggle. He was living very simply and quietly, and he had no contact with the Nationalist government, which now operated from Canton. Whatever disasters the army or the government suffered, he could not be held responsible. He had achieved the enviable position of a ruler who no longer possesses any responsibility, being invisible and invulnerable, but who works upon events in silence. Such a position had rarely been reached before even by the most determined and gifted Confucian sages.

From this idyllic mountain village the Generalissimo watched the events in China as though they were happening on another planet. Cooped up in Canton, without any effective power, the government ministers were quarreling among themselves, while the Kuomintang armies were retiring in disorder. Despairing of any further aid from the United States, the Generalissimo decided to seek it from the Philippines, lying immediately to the south of Formosa. Accordingly, in July he met President Elpidio Quirino at Baguio, and they drew up a joint statement on the necessity for an anticommunist alliance among the southeast Asian nations. It was not a document of any lasting importance, and no offers of aid came from the President of the Philippines.

For nearly six months the Generalissimo had taken no active part in affairs. Suddenly, while in the Philippines, he decided to visit Canton, which he had last visited in 1936. For a moment he seems to have toyed with the idea of returning to power, sweeping the entire government away and assuming command of the army, but the moment passed. In Canton he spoke as one who was greatly to be blamed for the disasters which had been inflicted upon China, inveighed once more against opium-smoking, and offered to die in defense of the city:

> I am ashamed to be back in Canton under the present circumstances of retreat and failure. I cannot but admit that I must share a great part of the defeat. I am appalled at the existence of gambling and opium-smoking under the very nose of the government. But we must hold Canton, our last port—the last place from which we can use both our navy and air force. I am ready to perish with the city.

A few days later he returned to Formosa, and then was off again to South Korea, where he spent two days with President Syngman Rhee discussing his anticommunist alliance. Nothing came of this venture. Another plan had occurred to him. He decided to fly to Chungking, the wartime capital, to see whether at this last moment it might not be possible to transform the province of Szechuan into a Nationalist bastion. Once more he lived in his famous hilltop residence, the Eagle's Nest, and gave orders, and behaved as though he was in charge. The clock had been turned back. Once more the enemy was behind the Ichang gorge, and once more he took the salute at military parades and addressed his soldiers on Monday mornings. Long ago he had planned to retreat to Sikang, the mountain fastness on the border of Tibet, if the Japanese advanced into Szechuan, and from time to time envoys were sent to parley with the tribal chieftains; so now once again envoys were sent into the hinterland, but this time the tribes were less accommodating.

Now, as though the fires that had been banked low were at last leaping into flame, he was continually on the move, giving orders to the army, the government, and the people. He paid a brief visit to Yunnan, another brief visit to Canton, and then he was back again in Formosa. The art treasures which had been housed in the great museum in Peking before the war had been carried overland to Chungking, to be hidden in caves out of the reach of Japanese bombs; now they were removed hurriedly to Formosa, out of the reach of the Chinese Communists. Meanwhile the Communists continued to advance steadily. They occupied Canton on October 15 without opposition. The city fell without fanfare, "with scarcely more than a quiet sigh," wrote the correspondent of the *New York Times*. But Kweichow, Szechuan, and Shensi were still in Nationalist hands. In theory Yunnan and Kwangsi, together with large areas of Kwangtung, were under the control of the government, but the government itself had vanished. President Li Tsung-jen had taken refuge in Nanning in Kwangsi. He was in no mood to continue the fight, and when the Generalissimo summoned him to Chungking, he replied:

> I am glad to learn that you have arrived in Chungking. I should have come up too, after receiving your cable. But my stomach ailment has become very much worse—I am very tired. So I have decided to leave for Hongkong today enroute to the United States for a thorough checkup, and if necessary an opera-

tion. Meanwhile I shall sound out the attitude of the United States toward China.

It was a strange letter, but not entirely unexpected. So many of the former members of the government were paralyzed by defeat. The Generalissimo could not prevent him from visiting America, but at least he could delay the visit; and the Chinese consulate in Hongkong was instructed to refuse a passport to the President of China. Eventually the President made a fruitless journey to the United States, where he was regarded as a man of straw without support in his own country or outside. Sometimes high tragedy is indistinguishable from farce, and the letters exchanged between the Generalissimo and the President, while the republic crumbled, belong to the comedy of disaster.

From time to time the President would send messages to Chungking, saying he intended to return and take up the reins of government. The letters were received with dismay, and never answered.

The Generalissimo had other things to occupy his attention. He still hoped that Chungking would prove to be the rock on which communist hopes would be shattered. The province of Szechuan was the richest in China; Yunnan might yet be saved; the capture of Canton was only one more incident in a long and costly campaign; and surely if the Communists were able to survive for so many years in Yenan, the Kuomintang could survive in Sikang.

Meanwhile the Communists were daily announcing the fall of famous cities. They had proclaimed the People's Republic of China with its new capital in Peking, and they were in no mood to tolerate the existence of a Kuomintang government on Chinese soil. On November 29 the advance guards of the Communists army were closing in on Chungking; distant gunfire could be heard in the Eagle's Nest. That evening the Generalissimo visited the military headquarters which had been his command post during the war against the Japanese; he found it deserted. A military map lay on the floor, and to prevent it from falling into enemy hands, he put a match to it. The next morning at dawn he flew to

Chengtu. If Chengtu could hold out, he planned to organize the guerrilla army which would reconquer China from the fastness of Sikang. But there was no longer any time for organizing armies. Chengtu was doomed by the advancing communist forces, and the guerrillas of Sikang were never more than a dream. Ten days after reaching Chengtu, accompanied by his son Chiang Ching-kuo, the Generalissimo flew to Formosa.

Once more he vanished into obscurity, into the silence of a mountain village near Sun Moon lake, in the central highlands of Formosa. There had been no last stand in China; his armies had melted away; and all the wars against the Chinese Communists had come to nothing. A few days later he received a telegram saying that all resistance had finally ceased. There was nothing he could do, and so he spent the rest of the day fishing in the lake.

FORMOSA

IN THE MONTHS immediately following the end of the war, the island of Formosa suffered one of its worst disasters. For fifty years, ever since the treaty of Shimonoseki, the island had been in the hands of the Japanese, who exploited the Formosans unmercifully. There were few schools and no colleges; anyone who resisted Japanese oppression was executed out of hand; and the only contacts permitted by the Japanese with the outside world were so closely regulated that scarcely any Formosans were able to leave the island. During those fifty years there were at least twenty uprisings, but little is known about them because the Japanese took care that little information should leave the country. When the war ended, the Formosans were delirious with joy. They killed as many Japanese as they could, and proclaimed their independence. They had forgotten that Chiang Kai-shek regarded Formosa as an integral part of China.

To remind them, the Chinese government sent an occupation force under the command of General Chen Yi, a veteran of Dr. Sun Yat-sen's Cantonese army. Formosans who had suffered intolerably under the Japanese now learned that they had merely exchanged one tyranny for another. Chen Yi was a very close friend of Chiang Kai-shek, and felt that he was above the law. The Formosans now found themselves at the mercy of an invader who took care that Japanese property should pass into Chinese hands and that no Formosan should be given a voice in the government. Corruption and nepotism held full sway, the governor acting as though the island was his private preserve. All the ills that affected the mainland—inflation, widespread poverty, smuggling, the secret police, military privilege, the concentration of wealth in a few hands—now erupted on an island where people had been accustomed to an orderly, if oppressive, government geared to a minimum of social improvement. The Chinese occupation was even more intolerable than the Japanese occupation. To add to the misery of the Formosans there was a cholera epidemic, and bubonic plague appeared for the first time in forty years.

On February 27, 1947, a small incident sparked the inevitable rebellion. A woman cigarette-seller was beaten to death by tax inspectors for not paying the proper taxes. A crowd gathered, and the inspectors' truck was set on fire. On the following day there were demonstrations in the streets of Taipei. The demonstrators were scattered by machine-gun fire. During the following days Nationalist soldiers and the secret police hunted down the demonstrators and everyone thought to be in sympathy with them, and since nearly everyone in Taipei was in sympathy with them, it was decided by the military government that only exemplary measures would be used. To prevent an uprising, a reign of terror was instituted. Trucks filled with government troops armed with machine guns swept through the streets, firing indiscriminately. Then when these measures appeared to infuriate the people still more, the military governor went on the radio and begged for calm, promising to pay compensation to the families of the dead, to open the rice stores, to withdraw the troops from the streets, and to punish the soldiers responsible for the massacres. None of these promises was kept, and the reign of terror continued.

On April 18, 1947, the American ambassador, Dr. Leighton Stuart, presented a full report on the massacres to the Generalissimo, who professed to have no knowledge of these incidents, though they had been reported at length in the foreign press. He agreed that perhaps General Chen Yi had exceeded his instructions, and four days later the general was replaced by Dr. Wei Tao-ming, a diplomat of considerable skill. Gradually, as the months passed, the scars began to heal.

According to the Generalissimo's official biographer, the Generalissimo cannot be held responsible for these incidents, because he knew nothing about them. Apparently there had been no communication between him and the military governor. The Kuomintang press sought to minimize the affair, proclaiming that nothing of any great importance had happened, that the American report was wildly exaggerated, and that in fact only a very small number of people had been killed. It was hinted that the well-meaning ambassador had been advised by communist sympathizers, and that this was only one more attempt by the American government to vilify the Kuomintang. The charges, however, were true, and in good conscience the Ambassador could not refuse to present the report. When General Wedemeyer arrived in China a few weeks later, he found nothing to suggest that the Kuomintang had changed its ways.

When the Generalissimo reached Formosa on December 12, 1949, he received no welcome from the people. He moved about quietly and secretly. A large and well-equipped army was in control of the island, for he had refused to throw his best American-trained forces into the struggle with the Chinese Communists. There was a force amounting to about a thousand tanks under the command of his younger son, Major General Chiang Wei-kuo. The original garrison had been augmented by troops ferried to the island from the coastal provinces; altogether there were about 800,000 soldiers on Formosa, some 600 airplanes, about 70 ships manned by a loyal navy, and in addition there were about 40,000 marines. One cruiser—the only cruiser in Kuomintang possession—had gone over to the Communists, but not long afterward it was sunk by a Nationalist bomber. The Generalissimo could congratulate himself that his navy and air force remained largely intact, and that he still possessed a standing army of formidable size. In addition he had two excellent naval bases at Tsoyin and Keelung on Formosa, and Tsinghai in the Chusan islands was heavily fortified, able to mount a continuing blockade on the port of Shanghai. He had guns on the island of Quemoy, which faced Amoy, and on the island of Mansan in the Pearl river delta, facing Canton. The island of Hainan was also in Kuomintang hands, with some forty thousand troops under the command of General Hsueh Yueh, the victor of the battle of Changsha. Most of his civil airplanes had gone over to the Communists, but civil aircraft could easily be bought on the international market. Surveying the effective strength of the forces under his command, he knew that the Chinese Communists would have the greatest difficulty in ousting him from his newly acquired fortress. Only a revolution on the island would remove the Kuomintang from power, and this, in the circumstances, was unlikely.

Some of these advantages proved to be only temporary, for the Chinese Communists were determined to sweep away the evidence of Kuomintang power close to the mainland. Hainan was the first to fall. It was separated from the mainland by a narrow strait, and was therefore open to invasion. The Communists massed a fleet of junks and landed in force in April 1950. The Kuomintang high command had to decide whether to continue fighting and risk the loss of General Hsueh Yueh's forces, or to add them to the army on Formosa. Finally it was decided that the advantages of remaining on Hainan were outweighed by the dangers, for the Communists possessed a sizable guerrilla force in the hills and were masters of the fifteen-mile-wide straits. General Hsueh Yueh fought his way to the south of the island, having lost the chief city, Huichow, after a "dispirited resistance" lasting six days. The survivors were taken to Formosa in troopships, and little more was heard about General Hsueh Yueh. It was generally felt that he might have managed the defense of the island with more skill and enthusiasm. Hainan, with its rich iron deposits and gold mines, was abandoned to the Chinese Communists.

The blockade of Shanghai by control of the Chusan islands had been one of the Generalissimo's more useful ideas. More than a hundred thousand troops were stationed on the islands, mostly at Tsinghai. These troops represented a far greater military capital than the forces which had been occupying Hainan, and the Generalissimo was under no illusions about the danger of maintaining so large an army so far from its base. The Chinese Communists were determined to prevent the blockade of Shanghai by every means possible, and they had thousands of junks at their disposal. Immediately after their success on Hainan, they employed the same strategy against the Chusan islands. A fleet of junks was assembled in Hangchow bay. This had been observed by spotter planes, and once more the Generalissimo had to make a difficult decision—whether to fight or to retire. Once more he decided to withdraw his troops. He claimed later that the preservation of so many well-trained and well-equipped troops was a strategic victory, but in fact it was a defeat, for his army would not have been able to withstand the full force of the Chinese Communist armada. His troops were rescued just in time, and he derived some satisfaction from the knowledge that nothing of any use to the enemy had been left behind. When the armada sailed out to capture the Chusans, Kuomintang bombers strafed them and the first landing parties were wiped out.

The dream of blockading the Chinese coast was fast melting away. About the same time the Nationalist troops were forced to abandon Mansan island, which commanded the approaches to Canton, and Tungshan island, off the coast of Fukien. There remained Formosa and the offshore islands of Quemoy and Matsu, which commanded the approaches to Amoy and Foochow. The possession of the offshore islands was of some symbolic importance, for they were very close to the mainland.

Many other problems confronted the Generalissimo. There was, for example, the problem of his own position, for though he gave orders to his ministers, commanded the army, and dominated the life of Formosa, he had no constitutional right to do any of these things. In theory he had retired from the government in January 1949. He was the head of the Kuomintang party, but there was nothing in the government statutes which permitted him executive authority. It was therefore arranged that the handpicked Legislative Yuan should petition him to resume the presidency.

On March 1, 1950, he resumed the exercise of presidential powers, and in his speech of acceptance he promised to make Formosa a model province:

> For more than forty years I have dedicated my life to the revolutionary cause and have long ago banished from my mind any thought of life and of death, of honor and of humiliation. My participation in or withdrawal from national affairs depends solely on the wish of the people. At this critical moment I cannot shirk my responsibility. All that I can do now is to make up for the things in which I have failed in the past, and to do my duty in planning for the future. It is my earnest hope that our patriotic peoples, at home and abroad, will present a united front, and that the rank and file of the three armed services will be imbued with enthusiasm for service, and the officials of all ranks will be loyal to the duties assigned them. Thus we fight together for the recovery of China's sovereignty.

It was a speech he had delivered many times before and would deliver many times again. Sixteen years later, when he assumed the presidency for his fourth term, there would be the same refusal to shirk his responsibility and the same disingenuous plea that he had merely bowed to the will of the people. Henceforward the constant theme of all his speeches was that he had assumed the presidency in order to redeem his errors.

There were many errors, and not the least of them was Chiang Kai-shek's disinclination to permit anyone else to share his power. Once in wartime Chungking the "Christian General," Feng Yu-hsiang, listened to him discussing his ailments. "I am suffering from continual headaches, dizzy spells, lumbago," the Generalissimo said. "I am fully aware that my powers are declining, and I think I deserve a long rest." Feng Yu-hsiang was amazed and delighted. "Obviously if you feel in this way," he said, "you should give your position to someone else." There was a long silence, and then the Generalissimo said, "I would step down if I thought there was anyone else who could carry out my ideas."

In Formosa the Generalissimo still regarded himself as the essential instrument of China's destiny. He was painfully aware that the Americans distrusted him and had not forgiven him for his defeat. President Truman had no high opinion of his abilities. In January 1950 the President declared that under no circumstances would the United States permit itself to be embroiled in the Chinese cockpit. He stated categorically that "the United States government will not provide military aid or advice to Chinese forces in Formosa." Aid to Formosa would be limited to economic assistance, which was given grudgingly with little hope that the money would be well spent.

The American attitude toward the Generalissimo changed decisively with the opening of the Korean war, when it was realized that Formosa occupied a position of crucial strategic importance. On June 28 General Douglas MacArthur was appointed commander-in-chief of all the allied forces in Korea. Three days later he flew to Taipei. It was a dramatic move, designed to demonstrate the importance of Formosa in the defense of eastern Asia. The Chinese Communists were planning to send an armada against Formosa; President Truman ordered the Seventh Fleet to patrol the Formosa Straits, thus effectively preventing the Chinese Communists from mounting their attack. In the following year military aid was offered. As a result of the Korean war the Generalissimo found himself, somewhat to his surprise, in the good graces of the United States. Yet he was still distrusted, and when he offered to send thirty-three thousand Kuomintang troops to Korea, the offer was politely rejected. He was tolerated, but not liked. He was respected, but not loved. He had committed too many errors to be permitted to enter the club as a full-fledged member; he was still on probation.

Formosa took no part in the Korean war. Neutralized and protected by the Seventh Fleet, it was permitted to enjoy a long breathing spell. The United States government was too preoccupied to devote much attention to Formosa, and the Formosans were content to remain in the quiet backwaters, almost forgotten by the outside world. It was an enviable situation, and they were properly grateful.

For the first time in many years the Generalissimo had time on his hands. In 1956 he completed a lengthy account of Chinese relations with Russia called *Soviet Russia in China*. Like *China's Destiny* the book was largely written by his secretaries. The central theme, endlessly repeated, is that the Chinese Communists were the servants of international communism, obedient to the orders of the Kremlin. It was a theme which could be substantiated only by a quite casual indifference to the evidence. He recounted the crimes committed by the Chinese and Russian Communists and the errors committed by the United States government, which were numerous, and attributable to the presence of Communists in high positions in the United States Treasury and Foreign Service. The Americans had been wrong to refuse his offer of Kuomintang troops to be used in Korea. These troops would have fought their way into Manchuria, and fighting on their own ground, they would have carried everything before them. "I believe," he wrote, "that the western powers' objection to the dispatch of an expeditionary force to Korea by the Republic of China was the *greatest cause for the stalemate in the Korean War*." He had not the least doubt that his troops would have toppled the Chinese Communists from power.

In *Soviet Russia in China* the Generalissimo had much to say about Lenin and Stalin, but very little about Mao Tse-tung, who is represented as a puppet dangling from Russian strings and incapable of hammering out any policies of his own. "Events have proved that there is no possibility for the Chinese Communists to leave Soviet Russia's fold," he wrote categorically, thus demonstrating that he had always misunderstood the nature of the Chinese Communist revolution. Mao Tse-tung had not come to power because he obeyed the Kremlin, but because he was a revolutionary in his own right, obedient to no one in his determination to bring about the downfall of a corrupt Kuomintang regime.

But while the Generalissimo was blind to his own faults, and incapable of understanding the springs of Mao Tse-tung's actions, he had many wise things to say about the nature of Russian Communist ambitions. He understood the Russian Communists better than he understood the Chinese Communists, and this was due perhaps to the fact that he had been in Russia and received frequent reports from his elder son, who had lived in the Soviet Union and married a Russian woman. Here, for example, he describes the aims of the Russian Communists:

> In order to achieve their inordinate scheme for world conquest, the Russian Communists chose the absolute forms of unlimited war. In their war against the free world they are limited by neither time or space. They can switch from one battlefield to another as from one form of warfare to another. They can carry out infiltration, propaganda, organization, political intrigue, subversion, and even armed uprising against their enemy on the inside, in coordination with their frontal attacks—economic, diplomatic, cultural, political, and psychological—on the outside. Every one of their moves is for the purpose of the decisive battle, and every advance is to be evaluated for its effect on the final outcome. They keep on advancing toward the target, namely, the final battle, unceasingly and without limitations in full expectation of attaining the ultimate objective.

On such matters he spoke with authority, sure of himself and of his conclusions. What is strange is that when he speaks about the Chinese Communists, he gives the impression of describing them at second hand, hesitantly, as though they had never entered the field of his experience. Mao Tse-tung is always referred to casually, as though he were a minor actor in the drama.

He had scarcely finished the book when Mao Tse-tung decided that the time had come to prepare for the long delayed invasion of Formosa by an attack on the offshore islands of Quemoy and Matsu. Shore-based batteries pounded the islands, and Chinese Communist airplanes bombed them, but the island defenses were well protected and the Nationalist navy had little difficulty in bringing up reinforcements. There were aerial dogfights, and for a few weeks the bombardment was maintained with extraordinary fury. Thereafter the battle for the islands assumed a symbolic character, with the shore batteries firing for a brief period every day, and then every other day, and then at long intervals. The Generalissimo proclaimed that the decisive battle for Quemoy had been won, but it would be more reasonable to say that there had been an inconclusive skirmish.

The Chinese Communists appeared to abandon hope of an easy conquest of Formosa. They could not deny its existence, but they could forget that it threatened them on a flank which would be difficult to defend if vast fleets were placed at the service of the Nationalists. On the seacoast they were vulnerable. They were vulnerable, too, in the air, for the Nationalists retained the mastery of the air space above the Formosa Straits, and they were able without any difficulty to drop spies and secret agents on the mainland by parachute. Three years later the Generalissimo explained to a visiting journalist that the *raison d'être* of Formosa lay precisely in the fact that Formosa was a part of China beyond the reach of the Chinese Communists, and he derived a lesson from the failure of the Hungarian revolution:

> Had there been a free Hungarian government either inside or outside the territory of Hungary when the Hungarian freedom fighters struck, the historical development of eastern Europe and even of the whole world would have followed an entirely different course. The crux of the problem, therefore, is not whether there will be an opportunity for the people on the Chinese mainland to rise in revolution against the Communists, but whether there will be enough resolution and sense of responsibility on the part of the free world to enable it to take full advantage of such an opportunity whenever it would present itself.

But though he spoke incessantly about reconquering the mainland, he always spoke in military and not in revolutionary terms. He never thought in social terms. He would explain patiently that when the Kuomintang returned to the mainland, everything would be as it was before, the communes would be abolished, Nationalist legality would be established, and the penitent Communists would be reintegrated into society. As for the landowners, they had a legal right to their land, and if the peasants wished to own the land, then they must buy it from the rightful owners. In some cases the government would be empowered to seize the land and divide it among the peasants, but only after proper compensation had been paid to the landlords.

As he grew older, his determination to reconquer the mainland only increased. It had become an obsession, and like all obsessions it was deeply personal, dangerous, and destructive. In the past he had often identified himself with the feudal princes of ancient China. Now as he grew older he saw himself as another Moses leading the people to the Promised Land, or another Christ suffering crucifixion for the sake of mankind.

At Easter, 1961, he delivered a sermon on the Resurrection to a small group of Christian friends. Characteristically he saw the Resurrection not as a promise of rebirth for individual Christians but as a promise of national revival. The individual vanished; only the nation had power to be born again. It was a weighty sermon, and the argument was pursued with an air of complete conviction and infallibility, as though no other interpretation was possible.

> Very clearly, Jesus went into Jerusalem ready to sacrifice himself because He wanted to redeem the Jewish people and mankind as a whole from sin and death. His sacrifice triumphs over all sins and death, from which man is thereby liberated. The Cross, therefore, is not only a symbol of Resurrection and the eternal life of Jesus, but also a turning point for national recovery and the liberation of mankind. In explaining to His disciples the meaning of His Resurrection from death, Jesus said: "Except a grain of wheat fall into the ground and die, it abideth alone; but if it die, it bringeth forth much fruit." This passage makes it apparent that life and Resurrection, here referred to, mean the rebirth of the whole national spirit and the resurrection of the whole of mankind. No other explanation can be more thorough or more lucid than this.

Unfortunately the explanation was neither thorough nor lucid, and it was only too clear that he had imposed his own conception of personal redemption and sacrifice on a text which could only with the greatest difficulty be interpreted in terms of "national recovery." In much the same way in his sermons he would identify Satan with the Chinese Communists, and prophesy their eventual destruction. At such times he would quote approvingly the text "Vengeance is mine, said the Lord."

THE SILENT ISLAND

UNDER THE KUOMINTANG, LIFE on Formosa continued according to rigid formulas worked out in the ancient past, with the military and the bureaucracy ruling in the name of an Emperor who was rarely seen and whose edicts were published at infrequent intervals. The rituals of worship were endlessly repeated, the courtiers moved solemnly through the palace courtyards on their mysterious errands, and from time to time there would be trumpet calls from the palace watch-towers, but what was actually happening within the palace, or whether indeed anything was happening at all, was unknown to the people. Power on Formosa was generated in silence and remoteness, and was all the more effective because it was shrouded in mystery.

In China the dead weight of the past falls heavily on the living. Even in revolutionary times the ancient rituals and gestures survive, and the minds of the revolutionaries are saturated in the traditions of the long distant past. So we find Mao Tse-tung behaving not like one of the relatively cultured and tolerant emperors of the eighteenth century but like one of the barbaric

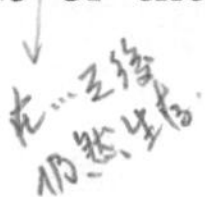

chieftains who are elevated to the throne after they have conquered the Chinese armies, while Chiang Kai-shek more closely resembles those emperors who come at the end of a declining dynasty, who go through the motions of governing with weariness and unconcealed distaste for the small details of government which affect the lives of ordinary people, and grow more inflexible as their real power diminishes. Both Mao Tse-tung and Chiang Kai-shek belonged to the imperial tradition.

So it came about that they suffered from the same poisons which infected imperial China, and they made very little effort to conceal their exalted, semi-divine status, encouraged the formation of their own dynasties, gave their relatives high offices, surrounded themselves with time-serving officials whose sole duty was to make the appropriate gestures at the right moment, cultivated their own legends and insisted that no other legends should be cultivated, portrayed themselves as saviors and liberators when in fact they had merely imposed themselves on the country by force of arms, and ruled by edict. There was never any real dialogue with the people, and indeed such a dialogue was prohibited by the nature of the imperial process, for the all-knowing Emperor is expected to know everything that goes on in the minds of the people. Because the dialogue had broken down, or was never begun, there were no checks and balances which would ensure that his rule satisfied the people. The Emperor lived in a vacuum. He did not know, and could not know, what was happening in his country, and his edicts were often meaningless, unrelated to the real situation in the country. The similarities between Chiang Kai-shek and Mao Tse-tung were greater than their differences. What distinguished them was not their methods but the qualities of their minds.

On the island of Formosa all the virtues and defects of the ancient imperial system could be studied in miniature. Once again there was a towering bureaucracy, with the bureaucrats owing their positions to imperial favor. With almost no exceptions the bureaucrats were Chinese who had accompanied Chiang Kai-shek from the mainland, and were thus in somewhat the same position as the Manchus who came from across the border and ruled over the conquered people. No positions of power or influence were given to the native Formosans. The bureaucrats were underpaid, and expected to make up their living expenses by small-scale corruption. The Control Yuan, designed to prevent corruption, was powerless. Corruption was so widespread that it affected all departments of government at all levels, and it was especially prevalent among policemen, tax officers and school administrators, who demanded the payment of bribes from the teachers before they were given positions. Inevitably the poor suffer most and the efficiency of government is reduced by the sporadic, unplanned and oddly capricious nature of corruption. Every government official has his price, but there are so many sliding scales, so many reasons for increasing and diminishing the price even when it is established that no one knows how much he is expected to pay, only that he must pay until he is wrung dry.

Corruption was not of course the invention of the Kuomintang; and as it was practiced on Formosa it lacked the total effrontery of the warlords of the twenties and thirties, and their successors in the Ministry of Finance in war-time Chungking, where the art was practiced with breathtaking finesse even when the Japanese were at the gates and whole provinces were reduced to starvation. Under the Ching dynasty corruption was regulated and precisely calculated, as though an entire department of government had been installed to see that it worked fairly on rich and poor alike. In Formosa it worked with a kind of calculated, grotesque unfairness, and was all the more terrible because it was as pervasive as the air men breathed.

From time to time half-hearted efforts were made to stamp out corruption in high places. The mayor of Taipei was arrested for accepting bribes from the local bus administration; he was acquitted, and his judges were elevated to higher positions. There was nothing particularly noteworthy in the trial except that the mayor of Taipei, being *ipso facto* a high Kuomintang official, and a close friend of the Generalissimo, was surprised that anyone should have dared to arrest him. He defended himself vigorously, produced his books, showed that in the course of a long career in administration he had never taken a single bribe, and called on character witnesses to defend his moral character and incidentally his connections with the Generalissimo. His wife was not so lucky, for she was found guilty of embezzling $300,000. She was given a deferred jail sentence.

In this way the government succeeded in alienating the people, who neither trusted it nor felt any enthusiasm for its titular leader. Demoralized, without hope in the future, cut off from the mainland, living in isolation from the main currents of civilization, they learned to obey, pay bribes and live quietly and obscurely. The overwhelming might of the regime, exercised through the army and the secret police, enforced obedience. The revolutionary Kuomintang had degenerated into a comparatively small body of men exercising the rights of prison wardens.

Literature, the arts and the sciences suffered in exactly the same way that they suffered on the mainland; the bureaucrats were interested only in their own survival and were prepared to reward only those artists and scientists who helped to perpetuate them in power. Anyone who was not in complete sympathy with the regime was regarded as an enemy to be chastised; anyone who attacked the regime was regarded as a self-confessed Communist deserving of death or worse. Free speech was regarded as a crime, and freedom of assembly was never permitted. Like all authoritarian states, it was found necessary to employ hordes of informers, not to find out what the people were thinking, but in order to justify the arrests of people who were not thinking favorably about the government. It has been calculated that there are nearly a quarter of a million part-time and full-time informers on the island.

On the rare occasions when anyone protested that everything was not well on Formosa, punishment was always swift and salutary. The government would tolerate a certain amount of friendly criticism provided the intentions of the critic were simply to tender generalized advice with suitable quotations from the writings of Dr. Sun Yat-sen and the Generalissimo; on specific matters of conduct or government policy no advice was permitted. Nothing could be said about the personal lives of government officials, and their policies must always be praised. The inevitable result was that the press on Formosa was as deadly dull as the press on the mainland, and the newspapers in both places were in fact very similar.

Only the very bravest dared to attack the regime. During the war the government had permitted a small splinter group called the Democratic League to exist. It was honeycombed with informers and was never in any real sense a political party. In 1960 Lei Chen, the editor of the *Free China Fortnightly*, attempted with the help of a few friends to found a new party called the China Democratic Party in opposition to the Kuomintang. He was a former Kuomintang official, a poet and teacher, deeply sympathetic to the Formosans who had no representation in the government. He had powerful friends in Kuomintang circles, and seems to have believed that the government would tolerate the existence of a party which genuinely desired to raise the social level of the people very much as a conservative government in England would tolerate the existence of a labour party. The times were ripe for change, the younger Kuomintang officials were becoming restive, and there were some indications that the Generalissimo himself would regard the new party as "acceptable." The trouble was that no one on the island really knew what was "acceptable" or "unacceptable," since the government had never offered to draw up any guide-lines and derived considerable advantage from the fact that it was the final arbiter and could make its decisions when and as it pleased. The China Democratic Party was founded amid fanfare and died a few days later when all its members were placed under arrest. Significantly the arrests were made by the military at the direct orders of the Generalissimo.

Lei Chen was arrested on September 4, 1960, and for the rest of the month was forced to submit to searching cross-examinations by military judges who had convinced themselves that he was secretly plotting the downfall of the Kuomintang government. He was treated as though he was a Communist agent. One of his colleagues confessed that in 1953 he had attempted to subvert him and bring him over to the Communist camp. It was noted that Lei Chen had not informed against his colleague, and was therefore liable to severe punishment. His articles in the *Free China*

Fortnightly were carefully examined and shown to be full of subtle condemnations of the government and clever misinterpretations of government intentions. In October he was brought up for trial before a military court. No lawyers could be found to defend him. It was not that the lawyers were in disagreement with him; they simply dared not defend a man who was already convicted in the eyes of the government. The charges were sedition, conspiracy and attempted overthrow of the government; the death penalty was demanded. A merciful judge sentenced him instead to ten years imprisonment followed by seven years' deprivation of his rights as a citizen. His colleague, the self-confessed Communist agent, received twelve years imprisonment. With one savage blow the government destroyed the *Free China Fortnightly* and the China Democratic Party.

As usual in such cases many problems were left unsolved. The Generalissimo, who had ordered the arrest and was in complete charge of the investigation, had very little to gain, and much to lose, by arresting a man who was regarded with favor by the Americans. On September 11, nine days after Lei Chen's arrest, he was asked by American correspondents about the forthcoming trial. The Generalissimo said that Lei Chen would be proved guilty of aiding and abetting the Chinese Communists. It was a simple statement, announced with absolute authority. In much the same way Stalin would bring dissenters to trial and condemn them long before the final verdict was announced. The Generalissimo was saying that Lei Chen had been condemned more than three weeks before he was made to appear before a military court.

The real crime of Lei Chen was never mentioned during the trial. It was a crime without a name, though everyone on the island was familiar with it. It was not *lèse majesté*, which implies a deliberate offense against the person of the supreme ruler, and it was not conspiracy, for there were no conspirators, and it was not the crime of bringing into existence a political party in opposition to the government, for the party had not been permitted to exist. But while there was no name for the crime, there was a word which resembled it. This word was "despair."

In prison Lei Chen was a model prisoner, permitted to read

and study. He was given writing materials and allowed to accumulate a small library of books. From time to time his wife was given permission to visit him. On April 1, 1963, a poem written by him in prison was published by the weekly magazine *Time and Tide:*

Be kind to enemies and friends; listen more and speak less.
Tolerate others, restrain yourself; freedom will be seen and democracy be practiced.
Accept criticism and correct mistakes, don't complain, don't blame, don't shirk, don't exaggerate, speak less and do more.
Don't speak against others, don't speak highly of yourself.
Let bygones be bygones, whatever will be will be.
Be faithful and diligent.
Tilling without harvesting.
Keep yourself straight, ignore others' talk.
Do whatever should be done, look upon death as going home.
These are the principles for one to live by, to deal with people or to rule a nation.

The poem became famous, for it seemed to belong to that small category of poems which within the space of a few lines crystallize a whole epoch. The haunting cadences spoke of a time when the human will no longer possesses any resources, when there is no hope anywhere, and where a man must be content with mere survival. In resignation the poet realizes that his life must be devoted to "tilling without harvesting," and that only death awaited him.

But there was another reason for the poem's fame, which was even more to the poet's credit. Hidden within the melancholy verses there was a note of irony, of self-vindication, and even of malice. He was saying that he hoped the rulers of the nation would be tolerant and restrained, accepting criticism, being always diligent and faithful and never praising themselves. He hoped, but he had not much hope. So he wrote these verses in despair for himself and his people, hoping against hope.

Time and Tide, the magazine in which the poem appeared, was immediately banned, and Mrs. Lei, who was a member of the Control Yuan, and who had smuggled the poem from the prison, was denied all visiting rights to her husband. In this way the government found satisfactory excuses for punishing *Time and*

Tide, the Control Yuan and the wife of the imprisoned editor. The magazine was banned for a year, and six months later, as the result of intervention by some foreign dignitaries who visited Formosa for the celebrations commemorating the birth of the Republic, Mrs. Lei was permitted to visit her husband once a month. The government was bowing to foreign pressure, but with ill-grace and without any indication that Lei Chen's case would ever be reopened.

The jails were full of political prisoners, for the government was convinced that a large number of Communists had infiltrated the island. Once a man had been arrested and described as a "red hat," there was little prospect that he would ever emerge from jail. The most dangerous political prisoners were held on Green Island off the coast of Formosa. From this well-guarded island escape was virtually impossible.

The Generalissimo was accustomed to keeping a close watch on his prisoners. He never forgot them and never forgave them. The most distinguished of his prisoners was the "Young Marshal," Chiang Hsueh-liang, who had arrested him in Sian so long ago that he seemed to belong to ancient Chinese history. The "Young Marshal" had made himself a voluntary prisoner and from the moment he reached Nanking, he became the private prisoner of the Generalissimo, kept under permanent house arrest, allowed to see only those people who received permission from the highest authority, his books and his reading matter all carefully examined by the guard set over him. At the beginning his guard was a lieutenant, but as the years passed he rose to the rank of major-general. On rare occasions the "Young Marshal" could be seen in the streets of Taipei on his way to a movie theater, his guard by his side. It was rumored that he had been working for more than thirty years on a general history of the Sung dynasty, a period not altogether unlike his own, but since he had never shown any sign of literary talent, there is some doubt whether the history was ever written.

Taipei was full of ghosts, for Chinese politicians are often long-lived. One could see men who had taken part in the 1911 revolution hobbling along its streets. The venerable Yu Yu-jen, for so long the ineffective head of the Control Yuan, an enchanting scholar and the greatest calligraphist of his time, continued to appear at public functions when he was well into his eighties. He had a long white silky beard and resembled a Taoist saint, and by his presence he gave dignity to any gathering he attended. Hu Shih, the great literary critic and one of the founders of the May Fourth movement which attempted in the early nineteen twenties to introduce a kind of revolutionary sanity into Chinese life, spent his last years on Formosa. But not many of the intellectual giants chose to remain with the Nationalists. Most of the eminent scientists and artists chose to remain on the mainland or to emigrate to the United States. In the stifling intellectual atmosphere of Formosa there were altogether too few rewards for men of outstanding ability.

The brain drain rarely occupied the attention of the government, which was inclined to regard the emigration of the best scholars and scientists with indifference, perhaps because the government had very little contact with them. The inevitable result was that schools, colleges, hospitals and research facilities were maintained at a level of minimum efficiency. It was calculated that between 1962 and 1967 nearly 15,000 engineers, technicians, scientists, doctors and teachers left for better-paying jobs abroad, most of them going to the United States, very few going to the mainland, for the Communists naturally distrusted anyone educated on Formosa. Significantly, most of these highly trained specialists were Chinese, not Formosans.

By 1968 the government was beginning to feel the effects of the brain drain and some belated attempts were made to halt it. The Generalissimo ordered the construction of 78 junior high schools and groundbreaking ceremonies were held throughout the island, while special inducements were offered to scientists and educators who might be tempted to take jobs abroad. But neither the new high schools nor the special inducements were on a scale large enough to influence the course of events. Formosa remained a cultural desert, the informers, the secret police and the corrupt bureaucracy reaching out among the talents and subjecting them to a cold embrace. The secret ambition of nearly all the talented scholars and scientists was to leave the island and never return.

One of the reasons why they lack any loyalty to the island lies in the official propaganda, which insists that Formosa is merely a temporary residence of the government which will soon be installed on the mainland. While Chiang Kai-shek repeatedly vows to "drink gall and sleep on faggots" until the mainland is reconquered, there is little belief among the Chinese on the island that the reconquest will ever take place. The Chinese Communist empire may disintegrate, but the disintegration will not come about as the result of Chiang Kai-shek's endeavours, and no Kuomintang army is likely to land on the mainland or even maintain a beachhead. The knowledge that the mainland is forever unapproachable has a debilitating and frustrating effect on the Chinese, who have an intense affection for the sights and sounds of their native country. On their identity cards the town and province they came from are recorded, a perpetual reminder that their chief loyalty is to the mainland, not to Formosa.

In the Generalissimo's eyes Formosa was merely a stepping stone, a brief halt on the journey which would once more bring him to Nanking. In the eyes of the American military strategists Formosa was a staging area for a war of nerves against the Chinese Communists. If the mainland could not be reconquered, at least it could be reminded that there were anti-Communists close to its shores. From the spring of 1951 onward there has been an American military presence on the island. Known as MAAG, which stands for Military Assistance Advisory Group, this military presence has assumed a major role in the economy and government of the island. Enormous sums were spent on armaments for the defence of the island, and on training and equipping the Nationalist army. In a fifteen year period the American government poured $2.5 billion dollars in military aid into Formosa. A considerable proportion of this money was inevitably lost to corrupt officials, but enough remained to produce an efficient and well-armed army. In addition the American government gave Formosa during the same period $1.5 billion in economic assistance. Since the gross national product of Formosa in 1951 amounted to only

$880 million, it was evident that the American taxpayer was paying the lion's share of the cost of supporting the military machine and the economy of Formosa. There is some doubt whether the money was well spent, for such fantastic sums could be excused only on the grounds that Chiang Kai-shek was organizing a huge invasion force prepared to attack and conquer the mainland. If the army was merely to be a defensive force, it was useless, since the defence of the island could be ensured by the Seventh Fleet.

As American dollars poured into the island, the gross national product quickly increased until in 1965 it reached $2.4 billion. This was proof, if proof were needed, that a backward economy could be transformed in a few years into a flourishing one by the injection of vast subsidies. Inflation was controlled, interest rates gradually went down, and by 1965, when economic aid tapered off, the economy of the island was in good shape. The Kuomintang economic experts had learned their lesson, and the calamitous mistakes made in Chungking were not repeated.

Although the government of Formosa could not have survived without American aid, the Generalissimo continued to distrust Americans. He was suspicious and uncomfortable in their presence, realizing that they viewed him with detachment as a necessary evil to be tolerated and encouraged only because no other anti-Communist leader was available. His strengths and his weaknesses were only too well known. From time to time he would make demands which could not be fulfilled, and he would remind the American military advisers that he had fought the Communists for forty years and therefore knew more about them than the Americans, who had never sought his advice. He was surprised that the Americans did not spend more money on equipping his soldiers.

On March 20, 1957, a strange incident took place in the garden of an American army sergeant's house in Taipei. A prowler who had entered the house and was escaping with some documents was ordered by the sergeant to halt. It was late at night, and the sergeant could not see the man clearly, although he knew that the man attempting to run away was a Chinese. The man refused to halt and the sergeant shot him dead. The incident was immediately reported to the military police. The sergeant was arrested and tried by a military court. Extensive inquiries were made, the exact circumstances of the shooting were studied in great detail, and on May 24, two months after the incident, the sergeant was acquitted. He was then flown out of the island.

During the course of the trial the identity of the prowler was established. It was learned that he was an officer in the reserve and an official in the secret police. He held the rank of major in the security forces which were under the direct command of the Generalissimo's elder son, Chiang Ching-kuo.

On the following day, shortly before one o'clock in the afternoon, a woman began to scream hysterically outside the gates of the American Embassy in Taipei. She claimed to be the wife of the dead Chinese, and loudly demanded compensation money. A crowd gathered, and soon a mob was pouring into the Embassy compound. Cars were overturned, the American flag was hauled down, and anyone found in the courtyard was mercilessly attacked. The crowd then stormed into the Embassy itself, destroying everything in its path. Files were ransacked, cipher books were opened, and confidential documents were stolen. The Americans were able to take some photographs of the people leading the mob, and were not surprised to discover that they included known members of the secret police. At best the secret police was wreaking vengeance on the Americans; at worst there was a concerted plot to open the secret files of the Embassy.

The rioting, which began at about 1:30 P.M., went on until nightfall. No attempt was made by Chiang Ching-kuo's security forces to put an end to it. Both the Embassy and the American Information Center were sacked. The American ambassador, Karl Rankin, had been on a visit to Hongkong. He flew in to Taipei while the rioting was still going on and immediately went to his Embassy, arriving on the scene during a brief lull. By this time a handful of officers of the security force had made their appearance; they warned the ambassador that they could not guarantee his safety if he entered the Embassy. He was therefore forced to be an unwilling spectator of the looting. Since there was nothing he could do, and the Chinese were threatening further violence during the night, he left the Embassy, sent a radio report of the incident to the Secretary of State, visited the hospital where the wounded had been taken, and spent the night telephoning high government officials. The Generalissimo could not be reached; he was in his mountain retreat at Sun Moon Lake. The commanders of the Nationalist army had flown to the off-shore islands. Government ministers did not answer the telephone. By an extraordinary coincidence everyone in authority had decided to spend that Friday evening out of town.

At daybreak the ambassador returned to his Embassy to find that the looters had fled, and there was now a cordon of security police around the building. During the night someone had evidently attempted to restore some order in the building, although papers and documents were still strewn along the corridors and in the offices. By the end of the morning the ambassador concluded that the codebook remained intact and no documents of importance had been stolen. Reporters were inclined to regard the ambassador's statement as a face-saving device, and it was generally assumed that the security forces had discovered all they wanted to know.

Exactly why the Embassy was looted was never discovered, and none of the theories advanced appeared to fit all the facts. There was not the least doubt that the attack was carefully planned and coordinated by the security forces, but there was considerable doubt about the motive. For some days previously Taipei had been full of rumors about an intended attack on the Embassy, but these rumors were thought to be too ridiculous to be believed and no special precautions were taken.

Mr. Rankin protested vigorously and received the apologies of the government. An indemnity was paid, and the Americans and Chinese injured during the attack were given bonuses. Only a few people remembered that the Chinese Nationalists had been scrupulous in their treatment of embassies, and only once before had Chiang Kai-shek given instructions to raid a diplomatic mission. That was the Russian Consulate in Shanghai. The raid took place in 1927, exactly thirty years before.

American patience was strained, but the State Department

did not regard a mere raid on an Embassy as sufficient reason for changing its policy toward Nationalist China. But more and more attention was now being directed at Chiang Ching-kuo, the head of the security police and the secret services, which reached out into all levels of life on the island. The government, the party, the army and the schools were all under his strict supervision; and while the Generalissimo remained remote and unapproachable, frequently spending weeks in seclusion at his retreat on Sun Moon Lake, his son remained in Taipei, carrying out his protective duties. He had a Russian wife and had lived for a long period in the Soviet Union. His temper was abrupt and authoritarian. Once he boasted that on an average he had broken up thirteen "communist conspiracies" every month over a period of three and a half years. This meant that he had destroyed 546 "communist cells," and since each "cell" can be expected to include about five men, he was claiming that he was responsible for about 2,500 executions. But his police powers did not extend merely over three and a half years. He arrived in Formosa in 1949 and from the moment of his arrival he was given extraordinary powers over the lives of the people on the island. There was no appeal from his sentences. He was a law unto himself, and the islanders lived in fear of him.

Chiang Ching-kuo was the heir apparent, the dynastic successor to his father. He wielded more effective power than anyone else on the island, and he was responsible to no one except his father. Nepotism within the Kuomintang had been a perpetual scandal on the mainland, but no one had ever dreamed that the Generalissimo seriously intended to found a dynasty. As Chiang Ching-kuo emerged more and more frequently into the limelight, assuming some of the ceremonial tasks formerly assumed by his father and traveling on important missions abroad as his father's representative, the Generalissimo's intentions became clear. The succession was already secured, and for still another generation the island would be ruled by someone bearing his name.

Recently, as so often in the past, the Generalissimo decreed that there should be no celebrations on his birthday. A birthday, he explained, was an occasion for much sorrow, since it commemorated a mother's suffering in childbirth. Predictably his orders were disobeyed and official funds were distributed to pay for the celebrations which took place in all the towns and villages of Formosa. The great dignitaries went to pay him tribute and to offer scrolls, the dragon dancers pranced through the streets, and there were special performances in the opera houses. His achievements were proclaimed by the village mayors, and officers addressed their troops, urging every soldier to imitate the virtues of the Generalissimo. In an official proclamation the Vice-President, Yen Chia-kan, a former finance minister, announced that "the Generalissimo's achievements in promoting nationalism, democracy and the people's livelihood have made him the most important man in the whole world."

THE ANCIENT OF DAYS

IN HIS OLD AGE Chiang Kai-shek showed few signs of changing. Like those strange gnarled rocks which the Chinese like to keep in their gardens, he seemed to be permanently settled in the landscape, while the world changed alarmingly around him. Defeat left no scars. The long thin face, refined by meditation and a rarely interrupted asceticism, was still unlined, although it acquired the brown parchment color of age. It was not only that he had weathered well, but it seemed in some curious way that he had never been weathered at all, that experience would never leave any imprint on his features, and that he was immune to the passing of time. The darkening of the face was merely the darkening of an old daguerrotype photograph.

On Formosa life went on exactly as it went on in Nanking and Chungking. His age, and the circumstances of exile, permitted him to become even more detached and unapproachable than before. As usual, he rose early, did his exercises by an open window, wrote up his diary, held cabinet meetings, and received foreign visitors in the house which had been set aside for him and which was called the Chiang Kai-shek Longevity Hall. Longevity indeed had become his chief claim to office. Almost alone, he represented a link with the days of the 1911 revolution. He was a survivor from an ancient past, and to many of the young Chinese on the island he seemed to acquire the legendary qualities of a venerable old age. Though he was not particularly admired, he was revered and venerated. Such veneration is traditionally accorded to the old in China; and photographs of the old man surrounded by his grandchildren, looking harmless and benevolent, were continually printed in the newspapers. In the ministerial offices a far more youthful portrait gazed down from the walls.

Yet there was no indication that old age had mellowed him, or changed his opinions, or permitted any new ideas to enter his head. He still ruled like a feudal chieftain, giving high positions to his relatives, his favorite generals, and his two sons. They could commit no wrong, and were never called to account. Corruption was widespread; the army ruled; the secret police were everywhere. The dynastic principle, which had been established in Nanking, was reaffirmed when his elder son was groomed for the succession. Highly placed Kuomintang officials, who had lost their properties on the mainland, were rewarded with vast holdings in Formosa. No effective opposition party was permitted to exist, and there was only a minimum of social progress.

A man can live by a single idea all his life and draw strength from it, but he cannot expect to be applauded for living by an idea which has lost its usefulness. The Generalissimo still lived according to the Confucian ethic he had learned from his mother, and it never seems to have occurred to him that any other way of life was possible. The "superior man" ruled, and all the others must obey him. It was a simple ethic, but it suffered from an ineradicable defect—it had no relationship to the facts of modern life. He never came to understand how the Chinese Communists rose to power. In his view there had been a vast conspiracy engineered from Moscow, and Mao Tse-tung was merely a Moscow-appointed puppet. Nowhere in his writings or speeches is there any awareness of the fact that the Chinese people had risen in their millions to rid themselves of the Kuomintang bureaucracy and a corrupt government, preferring the unknown perils of communism to the known perils of living under relentlessly predatory Kuomintang generals.

Because he failed to understand the reasons which brought the Chinese Communists to power, his propaganda addressed to the mainland had a strange air of unreality. He depicted the Chinese Communists as being terrified by the prospect of imminent invasion from Formosa. Did not all the Chinese on the mainland secretly support the Kuomintang? Was not the rule of benevolence infinitely preferable to the rule of violence? The Chinese Communists boast of their numbers and their power, but their boasting is merely the mask of an inner weakness. So he declared in a speech delivered in January 1966:

> There is a saying by an ancient sage: "The security of a nation depends on the rightness of its course, not on its strength; the survival of a country depends on the substance of its forces, not on its numerical strength." The Peking regime often boasts of the numerical strength of its forces. It is true that they outnumber us. But compared with our well-trained, singleminded forces, the Chinese Communists are inferior. The Chinese Communists are now forsaken even by their own kith and kin because they have come to regard the whole of mankind as an enemy. In contrast we have received unceasing assistance and support from our allies and friends, because we consider that benevolence is our duty. Thus our strength is substantial, whereas that of the enemy is flabby. Moreover, all the six hundred million people on the mainland are supporting our national cause deep down in their hearts. This shows that we, and not the enemy, are superior numerically. It also means that the current situation is turning more strongly in our favor.

In his speeches he continually derided the megalomania of the Chinese Communists, their "bloodstained and abominable people's communes," their factional quarrels, and their changing slogans. They possessed no well-integrated theory of government, and they reduced the young to mindless servitude. They had no roots among the people and represented nothing more than a small clique of power-mad adventurers who were far more interested in conquest than in social advancement. The communes especially distressed him, and they were therefore placed at the head of the crimes committed by the Chinese Communists. In the Ten Pledges which he offered for the consideration of the Chinese living on the mainland, he promised that the first task of the advancing Kuomintang army would be to destroy the communes. Of the Ten Pledges, six relate to civilians and four to members of the communist cadres and armed forces. The first six pledges read:

(1) The tyrannical "people's communes," devised by the communists for the sole purpose of enslavement and oppression of the people, shall be abolished and the free life of the people shall be restored.
(2) Everyone shall be allowed to retain the land he tills.
(3) Everyone shall have food, clothing, and daily necessities free of arbitrary control.
(4) Everyone shall be free to choose the kind of occupation he prefers and enjoy the fruits of his honest labor without interference from the government.
(5) According to the provisions of the constitution, the people shall have full freedom of religion, academic study, assembly, association, residence, and movement. Regardless of their political stand in the past, all political groups or civilian organizations that now take part in the anticommunist task shall be able to enjoy equality and legitimate rights and interests within the republic's constitutional framework.
(6) Class discrimination and revenge for personal feud shall be strictly prohibited. High moral standards and law and order shall be restored.

There followed four pledges to the communist cadres and armed forces, promising rewards to all those who came over to the anticommunist revolution, without indicating the precise nature of the rewards. The last pledge was addressed to all cadres of the Communist Party and the Communist Youth Corps, and promised that if they came over to the side of the Nationalists "their past shall not be held against them, and their lives, property, and family shall be protected."

The Ten Pledges were followed by Three Assurances, which

stated in even vaguer terms that the Chinese Communists would be pardoned for their crimes and enjoy equal status with the Nationalists. An exception was made for the "hardcore leaders," who were presumably to suffer punishment at the hands of the duly constituted legal authorities.

The Ten Pledges and the Three Assurances were offered to the Chinese living on the mainland with the utmost seriousness. They were broadcast continually from the Taipei radio and scattered over the mainland in millions of copies by airplane. Unfortunately they lacked conviction. No one could believe that the Kuomintang government would restore high moral standards and law and order, or that it was capable of ensuring that everyone would have food, clothing, and daily necessities; for it had failed lamentably in rendering these services to the people on the mainland and in Formosa. Nor could anyone believe that the Chinese Communists would be treated with kindness by the conquering Nationalists. There was only one clause which could possess an appeal to the peasants on the mainland. This was the clause which stated that "everyone shall be allowed to retain the land he tills." But during the entire twenty-two years of Kuomintang rule in China no serious effort was ever made to put this law on the statute book, and it was beyond belief that in his old age the Generalissimo had suffered a change of heart or turned his back on the landowners. There were few small peasants who owned the land they tilled on Formosa. Was it to be expected that the Kuomintang would offer the peasants the title deeds of the land when it returned to China?

The Ten Pledges were intended to be the battle cry of the new China, but they offered nothing new. There was no evidence that anyone had worked out a new revolutionary philosophy which could inspire the masses. These pledges were written by the Generalissimo and told more about his state of mind than about the future course of the Kuomintang. He was a very old man, and he no longer possessed the ability to think clearly. He represented himself in his pledges and assurances as a long-suffering man filled with benevolence and the spirit of forgiveness, determined to destroy the communes and to give every peasant his patch of land.

Significantly, he did not include in the rights granted to the people under Kuomintang rule the right to free speech. Implicit in all these pronouncements was the promise that the Kuomintang, if it returned to the mainland, would continue to repeat its errors, and the Chinese Communists had little to fear from the Kuomintang propaganda.

As he surveyed the triumphs of Kuomintang rule in Formosa, the Generalissimo sustained himself with the belief that he had committed no errors and that in God's good time he would lead his army to the aid of his embattled compatriots on the mainland. He saw himself as the indispensable instrument of victory and permitted no one else to share his high position or his responsibilities. On March 25, 1966, he addressed the National Assembly in Taipei, as he prepared to enter his fourth term as president of the Republic of China:

> As I am approaching eighty, I would prefer retirement and a return to private life. But I have been encouraged by the constant thought that I should redeem myself for what I have thus far failed to do for the nation. I feel that my obligations remain unfulfilled so long as the Chinese mainland is not recovered. The desperate cries and groans of our mainland compatriots, living lives of deprivation and agony and waiting for deliverance, have made me even more determined not to shirk my duty or avoid further sacrifices in order to vindicate our national honor.
>
> I shall be prepared to bear without complaint the burden of the heaviest duties and to face the severest trials and tribulations, and I shall permit myself to be guided in my actions by a clear conscience and the utmost sincerity. I shall join together with our compatriots, military and civilian alike, in striving to overcome the heaviest odds in order to win the final victory of our anticommunist revolution. In this way we shall overthrow the tyrannical regime and punish the rebels and demolish the Chinese Communist satrapy both from within and without in a coordinated struggle. I shall try my best to be worthy of the trust of the people.

The National Assembly acclaimed him and gave him emergency powers "to direct the final phase of the struggle against the communists," and a new ministry was created to deal with the problems of civil government in the reconquered territories. The Generalissimo claimed that his emergency powers "strengthened the source of national authority"; in fact they merely confirmed him in the dictatorial powers which he had wielded for nearly forty years. No other dictator had ruled for so long. Stalin had ruled with absolute power for only a quarter of a century. It seemed likely that the Generalissimo would rule for a full half-century.

He would grow older, bent and frail, leaning more and more heavily on his thick bamboo cane, and always the strings of power would be held tightly in his hands. He would claim that his greatest triumph was that he had preserved Formosa for democracy and freedom, but these were words which he had never examined closely. Again and again he would repeat that he had been defeated on the mainland because the United States had failed to give him aid in time and because he was the victim of conspirators in Moscow, and it would never occur to him that he had made strategic errors or misunderstood the temper of the Chinese people. In his speeches he was always the man of virtue whose sole desire was to see that the Chinese lived virtuously.

Now that it was no longer possible to declare that the Chinese Communists were puppets held on the leading-strings of Moscow—for Mao Tse-tung had broken decisively with Khrushchev and had nothing but abuse for Khrushchev's successors—the Generalissimo abandoned the argument he had pursued ever since he observed the existence of the Chinese Communists. From being a puppet Mao Tse-tung became a mere brigand. "He has now at last thrown away his Marxist-Leninist cloak," the Generalissimo observed in October 1966, "and thereby he has exposed his true ugly face—the face of a brigand." He compared Mao Tse-tung to Huang Chao of the ninth century, to Li Chuang of the seventeenth century, and to the Boxers who attacked the Legation Quarter in Peking in 1900 in a xenophobic rage. They were all brigands, and Mao Tse-tung was merely following in their footsteps. He was "a brute devoid of any sense of gratitude or justice." He was another Hitler or another Shih Huang Ti, who destroyed the books and went on to destroy Chinese civilization. The speech was addressed to the Chinese Communist cadres on the mainland, and was aimed like the Ten Pledges at winning them over to the Nationalist cause. The Generalissimo pointed out that Mao Tse-tung had habitually abandoned all his closest comrades in arms when he no longer needed them. "In the end he destroys all his comrades in arms in this way, until he finds himself sitting alone on the communist throne, a lonely despot abandoned by everyone." The Generalissimo said nothing about his own treacheries or his own loneliness in the seat of power. He begged the Chinese Communists to submit to his leadership and to grant the Kuomintang one more opportunity to rule China, but the language he spoke was no longer comprehensible on the mainland.

So the days passed while he cultivated his roses and azaleas, read the Bible and Jowett's *Daily Reader* attentively, took long walks through a pine forest, and gave orders. He had reason to be content with his life. He was the man of destiny who had risen from humble beginnings to immense power, and there was never a moment when he was not aware of his authority, his precise understanding of the forces which worked on peoples and nations. For forty years he had used people as instruments for his own ambition, and never felt any remorse. It was a strange life, and he was fully aware of its strangeness and singularity.

In his own eyes nothing had happened to prove that he had ever been wrong. The communist conquest of China had taken place during his absence, and he bore no responsibility for it. Had he not faithfully observed the instructions of Dr. Sun Yat-sen and followed in the path ordained by the master? Had he not read Confucius and observed all the principles pertaining to "the superior man"? He had read the Bible, and found in both the Old and New Testaments infallible signs of the victory of good over evil. What was strange was that so much learning had led to so much bloodshed, for in his wars uncounted millions of Chinese peasants had died.

One day, walking in the rice fields near Chungking, he paused to watch some peasants planting the rice. They were knee-deep in mud, grimy and bent and old, the veins of their legs swollen, their faces scorched by the summer sun. He watched them for a long time, and then he said, "I might very easily have been one of them. Instead I command great armies and a vast country."

It might have been better for the Chinese if he had been a peasant living humbly and obscurely.

Chronology

1866	*November 12* Birth of Sun Yat-sen
1887	*October 31* Birth of Chiang Kai-shek
1893	*December 26* Birth of Mao Tse-tung
1895	*August 24* Death of Chiang Su-an
1898	*July–September* "The Hundred Days" of the Emperor Kuang Hsu's reforms
1900	*June 20* Dowager Empress declares war on "all the foreigners in the world." Boxer rebellion begins
1905	*September* Sun Yat-sen founds Tung Meng Hui
1907–1909	Chiang Kai-shek attends military academy in Tokyo
1908	*November 14* Death of Emperor Kuang Hsu
1908	*November 15* Death of Dowager Empress Tzu Hsi
1911	*October 10* Revolution breaks out at Wuchang
1912	*March 10* Yuan Shih-kai becomes Provisional President
1916	*May 18* Assassination of Chen Chi-mei
1916	*June 6* Death of Yuan Shih-k'ai
1921	*June 4* Death of Chiang Kai-shek's mother
1921	*July* Chinese Communist Party founded in Shanghai
1922	*June 16* Rebellion of Chen Chiung-ming against Dr. Sun Yat-sen
1923	*September 2* Chiang Kai-shek reaches Moscow
1923	*December* Chiang Kai-shek returns to China
1924	*June 16* Whampoa Military Academy founded, with Chiang Kai-shek as superintendent

1925 *March* 12 Death of Dr. Sun Yat-sen

1925 *August* 20 Liao Chung-kai assassinated

1926 *July* 9 Chiang Kai-shek becomes commander-in-chief of Northern Expeditionary Army

1927 *March* 20 Northern Expeditionary Army captures Shanghai

1927 *August* 12 Chiang Kai-shek resigns as commander-in-chief of Nationalist Army

1927 *September* 28 Chiang Kai-shek sails for Japan

1927 *November* 10 Chiang Kai-shek returns to Shanghai

1927 *December* 1 Chiang Kai-shek marries Mei-ling Soong

1928 *January* 4 Chiang Kai-shek resumes his command of the Nationalist Army and becomes chairman of the Military Council

1928 *June* 4 Chang Tso-lin killed by Japanese

1929 *December* 29 Mukden flies Nationalist flag

1930 *November* Chiang Kai-shek attempts first "encirclement" campaign against the Chinese Communists in Kiangsi

1931 *May–July* The second and third "encirclement" campaigns

1931 *September* 18 Japanese invade Manchuria

1932 *January* 28 Japanese attack Shanghai

1933 *October* Fourth "encirclement" campaign against Chinese Communists

1934 *February* 19 New Life campaign inaugurated

1934 *October* 15 Long March of the Chinese Communists begins

1935 *October* Chinese Communists arrive in Pao-an in Shensi

1936 *December* 16 Chiang Kai-shek arrested at Sian by the "Young Marshal"

1936 *December* 26 Chiang Kai-shek released, and flies with "Young Marshal" as his prisoner to Nanking

1937 *July* 7 Marco Polo Bridge incident

1937 *July* 28 Japanese enter Peking

1937 *November* 11 Shanghai falls to Japanese

1937 *December* 11 Japanese begin sack of Nanking

1938 *October* 22 Japanese reach Canton

1938 *October* 26 Japanese reach Hankow

1939 *February* Japanese occupy Hainan

1940 *March* 30 Wang Ching-wei installed in Nanking as puppet

1941 *December* 9 China declares war on Japan, Germany, and Italy

1942 *January* 14–17 Battle of Changsha

1942 *February* 9 Chiang Kai-shek visits India, and later meets Gandhi

1943 *January* 10 Unequal treaties renounced by allies

1943 *November* 22–26 Cairo Conference

1944 *May* Japan strikes at Hunan

1944 *November* Kweilin and Liuchow in Japanese hands; Chungking and Kunming threatened

1945 *April* 12 Death of President Roosevelt

1945 *August* 6 Atom bomb falls on Hiroshima

1945 *August* 8 Soviet Union enters the Pacific War

1945 *August* 14 Sino–Soviet Treaty

1945 *August* 28 Mao Tse-tung arrives in Chungking

1945 *October* 4 Chiang Kai-shek attacks Kunming

1945 *December* 15 General Marshall flies to China

1946 *January* 10 Cease-fire agreements between Nationalists and Chinese Communists worked out by General Marshall

1947 *January* 7 General Marshall leaves China

1947 *July* 9 General Wedemeyer sent by President Truman to report on Nationalist China's morale and military competence

1947 *September* 19 General Wedemeyer reports on his findings

1948 *March* 19 Yenan, the Chinese Communist capital, falls to Nationalist Army

1948 *April 22* Wei Tao-ming appointed Governor of Formosa, replacing General Chen Yi

1948 *September* Chinese Communists mount Manchurian campaign and occupy Shantung

1948 *December 3* Hsuchow falls

1949 *January 21* Peking falls. Chiang Kai-shek announces his retirement. Beginning of uninterrupted campaign for conquest of China by the Chinese Communists

1949 *October 1* Mao Tse-tung proclaims People's Republic of China

1949 *November 30* After brief visit to Chungking, Chiang Kai-shek flies to Chengtu, and then to Formosa

1949 *December 8* Taipei proclaimed national capital by Chiang Kai-shek

1950 *March 1* Chiang Kai-shek resumes presidential powers

1950 *April 16* Chinese Communists land on Hainan

1950 *June 25* War breaks out between North and South Korea

1954 *September* Chinese Communists bombard off-shore island of Quemoy

1957 *May 25* Mob storms American Embassy in Taipei

1958 *August–October* Matsu and Quemoy bombarded

1960 *September 4* Lei Chen arrested

1966 *May 20* Chiang Kai-shek inaugurated for fourth term as President

Select Bibliography

ABEND, HALLETT. *My Life in China*. New York, Harcourt, Brace & Company, 1943

BERKOV, ROBERT. *Strong Man of China*. Boston, Houghton-Mifflin Company, 1938

CHANG, H. H. *Chiang Kai-shek*. New York, Doubleday, Doran & Company, 1944

The Conferences at Cairo and Tehran 1943. Washington, D.C., U.S. Government Printing Office, 1961

FEIS, HERBERT. *Churchill, Roosevelt, Stalin*. Princeton, N.J., Princeton University Press, 1955

FISCHER, LOUIS. *The Soviets in World Affairs*. Princeton, N.J., Princeton University Press, 1960

CHIANG KAI-SHEK, GENERAL AND MADAME. *An Account of a Fortnight in Sian*. New York, Doubleday, Doran & Company, 1937

———. *The Destiny of China*. Translated by Wang Sheng-chih, Singapore, privately printed, n.d.

———. *Message to the Chinese Communist Party Personnel*. Tapei, Government Information Office, 1967

———. *Selected Speeches and Messages in 1961*. Taipei, Government Information Office, 1962

———. *Selected Speeches and Messages in 1966*. Taipei, Government Information Office, 1967

———. *Soviet Russia in China: A Summing Up at Seventy*. London, George G. Harrap, 1957

———. *The Vicissitudes of San Min Chu I and Communism*. Taipei, Government Information Office, 1967

CHIANG KAI-SHEK, MADAME. *This is our China*. New York, Harper and Brothers, 1940

HAHN, EMILY. *Chiang Kai-shek.* New York, Doubleday & Company, 1955

HEDIN, SVEN. *Chiang Kai-shek, Marshal of China.* New York, John Day, 1940

JACOBY, NEIL H. *U.S. Aid to Taiwan.* New York, Frederick A. Praeger, 1966

JAFFE, PHILIP (editor). *China's Destiny.* New York, Roy Publishers, 1947

KERR, GEORGE H. *Formosa Betrayed.* Boston, Houghton-Mifflin Company, 1965

LI CHIEN-NUNG. *The Political History of China 1840–1928.* Stanford, Calif., Stanford University Press, 1967

MANCALL, MARK (editor). *Formosa Today.* New York, Frederick A. Praeger, 1964

PELISSIER, ROGER. *The Awakening of China 1793–1949.* London, Secker & Warburg, 1967

SCOTT, A. C. *Literature and the Arts in Twentieth Century China.* New York, Doubleday & Company, 1963

SIÉ, C. K. *Le Maréchal Chiang Kai Shek: Son Enfance, Sa Jeunesse.* Berne, Collection Chekiai, n.d.

TONG, HOLLINGTON. *Chiang Kai-shek.* Taipei, Government Publishing Company, 1953

United States Relations with China. Washington, D.C., U.S. Department of State, 1949

WHITE, THEODORE H., AND ANNALEE JACOBY. *Thunder out of China.* New York, William Sloane Associates, 1946

Index